210 Home Plans

ONE STORY DESIGNS OVER 2000 Sq. Ft.

HOME PLANNERS, INC.

23761 RESEARCH DRIVE
FARMINGTON HILLS, MICHIGAN 48024
TELEPHONE: (313) 477-1854

Contents

Edited by: Net Gingras
Cover design by: D. M. Naidus

Index to Designs

One the Cover: Cover Designs can be found on the following pages: Front cover - Design 22534, page 67. Back cover - top, Design 22181, page 7; middle, Design 22236, page 137; bottom, Design 22220, page 121.

How to read floor plans and blueprints

Selecting the most suitable house plan for your family is a matter of matching your needs, tastes, and life-style against the many designs we offer. When you study the floor plans in this issue, and the blueprints that you may subsequently order, remember that they are simply a two-dimensional representation of what will eventually be a three-dimensional reality.

Floor plans are easy to read. Rooms are clearly labeled, with dimensions given in feet and inches. Most symbols are logical and self-explanatory: The location of bathroom fixtures, planters, fireplaces, tile floors, cabinets and counters, sinks, appliances, closets, sloped or beamed ceilings will be obvious.

A blueprint, although much more detailed, is also easy to read; all it demands is concentration. The blueprints that we offer come in many large sheets, each one of which contains a different kind of information. One sheet contains foundation and excavation drawings, another has a precise plot plan. An elevations sheet deals with the exterior walls of the house; section drawings show precise dimensions, fittings, doors, windows, and roof structures. Our detailed floor plans give the construction information needed by your contractor. And each set of blueprints contains a lengthy materials list with size and quantities of all necessary components. Using this list, a contractor and suppliers can make a start at calculating costs for you.

When you first study a floor plan or blueprint, imagine that you are walking through the house. By mentally visualizing each room in three dimensions, you can transform the technical data and symbols into something more real.

Start at the front door. It's preferable to have a foyer or entrance hall in which to receive guests. A closet here is desirable; a powder room is a plus.

Look for good traffic circulation as you study the floor plan. You should not have to pass all the way through one main room to reach another. From the entrance area you should have direct access to the three principal areas of a house—the living, work, and sleeping zones. For example, a foyer might provide separate entrances to the living room, kitchen, patio, and a hallway or staircase leading to the bedrooms.

Study the layout of each zone. Most people expect the living room to be protected from cross traffic. The kitchen, on the other hand, should connect with the dining room—and perhaps also the utility room, basement, garage, patio or deck, or a secondary entrance. A homemaker whose workday centers in the kitchen may have special requirements: a window that faces the backyard; a clear view of the family room where children play; a garage or driveway entrance that allows for a short trip with groceries; laundry facilities close at hand. Check for efficient placement of kitchen cabinets, counters, and appliances. Is there enough room in the kitchen for additional appliances, for eating in? Is there a dining nook?

Perhaps this part of the house contains a family room or a den/bedroom/office. It's advantageous to have a bathroom or powder room in this section.

As you study the plan, you may encounter a staircase, indicated by a group of parallel lines, the number of lines equaling the number of steps. Arrows labeled "up" mean that the staircase leads to a higher level, and those pointing down mean it leads to a lower one. Staircases in a split-level will have both up and down arrows on one staircase because two levels are depicted in one drawing and an extra level in another.

Notice the location of the stairways. Is too much floor space lost to them? Will you find yourself making too many trips?

Study the sleeping quarters. Are the bedrooms situated as you like? You may want the master bedroom near the kids, or you may want it as far away as possible. Is there at least one closet per person in each bedroom or a double one for a couple? Bathrooms should be convenient to each bedroom—if not adjoining, then with hallway access and on the same floor.

Once you are familiar with the relative positions of the rooms, look for such structural details as:
• Sufficient uninterrupted wall space for furniture arrangement.
• Adequate room dimensions.
• Potential heating or cooling problems—i.e., a room over a garage or next to the laundry.
• Window and door placement for good ventilation and natural light.
• Location of doorways—avoid having a basement staircase or a bathroom in view of the dining room.
• Adequate auxiliary space—closets, storage, bathrooms, countertops.
• Separation of activity areas. (Will noise from the recreation room disturb sleeping children or a parent at work?)

As you complete your mental walk through the house, bear in mind your family's long-range needs. A good house plan will allow for some adjustments now and additions in the future.

Each member of your family may find the listing of his, or her, favorite features a most helpful exercise. Why not try it?

How to choose a contractor

A contractor is part craftsman, part businessman, and part magician. As the person who will transform your dreams and drawings into a finished house, he will be responsible for the final cost of the structure, for the quality of the workmanship, and for the solving of all problems that occur quite naturally in the course of construction. Choose him as carefully as you would a business partner, because for the next several months that will be his role in your life.

As soon as you have a building site and house plans, start looking for a contractor, even if you do not plan to break ground for several months. Finding one suitable to build your house can take time, and once you have found him, you will have to be worked into his schedule. Those who are good are in demand and, where the season is short, they are often scheduling work up to a year in advance.

There are two types of residential contractors: the construction company and the carpenter-builder, often called a general contractor. Each of these has its advantages and disadvantages.

The carpenter-builder works directly on the job as the field foreman. Because his background is that of a craftsman, his workmanship is probably good—but his paperwork may be slow or sloppy. His overhead—which you pay for—is less than that of a large construction company. However, if the job drags on for any reason, his interest may flag because your project is overlapping his next job and eroding his profits.

Construction companies handle several projects concurrently. They have an office staff to keep the paperwork moving and an army of subcontractors they know they can count on. Though you can be confident that they will meet deadlines, they may sacrifice workmanship in order to do so. Because they emphasize efficiency, they are less personal to work with than a general contractor. Many will not work with an individual unless he is represented by an architect. The company and the architect speak the same language; it requires far more time to deal directly with a homeowner.

To find a reliable contractor, start by asking friends who have built homes for recommendations. Check with local lumber yards and building supply outlets for names of possible candidates.

Once you have several names in hand, ask the Chamber of Commerce, Better Business Bureau, or local department of consumer affairs for any information they might have on each of them. Keep in mind that these watchdog organizations can give only the number of complaints filed; they cannot tell you what percent of those claims were valid. Remember, too, that a large-volume operation is logically going to have more complaints against it than will an independent contractor.

Set up an interview with each of the potential candidates. Find out what his specialty is—custom houses, development houses, remodeling, or office buildings. Ask each to take you into—not just to the site of—houses he has built. Ask to see projects that are complete as well as work in progress, emphasizing that you are interested in projects comparable to yours. A $300,000 dentist's office will give you little insight into a contractor's craftsmanship.

Ask each contractor for bank references from both his commercial bank and any other lender he has worked with. If he is in good financial standing, he should have no qualms about giving you this information. Also ask if he offers a warranty on his work. Most will give you a one-year warranty on the structure; some offer as much as a ten-year warranty.

Ask for references, even though no contractor will give you the name of a dissatisfied customer. While previous clients may be pleased with a contractor's work overall, they may, for example, have had to wait three months after they moved in before they had any closet doors. Ask about his follow-through. Did he clean up the building site, or did the owner have to dispose of the refuse? Ask about his business organization. Did the paperwork go smoothly, or was there a delay in hooking up the sewer because he forgot to apply for a permit?

Talk to each of the candidates about fees. Most work on a "cost plus" basis; that is, the basic cost of the project—materials, subcontractors' services, wages of those working directly on the project, but not office help—plus his fee. Some have a fixed fee; others work on a percentage of the basic cost. A fixed fee is usually better for you if you can get one. If a contractor works on a percentage, ask for a cost breakdown of his best estimate and keep very careful track as the work progresses. A crafty contractor can always use a cost overrun to his advantage when working on a percentage.

Do not be overly suspicious of a contractor who won't work on a fixed fee. One who is very good and in great demand may not be willing to do so. He may also refuse to submit a competitive bid.

If the top two or three candidates are willing to submit competitive bids, give each a copy of the plans and your specifications for materials. If they are not each working from the same guidelines, the competitive bids will be of little value. Give each the same deadline for turning in a bid; two or three weeks is a reasonable period of time. If you are willing to go with the lowest bid, make an appointment with all of them and open the envelopes in front of them.

If one bid is remarkably low, the contractor may have made an honest error in his estimate. Do not try to hold him to it if he wants to withdraw his bid. Forcing him to build at too low a price could be disastrous for both you and him.

Though the above method sounds very fair and orderly, it is not always the best approach, especially if you are inexperienced. You may want to review the bids with your architect, if you have one, or with your lender to discuss which to accept. They may not recommend the lowest. A low bid does not necessarily mean that you will get quality with economy.

If the bids are relatively close, the most important consideration may not be money at all. How easily you can talk with a contractor and whether or not he inspires confidence are very important considerations. Any sign of a personality conflict between you and a contractor should be weighed when making a decision.

Once you have financing, you can sign a contract with the builder. Most have their own contract forms, but it is advisable to have a lawyer draw one up or, at the very least, review the standard contract. This usually costs a small flat fee.

A good contract should include the following:

• Plans and sketches of the work to be done, subject to your approval.

• A list of materials, including quantity, brand names, style or serial numbers. (Do not permit any "or equal" clause that will allow the contractor to make substitutions.)

• The terms—who (you or the lender) pays whom and when.

• A production schedule.

• The contractor's certification of insurance for workmen's compensation, damage, and liability.

• A rider stating that all changes, whether or not they increase the cost, must be submitted and approved in writing.

Of course, this list represents the least a contract should include. Once you have signed it, your plans are on the way to becoming a home.

A frequently asked question is: "Should I become my own general contractor?" Unless you have knowledge of construction, material purchasing, and experience supervising subcontractors, we do not recommend this route.

Most people who are in the market for a new home spend months searching for the right house plan and the ideal building site. Ironically, these same people often invest

Some credit unions are now allowed to grant mortgages. A few insurance companies, pension funds, unions, and fraternal organizations also offer mortgage money to their

For more information, write Farmers Home Administration, Department of Agriculture, Washington, D.C. 20250, or contact your local office.

How to shop for mortgage money

very little time shopping for the money to finance their new home, though the majority will have to live with the terms of their mortgage for as long as they live in the house.

The fact is that all banks are not alike, nor are the loans that they offer—and banks are not the only financial institutions that lend money for housing. The amount of down payment, interest rate, and period of the mortgage are all, to some extent, negotiable.

• Lending practices vary from one city and state to another. If you are a first-time builder or are new to an area, it is wise to hire a real estate (not divorce or general practice) attorney to help you unravel the maze of your specific area's laws, ordinances, and customs.

• Before talking with lenders, write down all your questions. Take notes during the conversation so you can make accurate comparisons.

• Do not be intimidated by financial officers. Keep in mind that *you are not begging for money*, you are buying it. Do not hesitate to reveal what other institutions are offering; they may be challenged to meet or better the terms.

• Use whatever clout you have. If you or your family have been banking with the same firm for years, let them know that they could lose your business if you can get a better deal elsewhere.

• Know your credit rights. The law prohibits lenders from considering only the husband's income when determining eligibility, a practice that previously kept many people out of the housing market. If you are turned down for a loan, you have a right to see a summary of the credit report and change any errors in it.

A GUIDE TO LENDERS

Where can you turn for home financing? Here is a list of sources for you to approach:

Savings and loan associations are the best place to start because they write well over half the mortgages in the United States on dwellings that house from one to four families. They generally offer favorable interest rates, require lower down payments, and allow more time to pay off loans than do other banks.

Savings banks, sometimes called mutual savings banks, are your next best bet. Like savings and loan associations, much of their business is concentrated in home mortgages.

Commercial banks write mortgages as a sideline, and when money is tight many will not write mortgages at all. They do hold about 15 percent of the mortgages in the country, however, and when the market is right, they can be very competitive.

Mortgage banking companies use the money of private investors to write home loans. They do a brisk business in government-backed loans, which other banks are reluctant to handle because of the time and paperwork required.

membership, often at terms more favorable than those available in the commercial marketplace.

A GUIDE TO MORTGAGES

The types of mortgages available are far more various than most potential home buyers realize.

Traditional Loans

Conventional home loans have a fixed interest rate and fixed monthly payments. About 80 percent of the mortgage money in the United States is lent in this manner. Made by private lending institutions, these fixed rate loans are available to anyone whom the bank officials consider a good credit risk. The interest rate depends on the prevailing market for money and is slightly negotiable if you are willing to put down a large down payment. Most down payments range from 15 to 33 percent.

You can borrow as much money as the lender believes you can afford to pay off over the negotiated period of time—usually 20 to 30 years.

The FHA does not write loans; it insures them against default in order to encourage lenders to write loans for first-time buyers and people with limited incomes. The terms of these loans make them very attractive. The interest rate is fixed by FHA at 13½ percent, and you may be allowed to take as long as 25 to 30 years to pay it off.

The down payment also is substantially lower with an FHA-backed loan. At present it is set at 3 percent of the first $25,000 and 5 percent of the remainder, up to the $60,000 limit. This means that a loan on a $60,000 house would require a $750 down payment on the first $25,000 plus $1,750 on the remainder, for a total down payment of $2,500. In contrast, the down payment for the same house financed with a conventional loan could run as high as $20,000.

Anyone may apply for an FHA-insured loan, but both the borrower and the house must qualify.

The VA guarantees loans for eligible veterans, and the husbands and wives of those who died while in the service or from a service-related disability. The VA guarantees up to 60 percent of the loan or $27,500, whichever is less. Like the FHA, the VA determines the appraised value of the house, though with a VA loan, you can borrow any amount up to the appraised value.

The Farmers Home Administration offers the only loans made directly by the government. Families with limited incomes in rural areas can qualify if the house is in a community of less than 20,000 people and is outside of a large metropolitan area; if their income is less than $15,600; and if they can prove that they do not qualify for a conventional loan.

New loan instruments

If you think that the escalating cost of housing has squeezed you out of the market, take a look at the following new types of mortgages.

The graduated payment mortgage features a monthly obligation that gradually increases over a negotiated period of time—usually five to ten years. Though the payments begin lower, they stabilize at a higher monthly rate than a standard fixed rate mortgage. Little or no equity is built in the first years, a disadvantage if you decide to sell early in the mortgage period.

These loans are aimed at young people who can anticipate income increases that will enable them to meet the escalating payments. The size of the down payment is about the same or slightly higher than for a conventional loan, but you can qualify with a lower income. As of last year, savings and loan associations can write these loans, and the FHA now insures five different types.

The flexible loan insurance program (FLIP) requires that part of the down payment, which is about the same as a conventional loan, be placed in a pledged savings account. During the first five years of the mortgage, funds are drawn from this account to supplement the lower monthly payments.

The deferred interest mortgage, another graduated program, allows you to pay a lower rate of interest during the first few years and a higher rate in the later years of the mortgage. If the house is sold, the borrower must pay back all the interest, often with a prepayment penalty. Both the FLIP and deferred interest loans are very new and not yet widely available.

The variable rate mortgage is most widely available in California, but its popularity is growing. This instrument features a fluctuating interest rate that is linked to an economic indicator—usually the lender's cost of obtaining funds for lending. To protect the consumer against a sudden and disastrous increase, regulations limit the amount that the interest rate can increase over a given period of time.

To make these loans attractive, lenders offer them without prepayment penalties and with "assumption" clauses that allow another buyer to assume your mortgage should you sell.

Flexible payment mortgages allow young people who can anticipate rising incomes to enter the housing market sooner. They pay only the interest during the first few years; then the mortgage is amortized and the payments go up. This is a valuable option only for those people who intend to keep their home for several years because no equity is built in the lower payment period.

The reverse annuity mortgage is targeted for older people who have fixed incomes. This very new loan instrument allows those who qualify to tap into the equity on their houses. The lender pays them each month and collects the loan when the house is sold or the owner dies.

Traditional Designs
With Early American Charm

Design 22181 2,612 Sq. Ft.; 45,230 Cu. Ft.

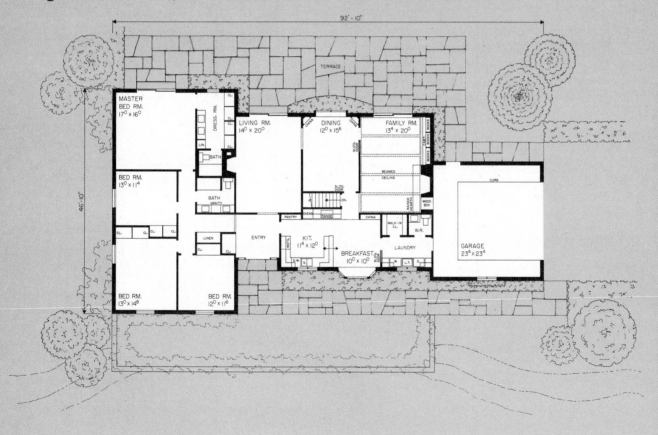

● It is hard to imagine a home with any more eye-appeal than this one. It is the complete picture of charm. The interior is no less outstanding. Sliding glass doors permit the large master bedroom, the quiet living room, and the all-purpose family room to function directly with the outdoors. The two fireplaces, the built-in china cabinets, the book shelves, the complete laundry and kitchen pass-thru to breakfast room are extra features. Count the closets. There are all kinds of storage facilities. Don't miss those in the beamed ceilinged family room. The oversized garage with its raised curb offers further storage possibilities. Although the illustration of this home shows natural quarried stone, you may wish to substitute brick or even siding. Note location of basement stairs.

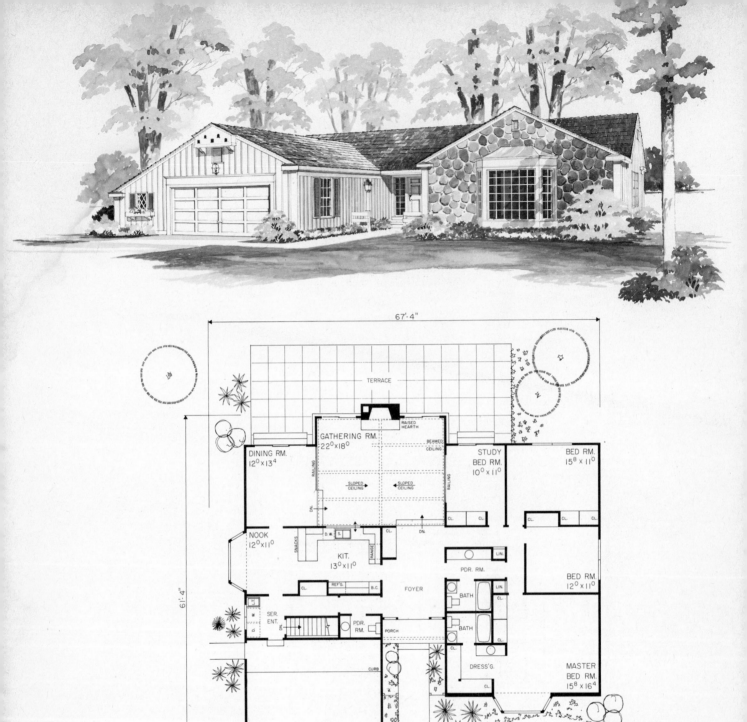

Design 22527 2,392 Sq. Ft.; 42,579 Cu. Ft.

● Vertical boards and battens, field-stone, bay window, a dovecote, a gas lamp and a recessed front entrance are among the appealing exterior features of this U-shaped design. Through the double front doors, flanked by glass side lites, one enters the spacious foyer. Straight ahead is the cozy sunken gathering room with its sloping, beamed ceiling, raised hearth fireplace and two sets of sliding glass doors to the rear terrace. To the right of the foyer is the sleeping wing with its three bedrooms, study (make it the fourth bedroom if you wish) and two baths. To the left is the strategically located powder room and large kitchen with its delightful nook and bay window.

● What a pleasing, traditional exterior. And what a fine, convenient living interior! The configuration of this home leads to interesting roof planes and even functional outdoor terrace areas. The front court and the covered porch with its stolid pillars strike an enchanting note. The gathering room will be just that. It will be the family's multi-purpose living area. Sunken to a level of two steps, its already spacious feeling is enhanced by its open planning with the dining room and study. This latter room may be closed off for more privacy if desired. Just adjacent to the foyer is the open stairwell to the basement level. Here will be the possibility of developing recreation space.

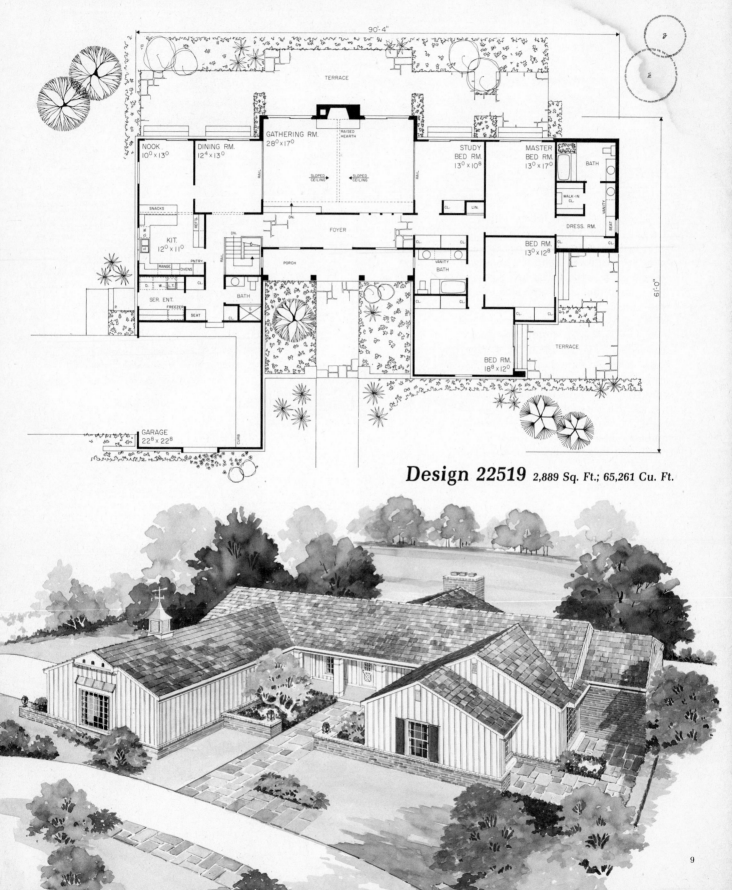

Design 22519 2,889 Sq. Ft.; 65,261 Cu. Ft.

Design 22766
2,711 Sq. Ft.; 59,240 Cu. Ft.

● A sizeable master bedroom with a dressing area featuring two walk-in closets, a twin lavatory and compartmented bath. Two-bedroom children's area with full bath and supporting study. Formal living and dining zone separated by a thru-fireplace. A spacious kitchen-nook with a cheerfully informal sun room just a step away through sliding glass doors. The service area has a laundry, storage, wash room and stairs to basement. An array of sliding glass doors leading to outdoor living on the various functional terraces. These are but some of the highlights of this appealing L-shaped traditional. Be sure to note the large number of sizeable closets for a variety of uses.

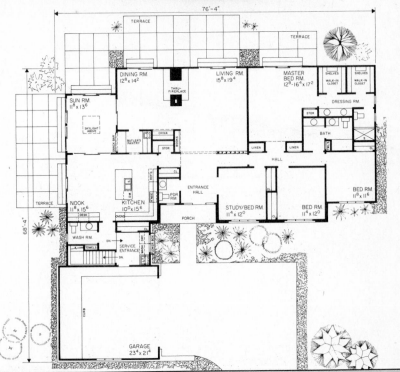

Design 22778
2,761 Sq. Ft.; 41,145 Cu. Ft.

● No matter what the occasion, family and friends alike will enjoy the sizeable gathering room. A spacious 20' x 23', this room has a thru fireplace to the study and two sets of sliding glass doors to the large rear terrace. Indoor-outdoor living can also be enjoyed from the dining room, study and master bedroom. There is also a covered porch accessible through sliding glass doors in the dining room and breakfast nook.

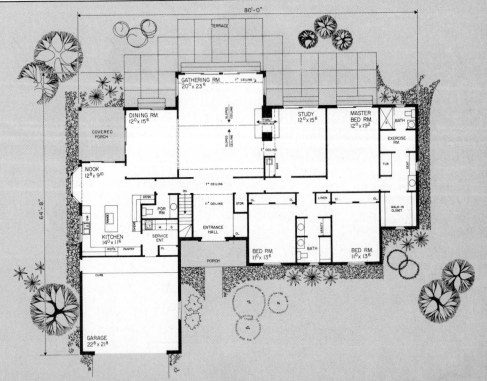

Design 22784
2,980 Sq. Ft.; 41,580 Cu. Ft.

● The projection of the master bedroom and garage create an inviting U-shaped area leading to the covered porch of this delightful traditionally styled design. After entering through the double front doors, the gallery will lead to each of the three living areas: the sleeping wing of two bedrooms, full bath and study; the informal area of the family room with raised hearth fireplace and sliding glass doors to the terrace and the kitchen/nook area (the kitchen has a pass-thru snack bar to the family room); and the formal area consisting of a separate dining room with built-in china cabinets and the living room. Note the privacy of the master bedroom.

Design 21149

2,040 Sq. Ft.; 35,290 Cu. Ft.

● The very shape of this traditional adaptation seems to spell, "welcome". A study of the floor plan reflects excellent zoning. The sleeping area consists of four bedrooms and two full baths. The formal area, located to the front of the house, consists of a separate dining room with built-in china cabinet and living room with fireplace and accompanying woodbox. Study the work center of the kitchen, laundry and wash room. An informal family room. It is only a couple of steps from the kitchen and functions with the outdoor terrace.

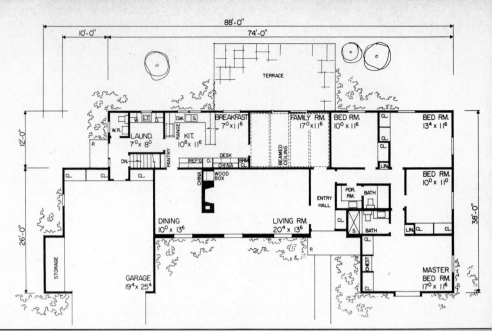

Design 22316

2,000 Sq. Ft.; 25,242 Cu. Ft.

● Here is a basic floor plan which is the favorite of many. It provides for the location, to the front of the plan, of the more formal areas (living and dining rooms); while the informal areas (family room and kitchen) are situated to the rear of the plan and function with the terrace. To the left of the center entrance is the four bedroom, two bath sleeping zone. Adjacent to the kitchen is the utility room with a wash room nearby. The garage features a storage room and work shop area with more storage.

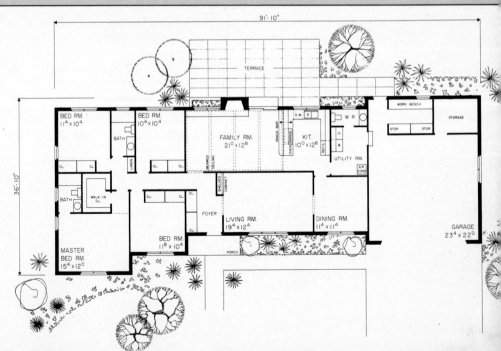

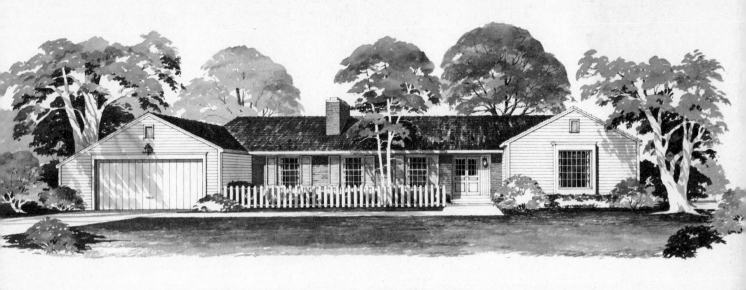

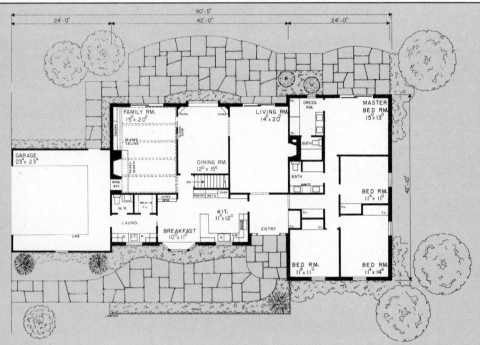

Design 22144
2,432 Sq. Ft.; 42,519 Cu. Ft.

● Have you ever wished you lived in a house in which the living, dining and family rooms all looked out upon the rear terrace? Further, have you ever wished your home had its kitchen located to the front so that you could see approaching callers? Or, have you ever wished for a house where traffic in from the garage was stopped right in the laundry so that wet, snowy, dirty and muddy apparel could be shed immediately? If these have been your wishes, this plan may be just for you.

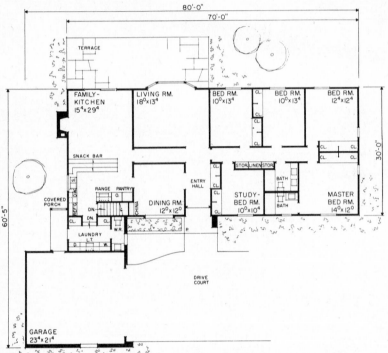

Design 21872
2,212 Sq. Ft.; 35,164 Cu. Ft.

● If exceptional exterior appeal means anything to interior living potential then this traditional home should have unlimited livability. And, indeed, it has! There are five bedrooms (and a study if you so wish), two full baths and loads of storage in the sleeping wing. The formal living zone highlights a quiet living room and separate dining room. Each completely free of cross-room traffic. For informal living there is the family-kitchen with a snack bar, fireplace and sliding glass doors to the terrace. The work center is outstanding with laundry and wash room nearby. There are plenty of cupboards and lots of counter space. The laundry, with more cupboards and twin closets, is nearby. Note wash room and covered side porch.

Design 21238
2,290 Sq. Ft.; 32,827 Cu. Ft.

● A popular floor plan concept with a charming, traditional exterior. The angular plan is one which functions most efficiently, for it is zoned for true convenience. The formal living and dining zone acts as a buffer between the quiet sleeping zone and the informal living and work center area. The spacious center entry hall looks down into the sunken living room. The durable and attractive slate floor carries into the separate dining room from the entry hall. For formal entertaining the dining room is but a few steps from the living room and kitchen.

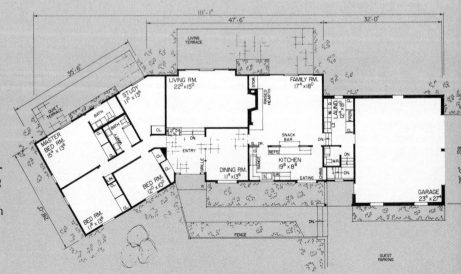

Design 21102
2,348 Sq. Ft.; 39,706 Cu. Ft.

● This quietly impressive home with curving front drive, covered front porch, delightful muntined windows, and panelled door flanked by patterned side-lites, houses a fine floor plan. The center entry hall joins another hall which runs the width of the home and routes traffic directly to each room. There are four bedrooms, two full baths, and plenty of storage potential in sleeping area. A covered rear porch off the master bedroom will be nice on hot, summer evenings. The living and dining rooms are sure to enjoy their privacy. The focal point of the plan, is perhaps the 27 foot family-kitchen. Don't miss the strategic location of the mud room. A snack bar provides a handy spot for the enjoyment of quick and easy meals.

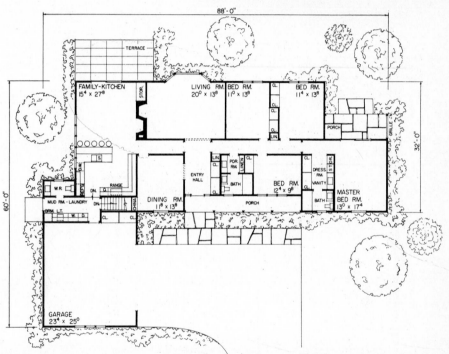

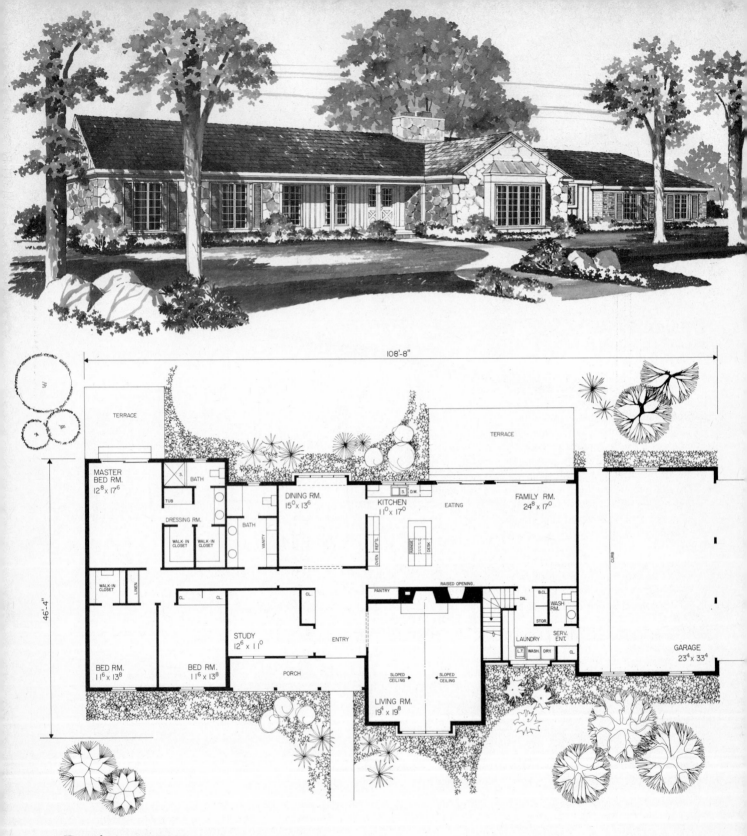

Design 22767 *3,000 Sq. Ft.; 58,460 Cu. Ft.*

● What a sound investment this impressive home will be. And while its value withstands the inflationary pressures of ensuing years, it will serve your family well. It has all the amenities to assure truly pleasurable living. The charming exterior will lend itself to treatment other than the appealing fieldstone, brick and frame shown. Inside, the plan will impress you with large, spacious living areas, formal and informal dining areas, three large bedrooms, two full baths with twin lavatories, walk-in closets and a fine study.

The kitchen features an island work center with range and desk. The two fireplaces will warm their surroundings in both areas. Two separate terraces for a variety of uses. Note laundry, wash room and three-car garage with extra curb area.

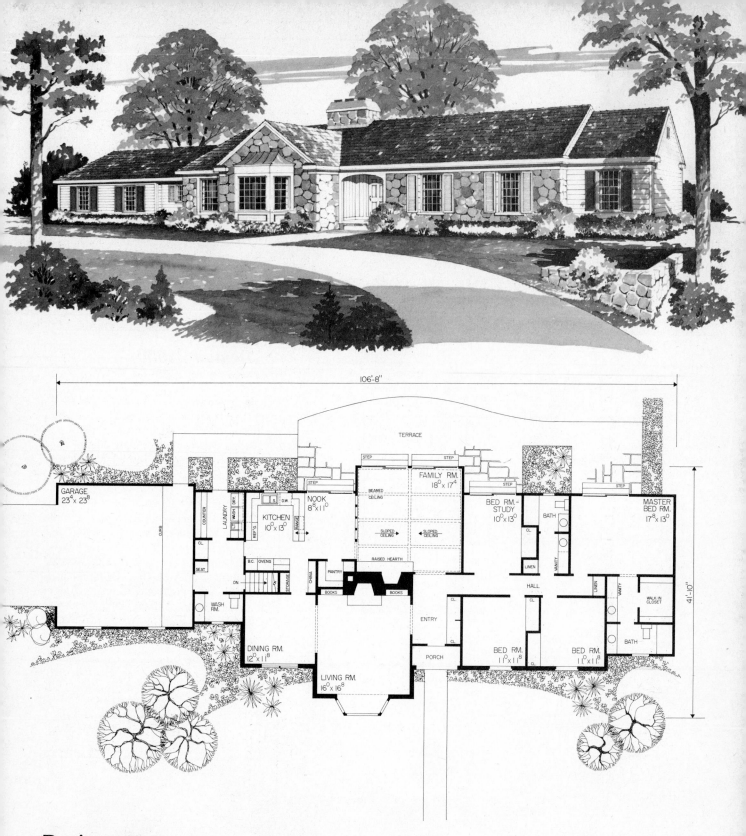

Design 22544 2,527 Sq. Ft.; 61,943 Cu. Ft.

● A fine blend of exterior materials enhance the beauty of this fine home. Here, the masonry material used is fieldstone to contrast effectively with the horizontal siding. You may substitute brick or quarried stone if you wish. Adding to the appeal are the various projections and their roof planes, the window treatment and the recessed front entrance. Two large living areas highlight the interior. Each has a fireplace. The homemaking effort will be easily and enjoyably dispatched with such features as the efficient kitchen, the walk-in pantry, the handy storage areas, the first floor laundry and extra washroom. The sleeping zone has four bedrooms, two baths with vanities and good closet accommodations. There's a basement for additional storage and recreation.

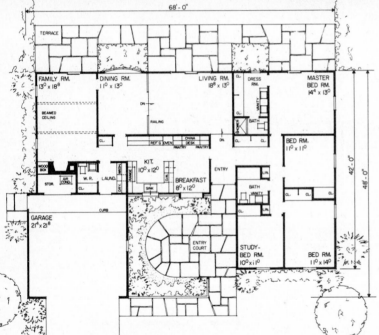

Design 21950
2,076 Sq. Ft.; 27,520 Cu. Ft.

● If you were to count the various reasons that will surely cause excitement over the prospect of moving into this home, you would certainly be able to compile a long list. You might head your list with the grace and charm of the front exterior. You'd certainly have to comment on the delightful entry court, the picket fence and lamp post, and the recessed front entrance. Comments about the interior obviously would begin with the listing of such features as: spaciousness galore; sunken living room; separate dining room; beamed ceiling family room; excellent kitchen with pass-thru to breakfast room; two full baths, plus wash room, etc.

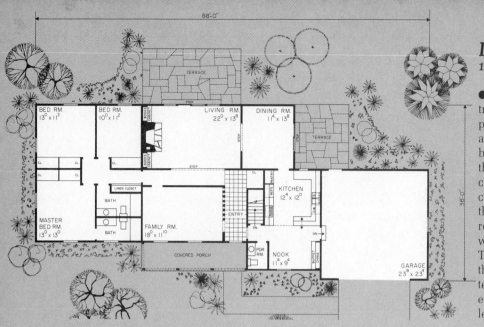

Design 22360
1,936 Sq. Ft.; 37,026 Cu. Ft.

● The charming characteristics of this traditional one-story are many. Fine proportion and pleasing lines assure a long and rewarding study. A list of them may begin with the fine window treatment, the covered front porch with its stolid columns, the raised panelled door, the carriage lamp, the horizontal siding, and the cupola. Inside, the family's everyday routine will enjoy all the facilities which will surely guarantee pleasurable living. The formal rear sunken living room and the dining room function with their own terraces. A 3½ foot high wall with turned wood posts on top separate the excellent family room from the entry hall.

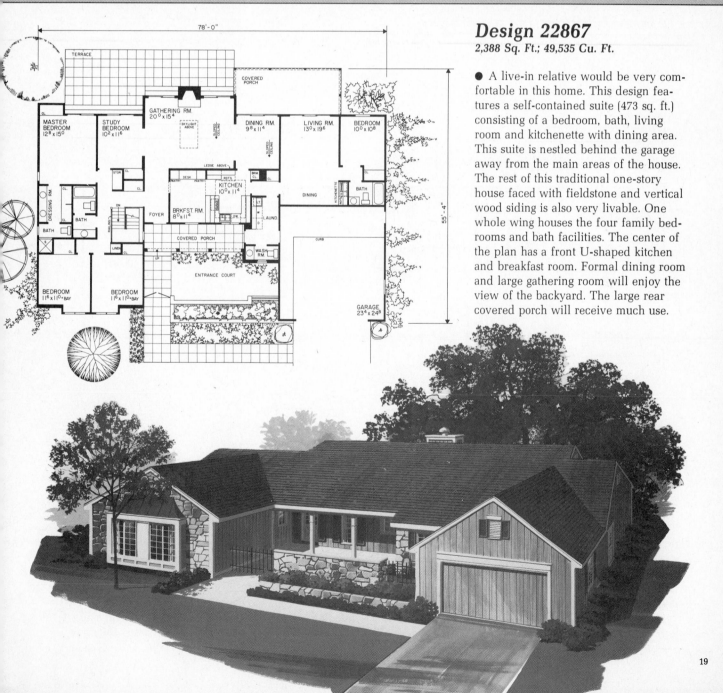

Design 22867
2,388 Sq. Ft.; 49,535 Cu. Ft.

● A live-in relative would be very comfortable in this home. This design features a self-contained suite (473 sq. ft.) consisting of a bedroom, bath, living room and kitchenette with dining area. This suite is nestled behind the garage away from the main areas of the house. The rest of this traditional one-story house faced with fieldstone and vertical wood siding is also very livable. One whole wing houses the four family bedrooms and bath facilities. The center of the plan has a front U-shaped kitchen and breakfast room. Formal dining room and large gathering room will enjoy the view of the backyard. The large rear covered porch will receive much use.

Design 22204 2,016 Sq. Ft.; 34,289 Cu. Ft.

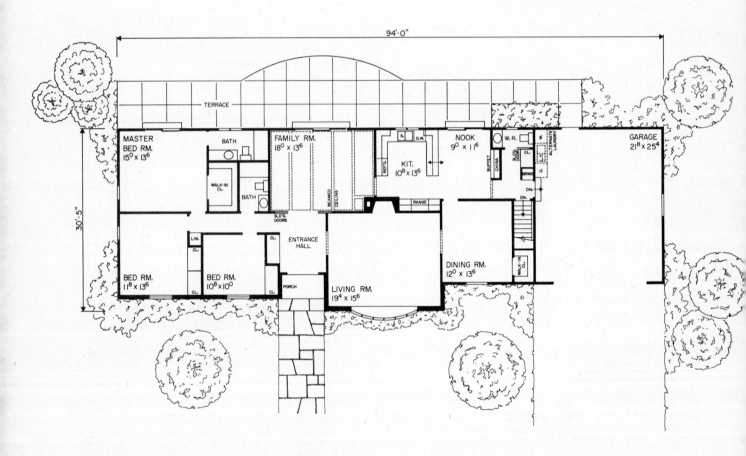

● Your life's investment could hardly be more wisely made than for the choice of this delightful traditional as your family's next home. Over the years its charm will hardly diminish. It will be as impressive as ever. This is a favorite plan of many. It establishes a quiet sleeping zone, a formal living-dining zone to the front, and an informal family-kitchen zone to the rear. Sliding glass doors permit the master bedroom, the family room, and the breakfast nook to have easy access to the rear terrace. Entering the house from the garage, all will appreciate the proximity of the closets, the wash room, and the basement stairs. Don't overlook the beamed ceiling.

Design 22208 2,522 Sq. Ft.; 32,939 Cu. Ft.

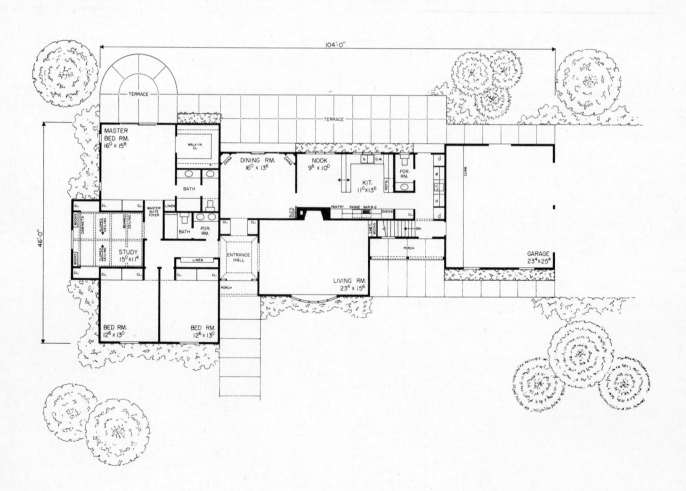

● You really won't need a half acre on which to build this exquisitely proportioned home. Its very breadth will guarantee plenty of space to the front, thus providing a fine setting. The pedimented gables, the horizon-tal siding, the corner boards, the window and door treatment, the two co-vered porches, and the cupola set the note of distinction. An excellent fea-ture is the service entrance adjacent to the garage. The bedroom wing is positively outstanding. In addition to the three bedrooms and two baths, there is the private study. It has slop-ing beamed ceilings, book shelves, cabinets and two closets. Notice that both baths are compartmented.

Design 21835

2,144 Sq. Ft.; 33,310 Cu. Ft.

● Cedar shakes and quarried natural stone, are the exterior materials which adorn this irregularly shaped traditional ranch home. Adding to the appeal of the exterior are the cut-up windows, the shutters, the pediment gable, the cupola and the double front doors. The detail of the garage door opening adds further interest. Inside, this favorite among floor plans, reflects all the features neccessary to provide complete livability for the large family. The sleeping zone is a 24' x 40' rectangle which contains four bedrooms and two full baths. A dressing room with a vanity and a wall of wardrobe storage highlights the master bedroom. Both the informal family room and the formal living room have a fireplace.

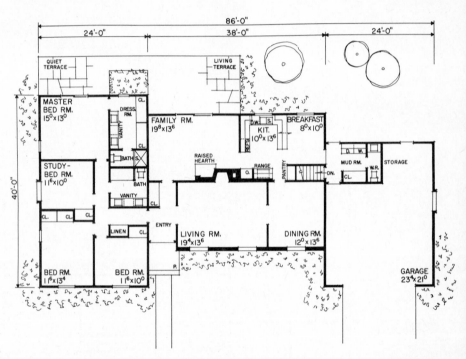

● Whatever the setting, here is a traditional, one story home that is truly impressive. Zoned in a most practical manner, the floor plan features an isolated bedroom wing, formal living and dining rooms and, across the rear of the house, the informal living areas.

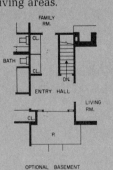

OPTIONAL BASEMENT

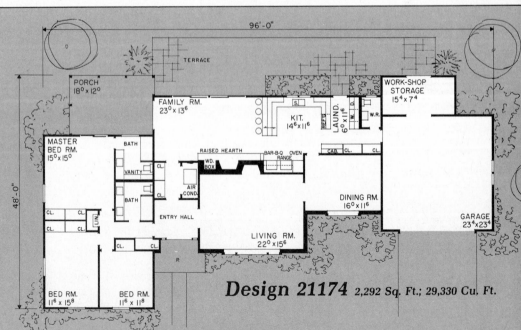

Design 21174 *2,292 Sq. Ft.; 29,330 Cu. Ft.*

Design 21786
2,370 Sq. Ft.; 37,170 Cu. Ft.

● Like this? If the answer is, yes, it is easy to understand. This is an extremely appealing design, highlighted by its brick masses, its window detailing, its interesting shape, and its inviting covered front entrance. The foyer is centrally located and but a step or two from all areas. The house, while it features all the facilities for family living, assures a full measure of privacy for all. The bedroom wing is distinctly defined. The quiet, sunken living room is off by itself. There is a separate, formal dining room. The family room is one which will function alone and cater to numerous activities. The kitchen, with its eating space, is of good size. The mud-room area is a true convenient living feature.

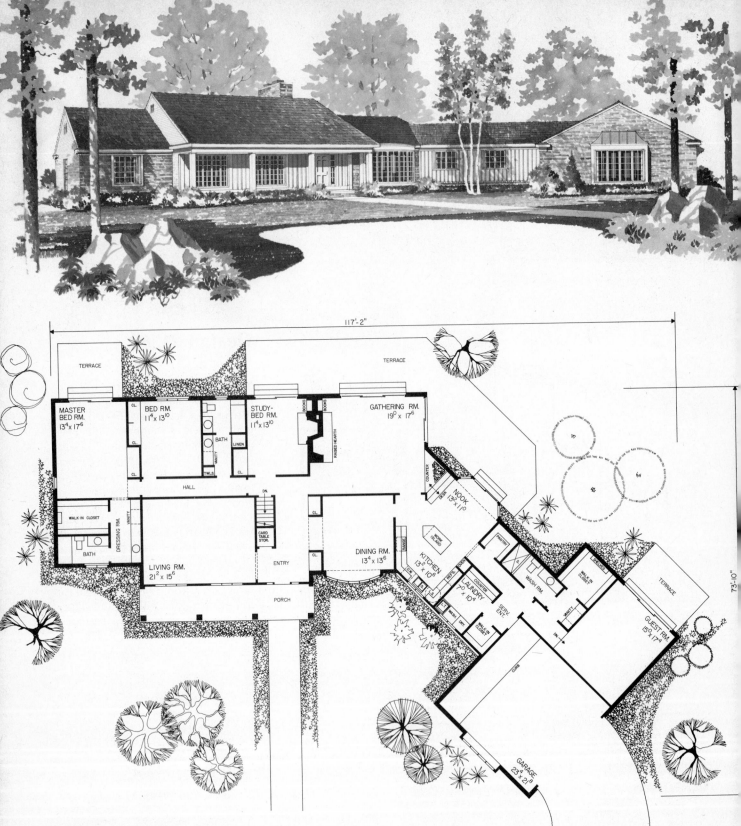

Design 22739 3,313 Sq. Ft.; 65,230 Cu. Ft.

● If you and your family are looking for new living patterns, try to envision your days spent in this traditionally styled home. Its Early American flavor is captured by the effective window and door treatment, the cornice work and the stolid porch pillars. Its zoning is interesting. The interior leaves nothing to be desired. There are three bedrooms and two full baths in the sleeping area. A quiet, formal living room separate from other living areas. The gathering and dining rooms are adjacent to each other and function with the excellent kitchen and its breakfast eating area. Then, there is an extra guest room sunken one step. A live-in relative would enjoy the privacy of this room. Full bath is nearby. This is definitely a home for all to enjoy.

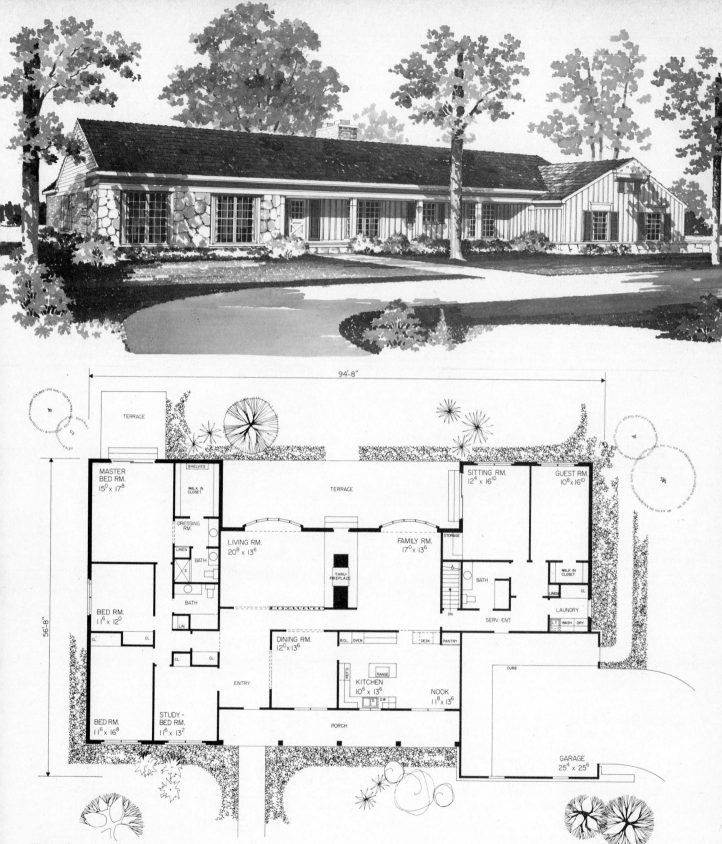

Design 22768 *3,436 Sq. Ft.; 65,450 Cu. Ft.*

● Besides its elegant traditionally styled exterior with its delightfully long covered front porch, this home has an exceptionally livable interior. There is the outstanding four bedroom and two-bath sleeping wing. Then, the efficient front kitchen with island range flanked by the formal dining room and the informal breakfast nook. Separated by the two-way, thru fireplace are the living and family rooms which look out on the rear yard. Worthy of particular note is the development of a potential live-in relative facility. These two rooms would also serve the large family well as a hobby room and library or additional bedrooms. A full bath is adjacent as well as the laundry. Note curb area in the garage for the storage of outdoor equipment.

Design 22209
2,659 Sq. Ft.; 45,240 Cu. Ft.

● Such an impressive home would, indeed, be difficult to top. And little wonder when you consider the myraid of features this one-story Colonial possesses. Consider the exquisite detailing, the fine proportions, and the symmetry of the projecting wings. The gracious and inviting double front doors are a prelude to the exceptional interior. Consider the four bedroom, two-bath sleeping wing. Formal entertaining can be enjoyed in the front living and dining rooms. For informal living there is the rear family room.

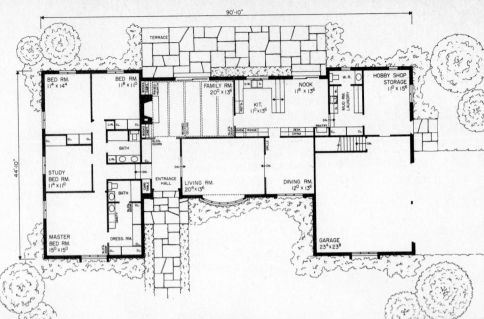

Design 22264
2,352 Sq. Ft.; 33,924 Cu. Ft.

● This U-shaped traditional will be a welcomed addition on any site. It has living facilities which will provide your family with years of delightful livability. The two living areas are located to the rear and function with the outdoor terrace. The outstanding kitchen is strategically located handy to the family room and the eating areas. A separate laundry area with fine storage and nearby powder room is a favorite feature. Note garage size and storage potential. Also notice stairway to attic.

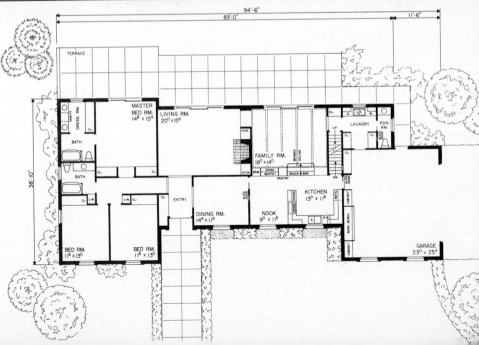

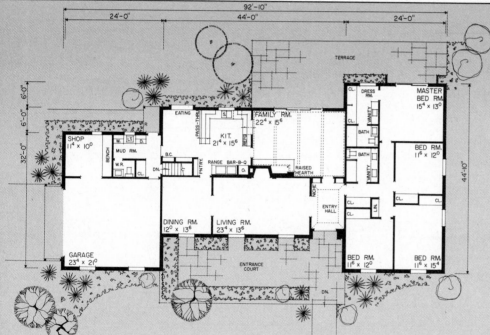

Design 21761
2,548 Sq. Ft.; 43,870 Cu. Ft.

● Low, strong roof lines and solid, enduring qualities of brick give this house a permanent, here-to-stay appearance. Bedroom wing is isolated, and the baths and closets deaden noise from the rest of the house. Center fireplaces in family and living rooms make furniture arrangement easy. There are a number of extras – a workshop, an unusually large garage, and an indoor barbecue. Garage has easy access to both basement and kitchen area. There are two eating areas – a formal dining room and a breakfast nook next to the delightful kitchen.

Design 22270
2,505 Sq. Ft.; 33,916 Cu. Ft.

● Four bedrooms, 2½ baths, spacious living areas, formal and informal dining areas, two fireplaces, separate laundry and outstanding storage facilities-these are but some of the highlights of this family oriented design.

Design 22271

2,317 Sq. Ft.; 30,115 Cu. Ft.

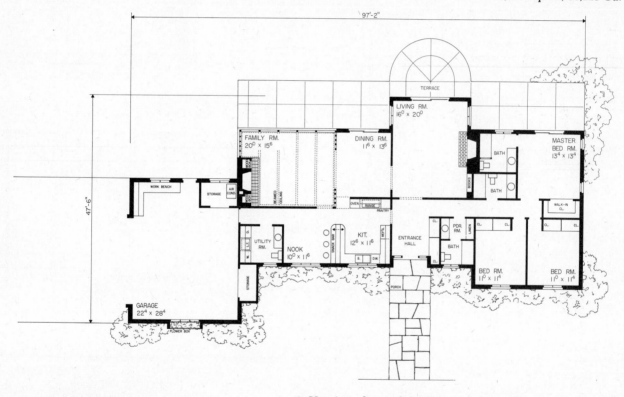

● Here's a plan with both formal and informal living areas functioning to the rear of the house. Among the features are the two fireplaces, three full baths, nook and snack bar, utility room and extra garage storage. Many other fine features are also included.

Design 22353
2,302 Sq. Ft.; 40,610 Cu. Ft.

● Here is an inviting Colonial Ranch home with matching pediment gables projecting toward the street. Deep double-hung windows flanked by shutters enhance the exterior charm. The massive chimney, the raised planter, the panelled front door, and the patterned garage door add their extra measure of appeal. The interior offers loads of livability. Note the sunken living room, the beamed-ceilinged family room, and the efficient kitchen strategically located between the breakfast nook and the formal dining room.

Design 22362
2,166 Sq. Ft.; 38,537 Cu. Ft.

● Here is a ground-hugging, tradition-al adaptation with plenty of exterior appeal and a fine functioning floor plan. Observe the interior zoning. The sunken living room will have plenty of privacy. The four bedroom sleep-ing area is a wing by itself. The U-shaped kitchen is strategically flan-ked by the two eating areas. Study the exceptional family room. Note pow-der room. The indoor-outdoor living relationships are excellent. The cov-ered rear porch will be a popular spot for summer outdoor eating and relaxation.

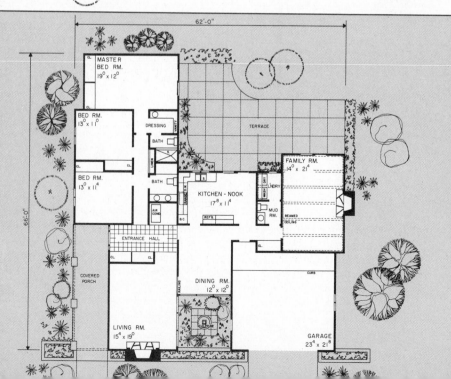

Design 22352
2,179 Sq. Ft.; 26,917 Cu. Ft.

● This enchanting hip-roof tradition-al has a distinctive air of its own. From the recessed gardening area be-tween the living room and garage to the master bedroom vanity, this plan is replete with features. Notice the covered front porch, the spacious kitchen, the quiet living room, the beamed ceilinged family room, the laundry/mud room, the sliding glass doors to terrace, etc. The planting court, so completely visible from the formal living and dining rooms, will be great fun for the amateur horticul-turist during the warm months.

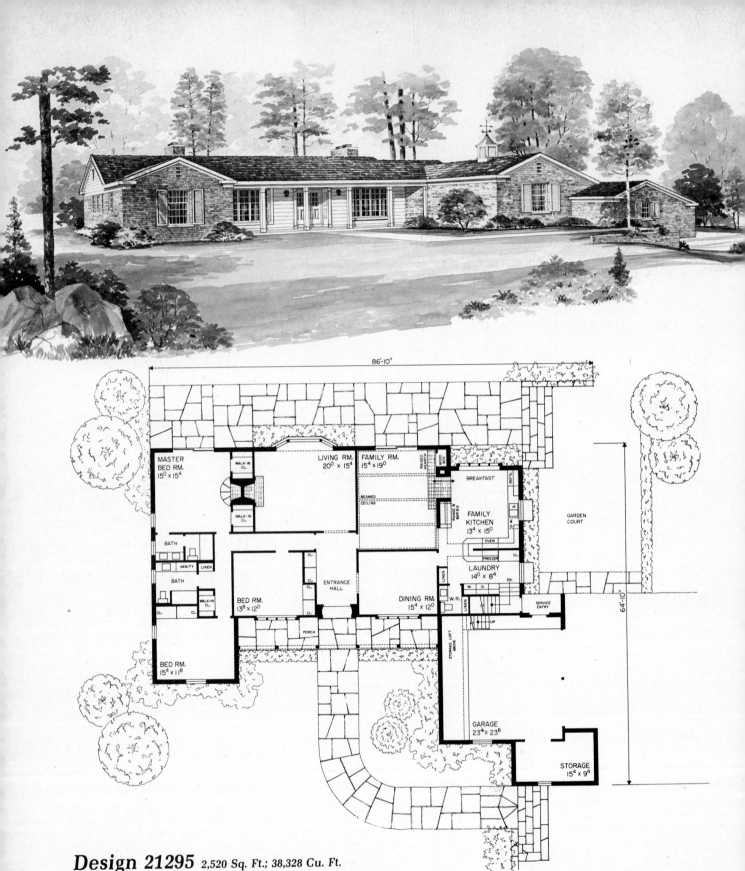

Design 21295 2,520 Sq. Ft.; 38,328 Cu. Ft.

● A custom home is one tailored to fit the needs and satisfy the living patterns of a particular family. Here is a traditional home which stands ready to serve its occupants ideally. The overhanging roof allows for the covered porch with its attractive wood columns. The center entrance leads to an interior which will cater to the formal as well as the informal activities of the family. Two fireplaces, back-to-back, serve the master bedroom and the quiet, formal living room. A two-way fireplace can be enjoyed from the large, beamed ceiling family room and the gaily, informal family kitchen. Note the laundry, the powder room and the garage storage. Of particular interest, is the storage room and the storage balcony. No storage problems here.

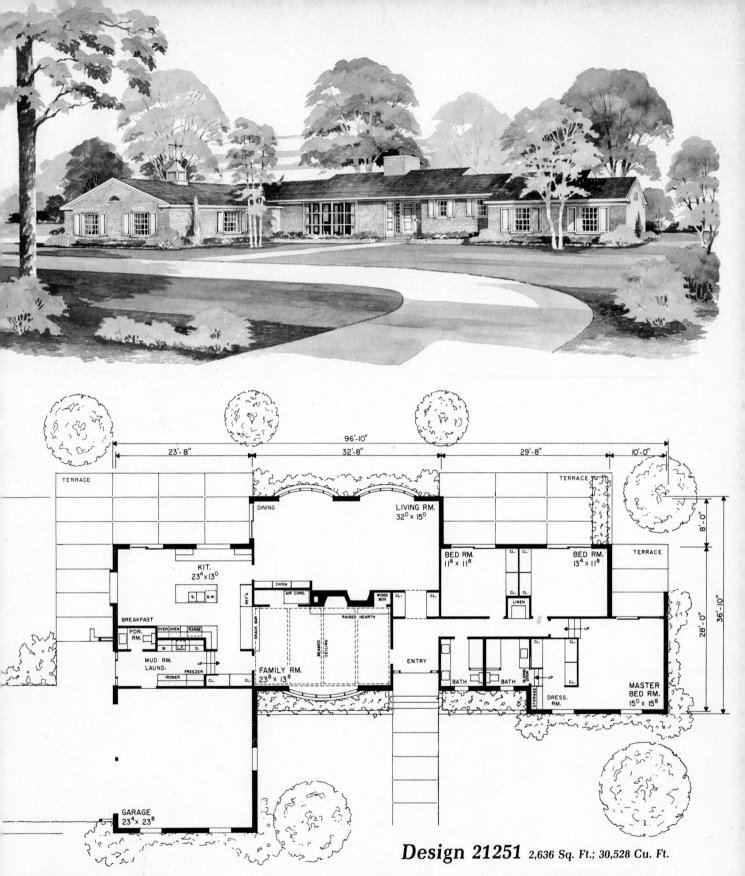

Design 21251 2,636 Sq. Ft.; 30,528 Cu. Ft.

● A custom home is one that can be identified by its note of distinction – both inside and out. This dramatic one-story home, with its traditional flavor, achieves that identity. Set back on a suburban site, it will be a showplace, indeed. Flanking the rais-

ed and covered front entry are two attractive planting areas. Separating the outstanding family kitchen/work center and the wonderfully private sleeping wing, are the spacious living areas. The informal living area, the family room, is handy to the fine

kitchen and overlooks the front yard through a bowed bay-window. The formal living area is 32 feet long – ideal for formal entertaining. Don't miss the two fireplaces and functional terraces. There are three terraces for varied uses.

Design 21924 2,504 Sq. Ft.; 42,498 Cu. Ft.

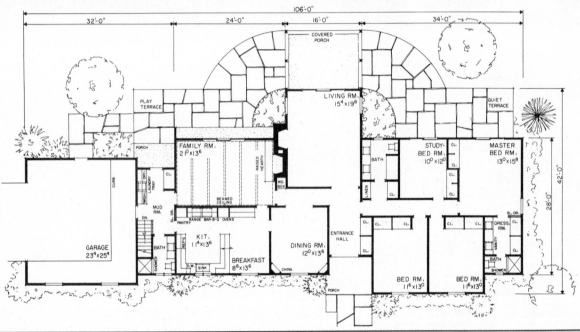

Design 21851 2,450 Sq. Ft.; 42,052 Cu. Ft.

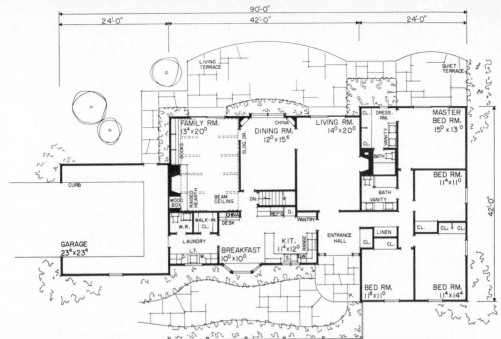

90'-0"

24'-0"   42'-0"   24'-0"

LIVING TERRACE   QUIET TERRACE

FAMILY RM.
13⁴ x 20⁰

DINING RM.
12⁰ x 15⁶

CHINA

LIVING RM.
14⁰ x 20⁰

DRESS. RM.

MASTER BED RM.
15⁰ x 13⁰

VANITY

BATH

BED RM.
11⁴ x 11⁰

BEAM CEILING

BOOKS

SLDG. DR.

CL.

CL.

BATH VANITY

42'-0"

CURB

LIVING

WOOD BOX

RAISED HEARTH

WALK-IN CL.

DN.

REF'G.

D.

CHINA DESK

PANTRY

ENTRANCE HALL

LINEN

CL.   CL.   CL.

GARAGE
23⁴ x 23⁴

LAUNDRY

W.R.

L.T.

D. W.

BREAKFAST
10⁰ x 10⁰

KIT.
11⁴ x 12⁰

S. RANGE

CL. CL.

BED RM.
11⁸ x 11⁰

BED RM.
11⁴ x 14⁴

FENCE

Design 21886 2,352 Sq. Ft.; 41,244 Cu. Ft.

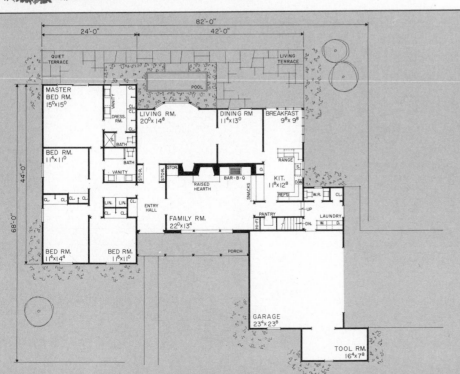

82'-0"

24'-0"   42'-0"

QUIET TERRACE   LIVING TERRACE

MASTER BED RM.
15⁰ x 15⁰

VANITY

DRESS. RM.

CL.

POOL

LIVING RM.
20⁰ x 14⁸

DINING RM
11⁴ x 13⁰

BREAKFAST
9⁸ x 9⁸

BATH

BED RM.
11⁴ x 11⁰

BATH

VANITY

STOR.

RANGE

S.

44'-0"

68'-0"

CL. CL.

LIN. LIN.

CL. CL.

ENTRY HALL

STOR.

STOR.

RAISED HEARTH

BAR-B-Q

SNACKS

KIT.
11⁸ x 12⁸

D.W.

REF'G.

W.R.

CL.

BED RM.
11⁴ x 14⁴

BED RM.
11⁸ x 11⁰

FAMILY RM.
22⁰ x 13⁴

HI-FI

PANTRY

UP

DN.

W. D.

LAUNDRY

PORCH

GARAGE
23⁴ x 23⁸

TOOL RM.
16⁴ x 7⁸

● Here are three designs each featuring four bedrooms and two plus baths. While each home has a basement, it also highlights a first floor laundry. The differing arrangements of the living, dining, and family rooms are most interesting. The kitchens function directly with the breakfast rooms, yet again, their locations vary. Raised hearth fireplaces are a focal point of the family rooms, while a second fireplace can be found in the living rooms. Note the side opening garages. Design 21851 has a handy tool room for heavy equipment.

Design 22783

3,210 Sq. Ft.; 57,595 Cu. Ft.

● The configuration of this traditional design is outstanding indeed. The garage-bedroom wing on one side and the master bedroom on the other create an inviting U-shaped entry court. This area is raised two steps from the driveway and has a 6 foot high masonry wall with coach lamps for an added attraction. Upon entrance through the double front doors one will begin to enjoy the livability that this design has to offer. Each room is well planned and deserves praise. The sizeable master bedroom has a fireplace and sliding glass doors to the entry court. Another sizeable room, the gathering room, has access to the rear terrace along with the dining room, family room and rear bedroom. Note interior kitchen which is adjacent to each of the major rooms.

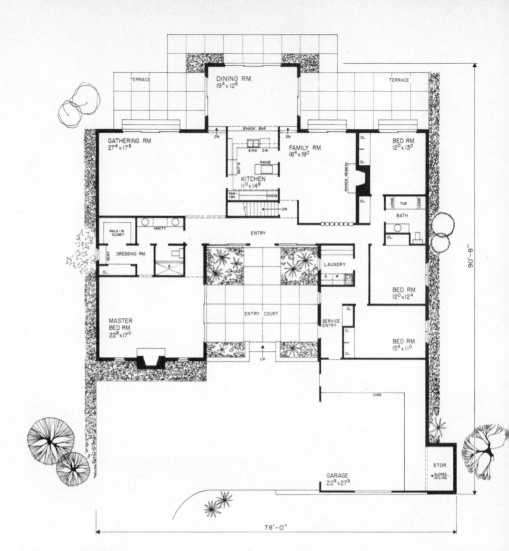

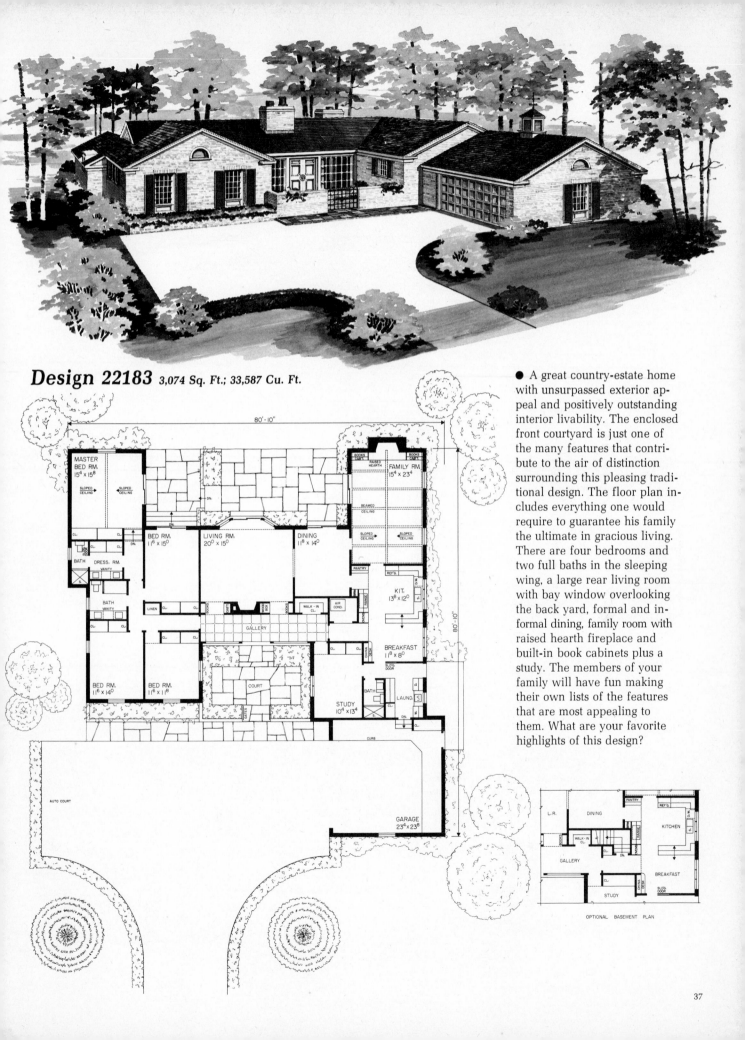

Design 22183 3,074 Sq. Ft.; 33,587 Cu. Ft.

Floor plan labels:

MASTER BED RM. 15⁴ x 15⁸
SLOPED CEILING
SLOPED CEILING
CL. CL.
BATH
DRESS. RM. VANITY
BATH VANITY
LINEN CL.
BED RM. 11⁶ x 15⁰
BED RM. 11⁶ x 14⁰
BED RM. 11⁶ x 11⁸
LIVING RM. 20⁰ x 15⁰
DN.
GALLERY
COURT
GATES
CURB
STUDY 10⁴ x 13⁴
DINING 11⁸ x 14⁰
WALK-IN CL.
AIR COND.
WOOD BOX
BOOKS
CL.
PANTRY
RANGE
REF'G.
D.W.
KIT. 13⁸ x 12⁰
CHINA CL.
BREAKFAST 11⁸ x 8⁰
SLD'G. DOOR
BATH
LAUND.
CL.
BOOKS CAB'T
RAISED HEARTH
FAMILY RM. 15⁴ x 23⁴
BOOKS CAB'T
BEAMED CEILING
SLOPED CEILING
SLOPED CEILING
AUTO COURT
GARAGE 23⁴ x 23⁸

80'-10"
80'-10"

OPTIONAL BASEMENT PLAN

Basement labels:
L.R.
DINING
PANTRY
REF'G.
KITCHEN
WALK-IN CL.
GALLERY
STUDY
CHINA CL.
BREAKFAST
SLD'G. DOOR

● A great country-estate home with unsurpassed exterior appeal and positively outstanding interior livability. The enclosed front courtyard is just one of the many features that contribute to the air of distinction surrounding this pleasing traditional design. The floor plan includes everything one would require to guarantee his family the ultimate in gracious living. There are four bedrooms and two full baths in the sleeping wing, a large rear living room with bay window overlooking the back yard, formal and informal dining, family room with raised hearth fireplace and built-in book cabinets plus a study. The members of your family will have fun making their own lists of the features that are most appealing to them. What are your favorite highlights of this design?

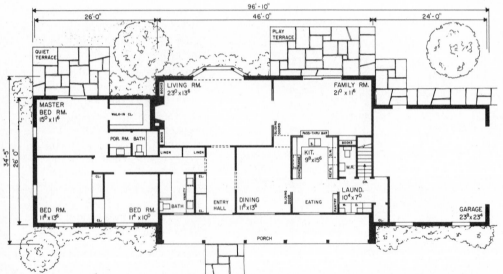

Design 22109
2,054 Sq. Ft.; 38,392 Cu. Ft.

● Long and low are characteristics of this traditional one-story. The main portion of the house is highlighted by the porch with its columns. The shuttered windows and doors add their note of distinction. The breadth of this design is emphasized by the addition of the two wings. One comprises the attached two-car garage. The other, the sleeping area made up of three bedrooms and two full baths. The master bedroom has its own compartmented bath, the huge walk-in closet, and sliding glass doors to its quiet terrace.

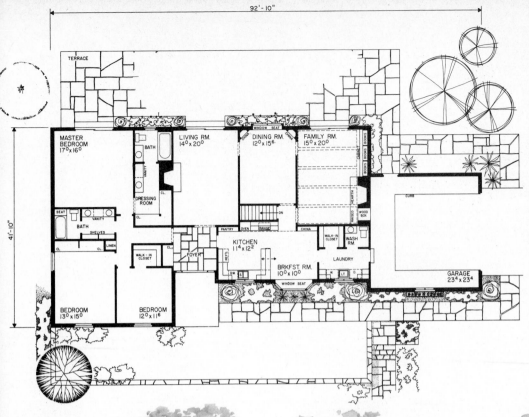

Design 22675
2,478 Sq. Ft.; 43,156 Cu. Ft.

● Many extra features have been designed into this delightfully traditional home. Book shelves and cabinets are in the family room, china cabinets and a window seat are in the dining room, a second window seat is in the breakfast room, a large dressing room with vanity is in the master bedroom and the list can go on. Two fireplaces, one in each of the living areas. If you like this design, but are in need of a four bedroom home, please see our Design 22181 on Page 7.

Design 21170
2,000 Sq. Ft.; 24,840 Cu. Ft.

● Footnote to perfection. This L-shaped traditional design tells a fine story of excellent proportion. Its appeal is its delightful simplicity. The large family will find its living patterns admirably taken care of by this attractive home. A family with many members needs well-organized space in which to move around. Here, traffic circulation will be orderly. The double front doors are recessed and protected by the roof overhang. From the formal entry hall traffic can flow directly to the living room, the family room-kitchen area, or to the sleeping area. The kitchen serves both the dining and family rooms equally well. The inside bath is conveniently accessible from the living areas and the bedrooms.

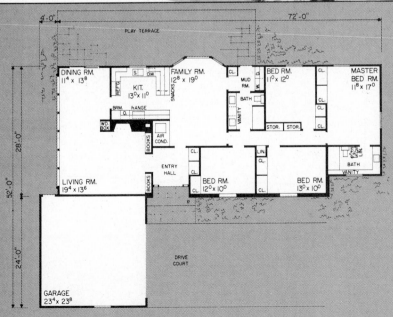

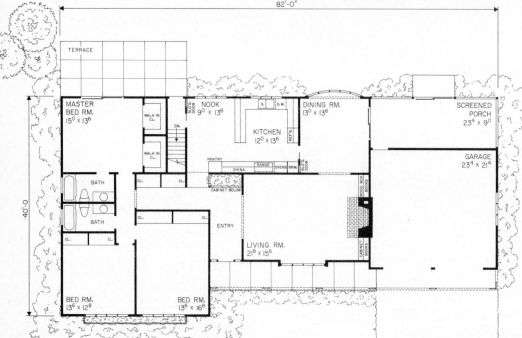

Design 22260
2,041 Sq. Ft.; 41,248 Cu. Ft.

● Upon entering thru the front door of this hip-roof traditional, one is taken by the built-in planter atop a practical storage cabinet. A look into the living room reveals an attractive fireplace flanked by book shelves, cabinet and wood box. A step into the master bedroom brings into view the twin walk-in closets and sliding glass doors to the rear terrace. Moving into the kitchen one observes the fine counter and cupboard space. This efficient work area is but a step from the informal nook and the formal dining room. Behind the garage is a large covered screened porch.

● For country-estate living. This L-shaped traditional home will be a worthy addition to any building site. Its pleasing proportions are almost breathtaking and seem to foretell the tremendous amount of livability its inhabitants are sure to enjoy. The zoning for pleasurable living could hardly be improved upon. The children's bedrooms function together in a wing with its own bath. There is a large master bedroom suite.

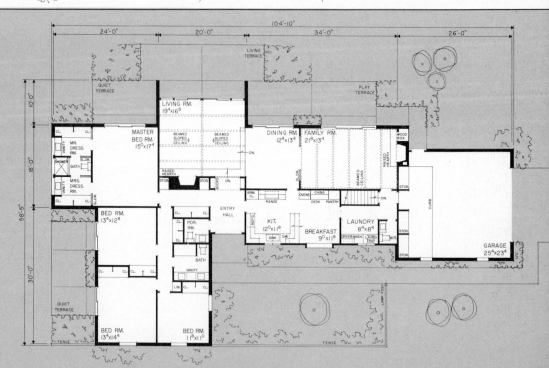

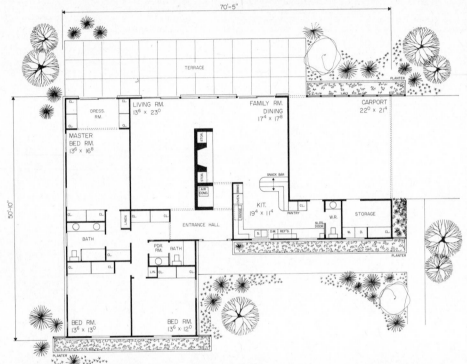

TERRACE

DRESS. RM.

LIVING RM.
13⁶ x 23⁰

FAMILY RM.
DINING
17⁴ x 17⁸

CARPORT
22⁰ x 21⁴

PLANTER

MASTER BED RM.
13⁶ x 16⁸

AIR COND.

SNACK BAR

KIT.
19⁴ x 11⁴

PANTRY

W.R.

STORAGE

CL.

LINEN

ENTRANCE HALL

SLD. DOOR

D.W.

REF'S.

W. D.

CL.

BATH

PDR. RM.

BATH

LIN.

PLANTER

BED RM.
13⁶ x 13⁰

BED RM.
13⁶ x 12⁰

PLANTER

70'-5"

50'-10"

Design 22268
2,183 Sq. Ft.; 23,475 Cu. Ft.

● Reminiscent of Florida, yet this appealing design need not to be built with a palm tree nearby to complete the picture. In fact, with minor modifications it would adapt well to the more northerly climates. The wide overhanging roof functions as a sun visor for the shuttered window. A delightful measure of appeal is added by the long, low planting areas. The double front doors open to the center entrance hall. It is here that efficient traffic patterns become apparent. Looking out upon the rear yard are two living areas. They are partially, and effectively, separated by the fireplace wall.

Design 21952   2,705 Sq. Ft.; 41,582 Cu. Ft.

Design 21929 2,312 Sq. Ft.; 26,364 Cu. Ft.

● There's more to this U-shaped, traditional adaptation than meets the eye. Much more! And, yet, what does meet the eye is positively captivating. The symmetry of the pediment gables, the window styling, the projecting garden wall, the iron gates, and the double front doors, are extremely pleasing. Once inside, a quick tour reveals plenty of space and a super-abundance of features. Each of the rooms is extra large and allows for fine furniture placement. In addition to the raised hearth fireplace, the family room highlights built-in book shelves, sliding glass doors and beamed ceilings.

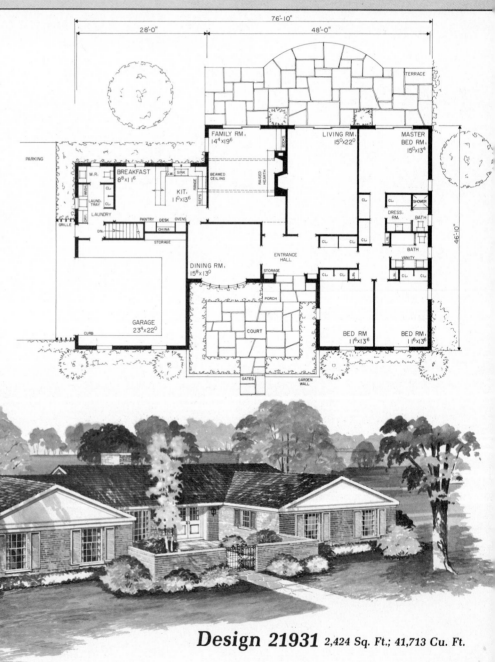

Design 21931 2,424 Sq. Ft.; 41,713 Cu. Ft.

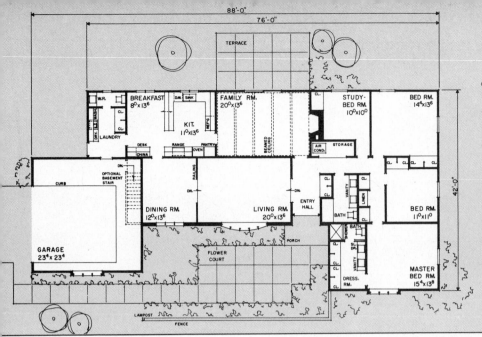

● This home will lead the hit parade in your new subdivision. Its sparkling, traditionally styled exterior will be the favorite of all that pass. And, once inside, friends will marvel at how the plan just seems to cater to your family's every activity. When it comes to eating, you can eat in the informal breakfast room or the formal dining room. As you come in the front door you may sit down and relax in the sunken living room or the beamed ceiling family room. Two full baths with built-in vanities, plus the extra wash room will more than adequately serve the family.

● Here is an exquisite U-shaped home that has an exciting story to tell about pleasureable indoor-outdoor living relationships. Wherever you may be standing in this four bedroom home, you will be a few steps from a set of sliding glass doors which open to outdoor terraces. The formal dining room, with its large bay of windows, will be a most pleasant place to eat. Also an informal breakfast nook with built-in pantry and china cabinets.

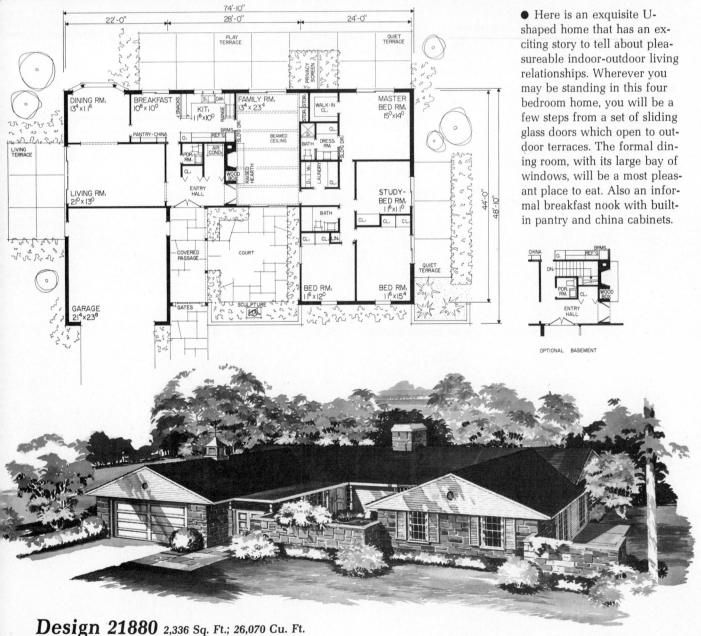

Design 21880 *2,336 Sq. Ft.; 26,070 Cu. Ft.*

Design 22269 2,652 Sq. Ft.; 29,470 Cu. Ft.

Design 21201 2,960 Sq. Ft.; 48,274 Cu. Ft.

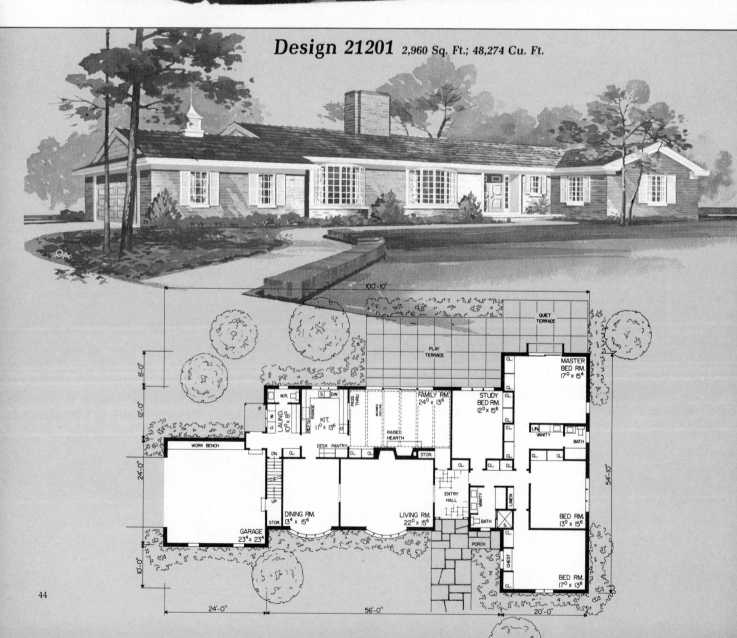

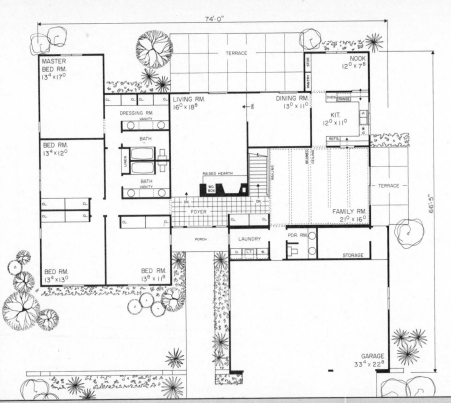

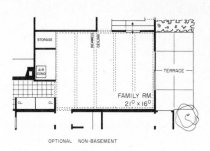

OPTIONAL NON-BASEMENT

● Here on these two pages are three totally different designs. Not only is there a great difference in their exterior character, there is a similar divergence in their size and the living patterns offered. Consider your family's living habits and how they may adapt to each of these three delightful homes. Which best suits your family's routine?

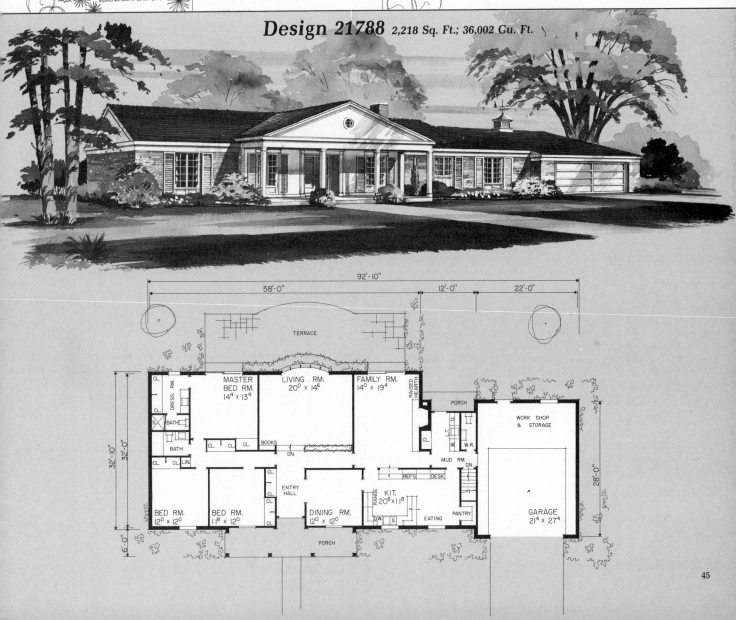

Design 21788 2,218 Sq. Ft.; 36,002 Cu. Ft.

Design 22259

2,016 Sq. Ft.; 43,337 Cu. Ft.

● Here is a 28 x 72 foot basic rectangle which houses 2,016 square feet of livability. Because of its rectangular shape it will be most economical to build. The projecting garage adds delightfully to the overall appeal and permits the utilization of a smaller building site. The covered front porch provides sheltered passage between the house and the garage. Inside there is a whale of a lot of livabiltiy. There are four bedrooms, two baths, laundry area, family room, large kitchen, spacious living and dining area. There is a fireplace flanked by book shelves and sliding glass doors to terraces.

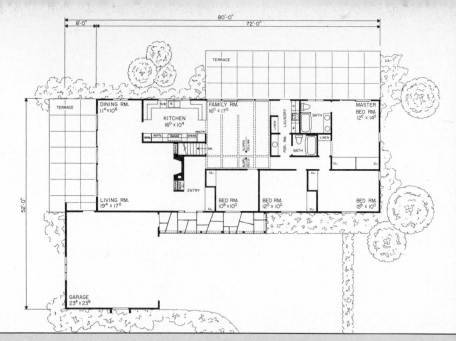

Design 22233

2,166 Sq. Ft.; 43,217 Cu. Ft.

● An L-shaped traditional with more than its full share of charm. There are features galore to recommend this home to the active family. In many ways the floor plan is unique. For instance, the covered front porch provides sheltered access to the garage from the foyer. Further, the location of the basement stairs makes that area equally accessible from house and garage. Also, observe the positioning of the laundry. It is, indeed a strategic one. Then, there is the placement of the kitchen only a step or two from the breakfast nook, and the family and dining rooms. While the family room with its beamed ceiling, and raised hearth fireplace will be in constant use, the living room will be a favorite spot, too. No cross room traffic in this floor plan.

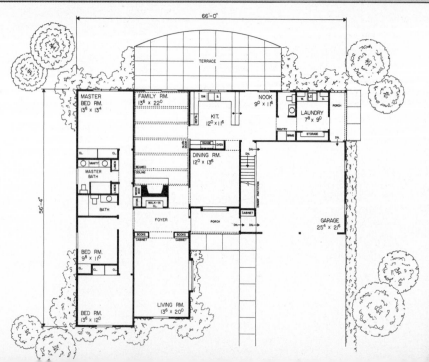

46

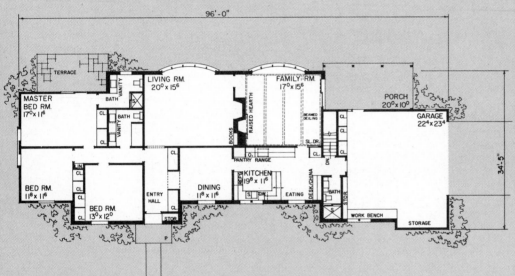

96' - 0"

TERRACE

MASTER
BED RM.
17⁰ x 11⁶

BATH

VANITY

LIVING RM.
20⁰ x 15⁶

CL

BATH

VANITY

CL

CL

BED RM.
11⁸ x 11⁶

LIN
CL

CL

CL

BED RM.
13⁰ x 12⁰

ENTRY
HALL

STOR.

P

CL

DINING
11⁸ x 11⁶

BOOKS

RAISED HEARTH

FAMILY RM.
17⁰ x 15⁶

BEAMED
CEILING

PANTRY RANGE

KITCHEN
19⁸ x 11⁶

DESK/CHINA

REF.

S

DW.

EATING

SL. DR.

CL

DW.

BATH

STOR.

WORK BENCH

PORCH
20⁰ x 10⁰

GARAGE
22⁴ x 23⁴

STORAGE

34'- 5"

Design 21144
2,064 Sq. Ft.; 29,579 Cu. Ft.

● Natural quarried stone, an interesting roof line, delightful window treatment, and a recessed front entrance give this traditional home an aura of quiet charm. Of particular interest inside are the multiple dining arrangements. There's a separate dining room for formal diners, a breakfast nook, and a snack bar. Both the family room and master bedroom have their outdoor living areas. Three full baths, two with stall showers, provide ample facilities. Each of the living areas feature an attractive fireplace — one with a raised hearth.

● A house that has everything is
generally hard to find. Yet, here is
one that seems to lack nothing that
will help guarantee many years of
the utmost in comfort and convenience. Behind this handsome facade
there is a heap of living potential.
Two full baths, one with stall shower, the other with a vanity, service
the four bedroom sleeping area.
The quiet living and dining rooms
are cheerful and spacious. Separating the U-shaped kitchen work
center from the family room is a
large storage unit featuring upper
and lower cabinets and a pass-thru
forming a snack bar.

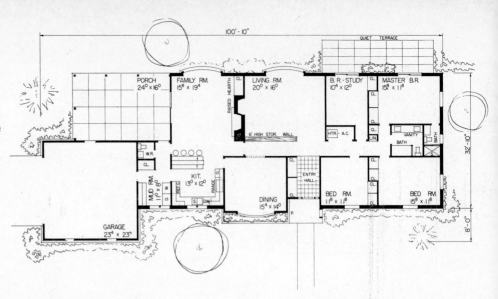

● A real charmer, is this traditional
ranch home with its horizontal siding, natural stone, delightful windows, recessed double doors, and
attached garage with planting box
and cupola. It is further enhanced
by excellent zoning. There is a quiet
sleeping area with four bedrooms,
two baths, and lots of closets. There
is the formal living room and separate dining room overlooking the
front yard. At the rear there is the
spacious family-kitchen area with
the laundry and extra wash room
nearby. For outdoor living there are
three separate, but related terraces.

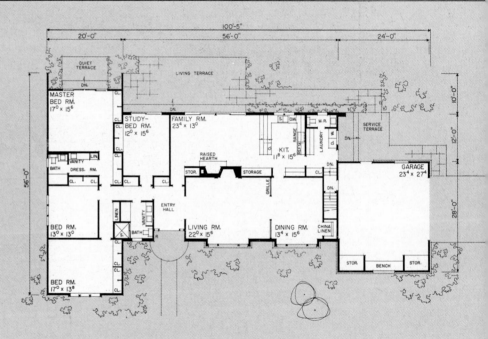

● Dream houses can take many
forms and reflect a variety of living
patterns. Here is one that has all the
prerequisites. Its exterior represents
good designs, while its interior fur-
nishes outstanding livability. The
gracious facade is highlighted by
delightful window treatment, inviting double front doors that are recessed, a long and dramatic roof
plane, and brick veneer construction. The side opening garage adds
to the majestic length of this
country-estate home. Inside there
are a multitude of features. The
rooms are large, well related to one
another, and each has its own outstanding feature or two.

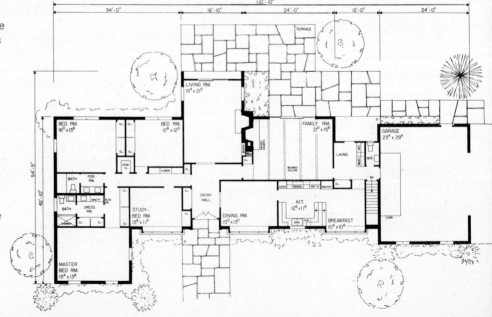

Design 21028 2,430 Sq. Ft.; 29,160 Cu. Ft.

Design 21744 2,914 Sq. Ft.; 49,027 Cu. Ft.

Design 21959 2,904 Sq. Ft.; 45,198 Cu. Ft.

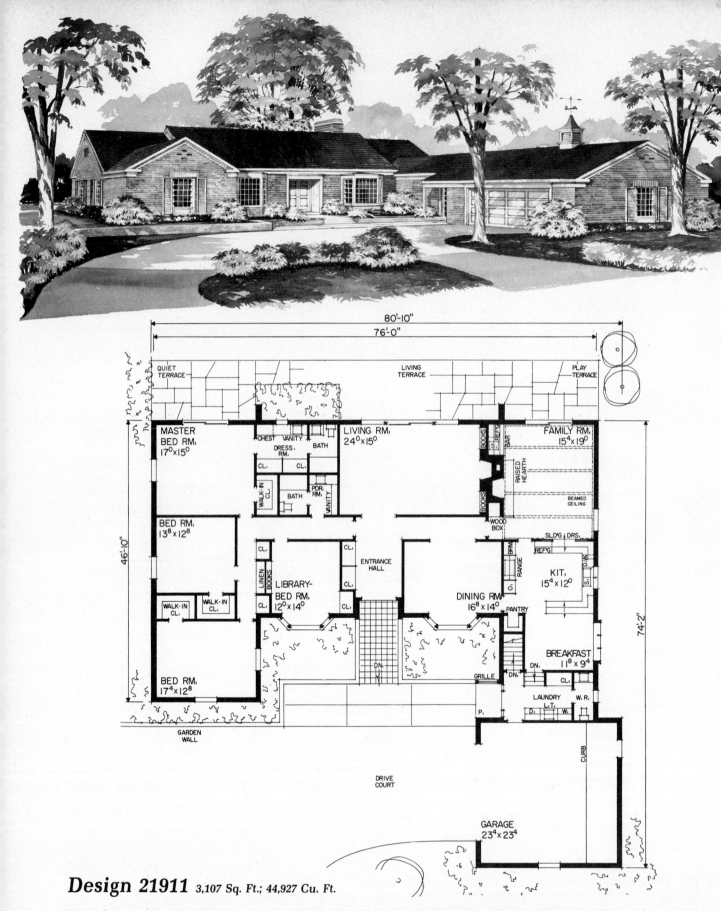

Design 21911 3,107 Sq. Ft.; 44,927 Cu. Ft.

● For luxurious, country-estate living it would be difficult to beat the livability offered by these two impressive traditional designs. To begin with, their exterior appeal is, indeed, gracious. Their floor plans highlight plenty of space, excellent room arrangements, fine traffic circulation, and an abundance of convenient living features. It is interesting to note that each design features similar livability facilities. Both may function as four bedroom homes . . .

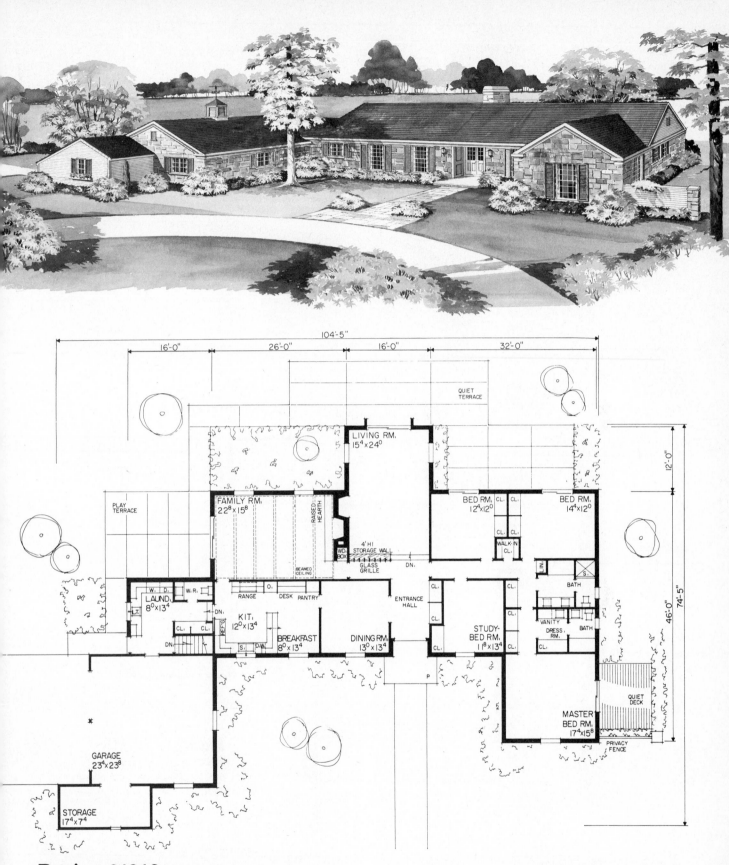

Design 21916 3,024 Sq. Ft.; 46,470 Cu. Ft.

● . . . or three bedroom with a study or library. There are first floor laundries, two fireplaces, formal and informal living and dining areas, fine storage potential, and delightful indoor-outdoor living relationships. You'll have fun listing the built-in features. The two family rooms have beamed ceilings and sliding glass doors to the play terraces. The two living rooms are spacious and enjoy a full measure of privacy. They are but a step from outdoor living.

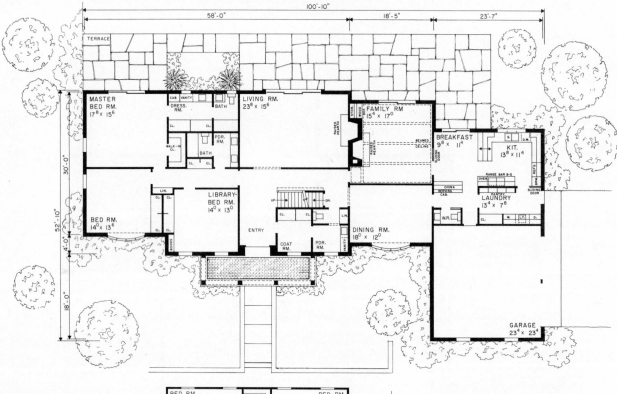

TERRACE

100'-10"
58'-0" **18'-5"** **23'-7"**

MASTER BED RM. 17⁸ x 15⁶

LIVING RM. 23⁸ x 15⁶

FAMILY RM. 15⁴ x 17⁰

BREAKFAST 9⁸ x 11⁴

KIT. 13⁸ x 11⁴

30'-0"

52'-10"

BED RM. 14⁰ x 13⁶

LIBRARY-BED RM. 14⁰ x 13⁰

DINING RM. 18⁰ x 12⁰

LAUNDRY 13⁴ x 7⁸

ENTRY

4'-0"

18'-0"

GARAGE 23⁴ x 23⁴

BED RM. 16⁴ x 11⁶

WALK-IN CL.

BED RM. 16⁶ x 11⁶

ATTIC STOR.

WALK-IN CL.

ATTIC STOR.

SAUNA BATH

BATH

ATTIC STOR.

Design 22133
3,024 Sq. Ft. — First Floor
826 Sq. Ft. — Second Floor
54,883 Cu. Ft.

● A country-estate home which will command all the attention it truly deserves. The projecting pediment gable supported by the finely proportioned columns lends an aura of elegance. The window treatment, the front door detailing, the massive, capped, chimney, the cupola, the brick veneer exterior and the varying roof planes complete the characterization of this impressive home. Inside, there are 3,024 square feet on the first floor. In addition, there is a two bedroom second floor should its development be necessary. However, whether called upon to function as a one, or 1½ story home it will provide a lifetime of gracious living. Don't overlook the compartment baths, the laundry and the many built-ins available.

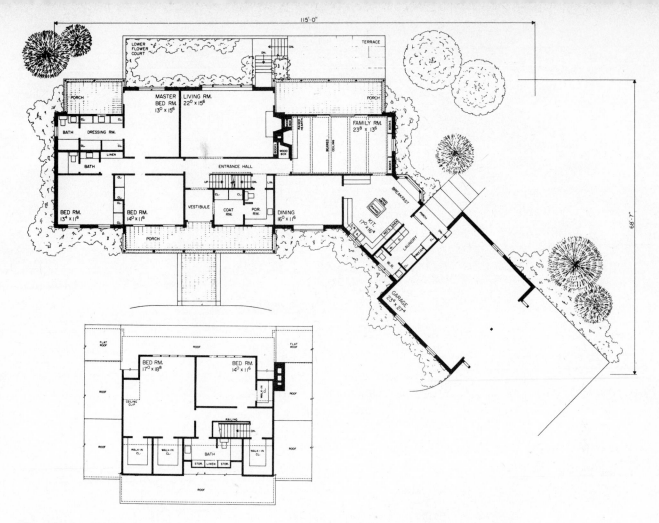

Design 21711 *2,580 Sq. Ft. — First Floor; 938 Sq. Ft. — Second Floor; 46,788 Cu. Ft.*

● If the gracious charm of the Colonial South appeals to you, this may be just the house you've been waiting for. There is something solid and dependable in its well balanced facade and wide, pillared front porch. Much of the interest generated by this design comes from its interesting expanses of roof and angular projection of its kitchen and garage. The feeling of elegance is further experienced upon stepping inside, through double doors, to the spacious entrance hall where there is the separate coat room. Adjacent to this is the powder room, also convenient from the living areas. Work area of kitchen and laundry room is truly outstanding. Designed as a five bedroom house, each is large. Storage and bath facilities are excellent.

Design 21060 3,190 Sq. Ft. — First Floor; 1,024 Sq. Ft. — Second Floor; 52,189 Cu. Ft.

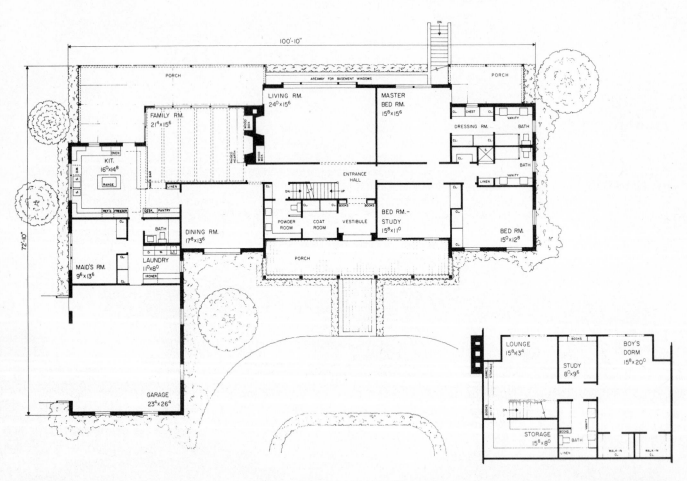

● Like some of the other designs of this section, this Colonial adaptation can be categorized as either a one or 1½ story home. However, you may opt to live in this home as a one-story. You may develop the second

floor as suggested above, or not at all, except for attic storage space. Truly a home of distinction for the large family. Study this plan carefully. List its many features for this is certainly a unique home with unrestricted liv-

ability. It will serve your family's formal and informal living patterns for many years. Don't overlook the bath facilities, or the extra maid's room — use it as a family hobby room if you wish.

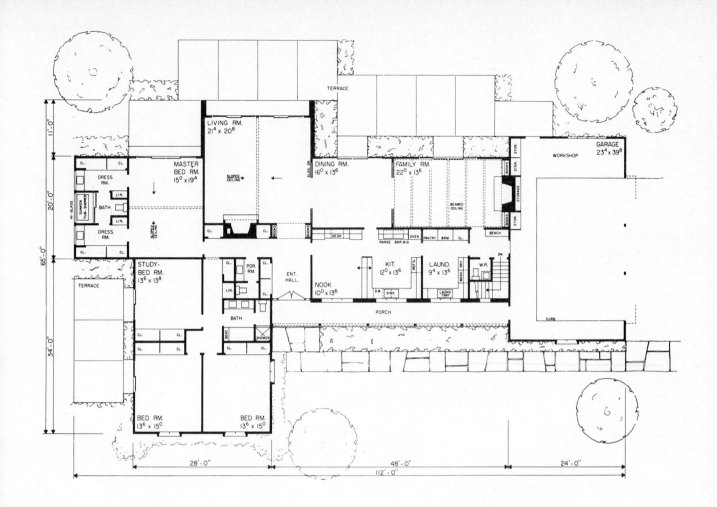

Design 21936 *3,280 Sq. Ft.; 54,619 Cu. Ft.*

● Country-estate living could hardly be better provided for than by this 3,280 square foot home. The arrangement of the numerous rooms places the major living areas to the rear where they enjoy their privacy and function with the outdoors. Count the sliding glass door units. Visualize the gracious indoor/outdoor living to be enjoyed by all the members of the family. Even the children's rooms have a terrace. The homemaker's work center overlooks the front yard and is efficient, indeed. There is a breakfast nook, a U-shaped kitchen, a separate laundry room, an extra wash room and a whole wall of storage facilities. Be sure you notice the powder room.

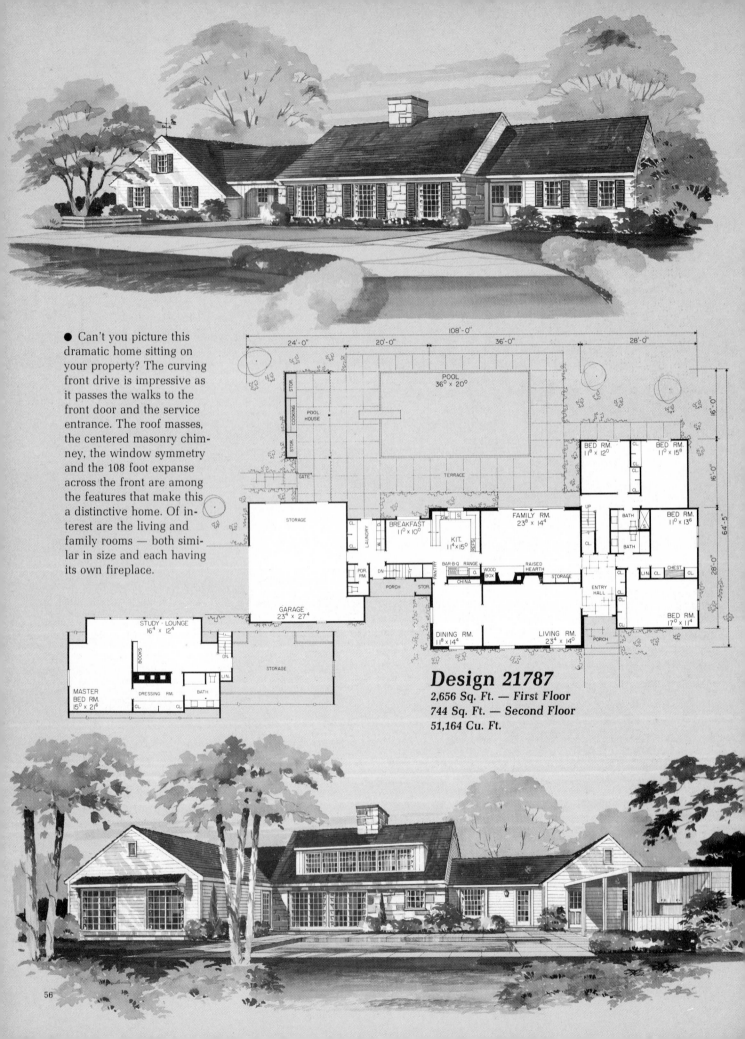

● Can't you picture this dramatic home sitting on your property? The curving front drive is impressive as it passes the walks to the front door and the service entrance. The roof masses, the centered masonry chimney, the window symmetry and the 108 foot expanse across the front are among the features that make this a distinctive home. Of interest are the living and family rooms — both similar in size and each having its own fireplace.

Design 21787

2,656 Sq. Ft. — First Floor
744 Sq. Ft. — Second Floor
51,164 Cu. Ft.

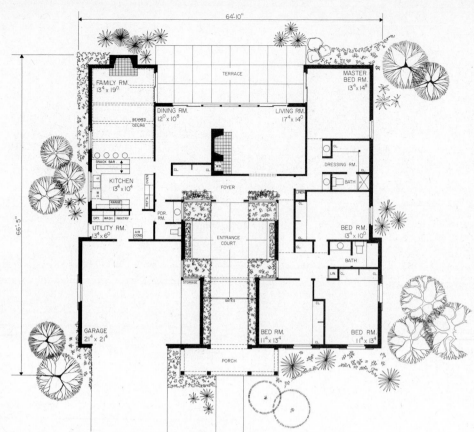

Design 22371

2,389 Sq. Ft.; 29,220 Cu. Ft.

● Here is a unique, brick veneer traditional home with a completely surrounded entrance court. The covered front porch with its well-proportioned columns, provides extra shelter for the covered walkway to the court. This pleasant area provides an effective approach to the double front doors. Glass panels foster the enjoyment of the planting areas from inside. The configuration of this house as it envelopes the court gives rise to interesting roof planes. The interior features an abundance of highlights. They include: two fireplaces, plenty of closets, two full baths plus powder room, beamed ceilinged family room, snack bar with pass-thru to efficient kitchen, utility room, and interior planting units. The recessed rear terrace is accessible through sliding glass doors from the four major rooms (family, living, dining and master bedroom).

Design 22777
2,006 Sq. Ft.; 44,580 Cu. Ft.

● Many years of delightful living will surely be enjoyed in this one-story traditional. The covered front porch adds a charm to the exterior as do the paned windows and winding drive. Inside there is livability galore. An efficient kitchen with island range and adjacent laundry make this work area very pleasing. A breakfast nook with bay window and built-in desk to serve the family when informal dining is called upon plus a formal dining room with sliding glass doors to the rear terrace. The large gathering room with raised hearth fireplace can serve the family on any occasion gracefully. The sleeping wing consists of two bedrooms and a study (or make it three bedrooms). The master bedroom includes all the fine features one would expect: a huge walk-in closet, a vanity, a bath and sliding glass doors to a private terrace.

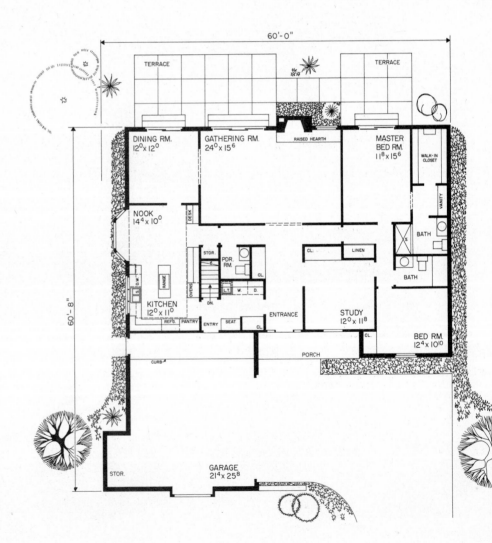

Contemporary Designs
For Lifestyle '80's & Beyond

80'-5"

71'-2"

BED RM.
11⁸ x 15⁰

BED RM.
11⁸ x 15⁰

SKYLIGHT

BATH

CL.

CL.

CL.

SLID. DOOR

CHEST

VANITY

CABINET

CABINET

BOOKS

BOOKS

TERRACE

TERRACE

BEAMED CEILING

FAMILY RM.
21⁴ x 15⁴

SLOPED CEILING

SLOPED CEILING

SNACK BAR

WORK BENCH

HER BATH

WALK-IN CL.

KIT.
13⁴ x 10⁴

PDR. RM.

STOR.

LINEN

SKYLIGHT

SKYLIGHT

AIR COND.

REFG.

RANGE

OVEN

DW.

STOR.

CL.

GARAGE
25⁴ x 21⁴

HIS BATH

MASTER BED RM.
14⁰ x 21⁴

WALK-IN CL.

DINING

GRILLE

FOYER

SLOPED CEILING

SLOPED CEILING

LIVING RM.
21⁴ x 26⁰

BEAMED CEILING

Design 22244
2,489 Sq. Ft.; 30,196 Cu. Ft.

● Contemporary design for those with a flair for individuality and a hankering for new patterns of living.

Design 22730
2,490 Sq. Ft.; 50,340 Cu. Ft.

● Here is a basic one-story home that is really loaded with livability on the first floor and has a bonus of an extra 1,086 sq. ft. of planned livability on a lower level. What makes this so livable is that the first floor adjacent to the stairs leading below is open and forms a balcony looking down into a dramatic planting area. The first floor traffic patterns flow around this impressive and distinctive feature. In addition to the gathering room, study and family room, there is the lounge and activity room. Notice the second balcony open to the activity room below. The master bedroom is outstanding with two baths and two walk-in closets. The attached three-car garage has a bulk storage area and is accessible through the service area.

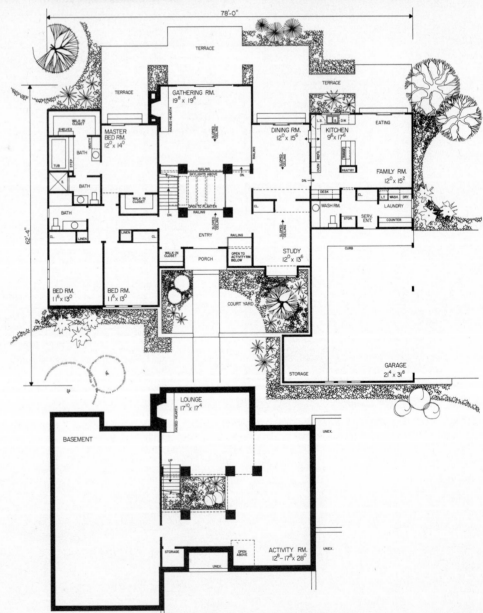

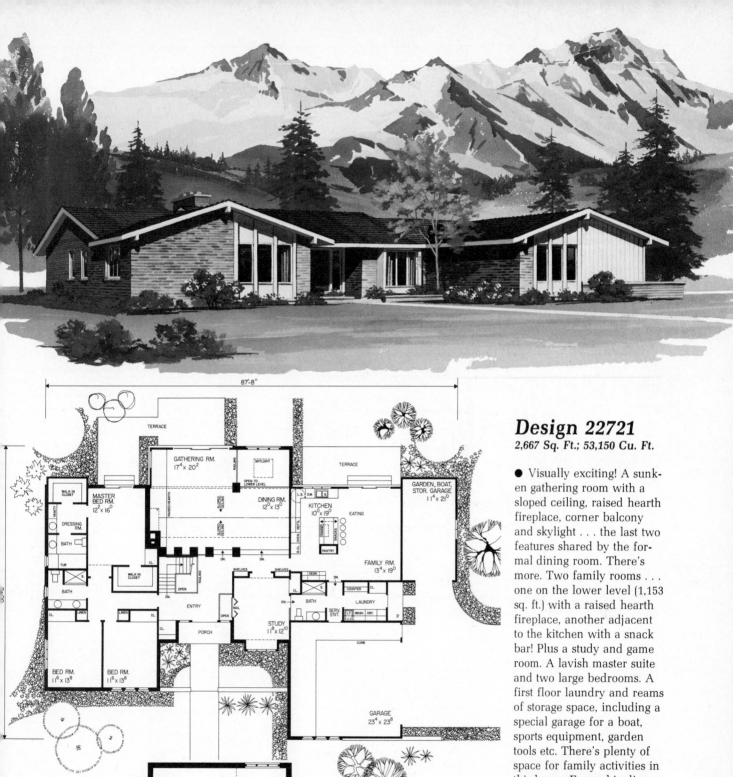

Design 22721
2,667 Sq. Ft.; 53,150 Cu. Ft.

● Visually exciting! A sunken gathering room with a sloped ceiling, raised hearth fireplace, corner balcony and skylight . . . the last two features shared by the formal dining room. There's more. Two family rooms . . . one on the lower level (1,153 sq. ft.) with a raised hearth fireplace, another adjacent to the kitchen with a snack bar! Plus a study and game room. A lavish master suite and two large bedrooms. A first floor laundry and reams of storage space, including a special garage for a boat, sports equipment, garden tools etc. There's plenty of space for family activities in this home. From chic dinner parties for friends to birthday gatherings for kids, there's always the right setting . . . and so much room that adults and children can entertain at the same time.

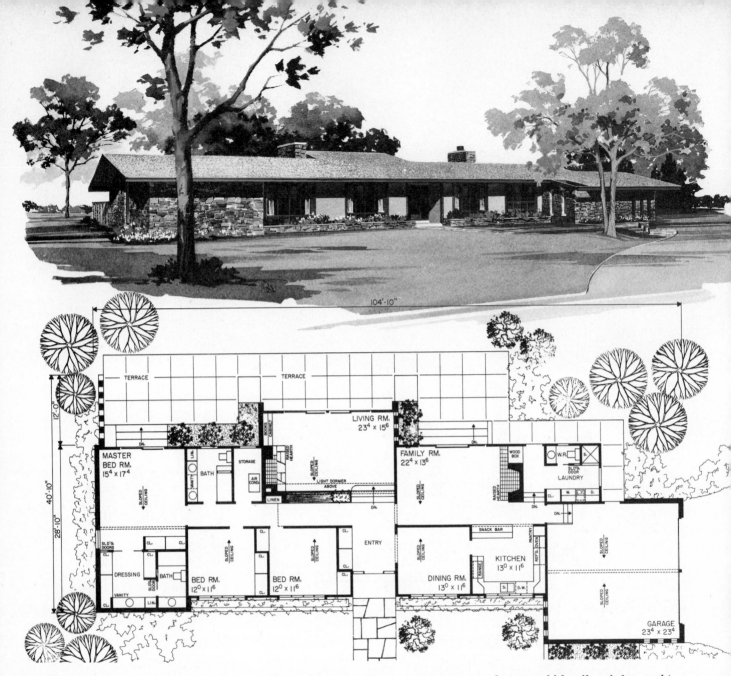

TERRACE   TERRACE

LIVING RM.
23⁴ x 15⁶

MASTER
BED RM.
15⁴ x 17⁴

BATH

STORAGE

FAMILY RM.
22⁴ x 13⁶

WOOD
BOX

W.R.

SLD'G
DOOR

LAUNDRY

LINEN

DRESSING

BATH

BED RM.
12⁰ x 11⁶

BED RM.
12⁰ x 11⁶

ENTRY

SNACK BAR

PANTRY

REF'G. OVEN

KITCHEN
13⁰ x 11⁶

DINING RM.
13⁰ x 11⁶

RANGE

GARAGE
23⁴ x 23⁴

104'-10"

40'-10"   28'-10"   12'-0"

Design 22255
2,356 Sq. Ft.; 24,145 Cu. Ft.

● Convenient living could hardly ask for anything
more. Study this design inside and out. It is positively
outstanding from every angle.

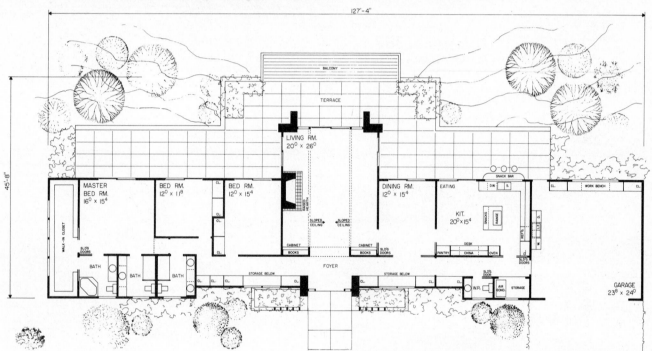

Floor plan labels:

BALCONY

TERRACE

127'-4"

45'-8"

MASTER BED RM. 16⁰ x 15⁴

BED RM. 12⁰ x 11⁸

BED RM. 12⁰ x 15⁴

LIVING RM. 20⁰ x 26⁰

DINING RM. 12⁰ x 15⁴

EATING

KIT. 20⁰ x 15⁴

SNACK BAR

WORK BENCH

GARAGE 23⁸ x 24⁰

WALK-IN CLOSET

SLD'G DOORS

BATH BATH BATH

RAISED HEARTH

SLOPED CEILING SLOPED CEILING

CABINET BOOKS CABINET BOOKS SLD'G DOORS

FOYER

STORAGE BELOW STORAGE BELOW

W.R. AIR COND. STORAGE SLD'G DOOR

PANTRY CHINA OVEN DESK

RANGE REF'S.

Design 22256 2,632 Sq. Ft.; 35,023 Cu. Ft.

● A dream home for those with young ideas. A refreshing, contemporary exterior with a unique, highly individualized interior. What are your favorite features.

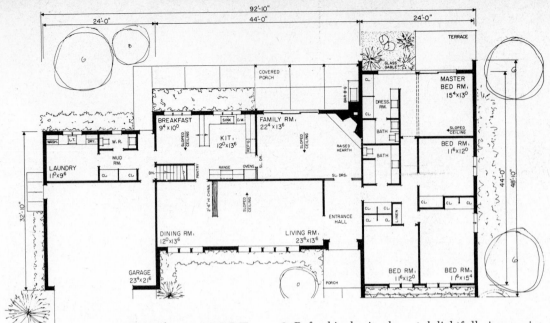

Design 21897
2,628 Sq. Ft.; 38,859 Cu. Ft.

● Refreshingly simple, yet delightfully impressive. The low-pitched roof has a wide overhang with the exposed rafter tails protruding at each gable end. Appealing architectural detailing highlights the projecting bedroom wing. Study the plan carefully. The livability is exceptional.

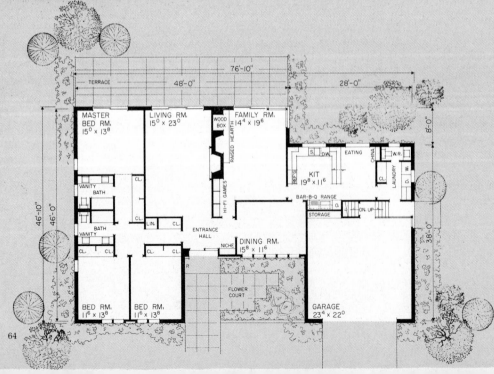

Design 21713
2,374 Sq. Ft.; 33,852 Cu. Ft.

● Are you among those who enjoy informal living, but prefer to keep pots and pans, dirty laundry, and youngsters just learning to feed themselves in the background? Then study this plan carefully. Kitchen and eating nook are neatly tucked in behind the garage, along with an adequately sized laundry and over 100 sq. ft. of eating space. The family room is well located to serve as a transition between the work areas and more formal living space. And the dining room is beautifully planned to overlook the courtyard garden.

Design 21703
2,924 Sq. Ft.; 46,303 Cu. Ft.

● It will be fun, indeed, deciding which of the three designs on these two pages is your family's favorite. Whatever your choice may be, your family will enjoy plenty of space. Observe the sunken master bedroom.

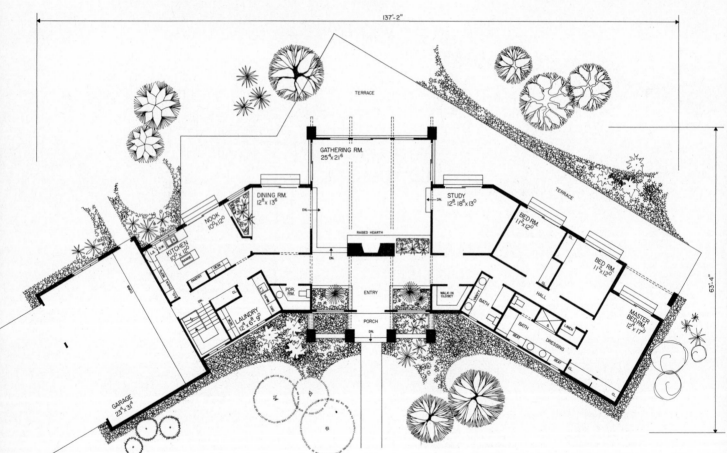

Design 22720 3,130 Sq. Ft.; 45,700 Cu. Ft.

● A raised hearth fireplace lights up the sunken gathering room which is exceptionally large and located at the very center of this home! For more living space, a well-located study and formal dining room each having a direct entrance to the gathering room. Plus a kitchen with all the right fea-tures . . . an island range, pantry, built-in desk and separate breakfast nook. There's an extended terrace, too . . . accessible from every room! And a master suite with double clos-ets, dressing room and private bath. Plus two family bedrooms, a first-floor laundry and lots of storage space. A basement too, for additional space. This is a liveable home! You can entertain easily or you can hide-out with a good book. Study this plan with your family and pick out your favorite features. Don't miss the dra-matic front entry planting areas, or the extra curb area in the garage.

Design 22534 3,262 Sq. Ft.; 58,640 Cu. Ft.

● The angular wings of this ranch home surely contribute to the unique character of the exterior. These wings effectively balance what is truly a dramatic and inviting front entrance. Massive masonry walls support the wide overhanging roof with its exposed wood beams. The patterned double front doors are surrounded by delightful expanses of glass. The raised planters and the masses of quarried stone (make it brick if you prefer) enhance the exterior appeal. Inside, a distinctive and practical floor plan stands ready to shape and serve the living patterns of the active family. The spacious entrance hall highlights sloped ceiling and an attractive open stairway to the lower level recreation area. An impressive fireplace and an abundance of glass are features of the big gathering room. Interestingly shaped dining room and study flank this main living area. The large kitchen offers many of the charming aspects of the family-kitchen of yesteryear. The bedroom wing has a sunken master suite.

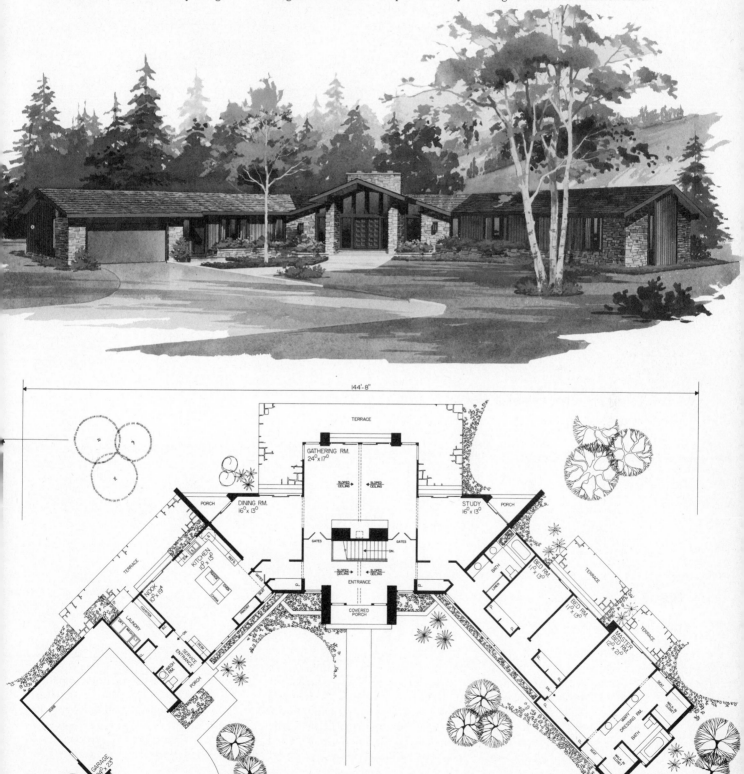

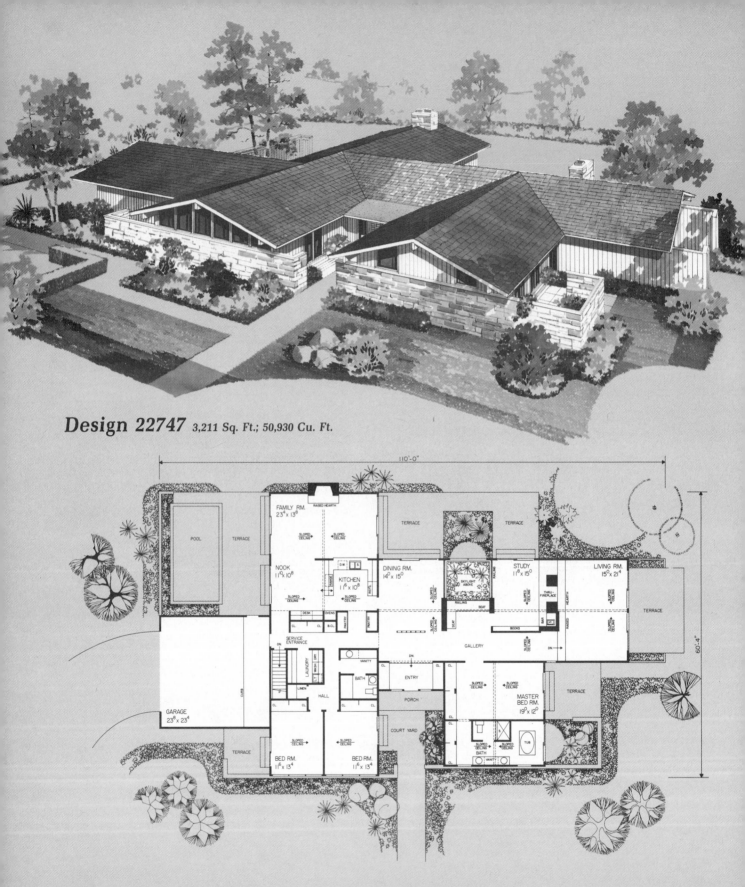

Design 22747 3,211 Sq. Ft.; 50,930 Cu. Ft.

● This home will surely provide its occupants with a glorious adventure in contemporary living. Its impressive exterior seems to foretell that great things are in store for even most casual visitor. A study of the plan reveals a careful zoning for both the younger and older family members. The quiet area consists of the exceptional master bedroom suite with private terrace, the study and the isolated living room. For the younger generation, there is a zone with two bedrooms, family room and nearby pool. The kitchen is handy also and serves the nook and family rooms well. Be sure not to miss the sloping ceilings, the dramatic planter and the functional terrace.

● Skylights in the kitchen! That's putting good design where you spend your time. There's more. A U-shaped work area, built-in range and oven, pantry and a spacious breakfast nook with sliding glass doors onto a dining terrace. Formal living and dining rooms with a shared fireplace and direct access to the terrace/garden court area. A luxury master suite with a dressing area, huge walk-in closet and private bath. Plus two large family bedrooms also with walk-in closets that open onto a third terrace. A first floor laundry with plenty of counter space and lots of convenient storage. The roof of the attached three-car garage extends to provide a dramatic covered walkway to the double front doors. This house has all the features that make life easy and delightful.

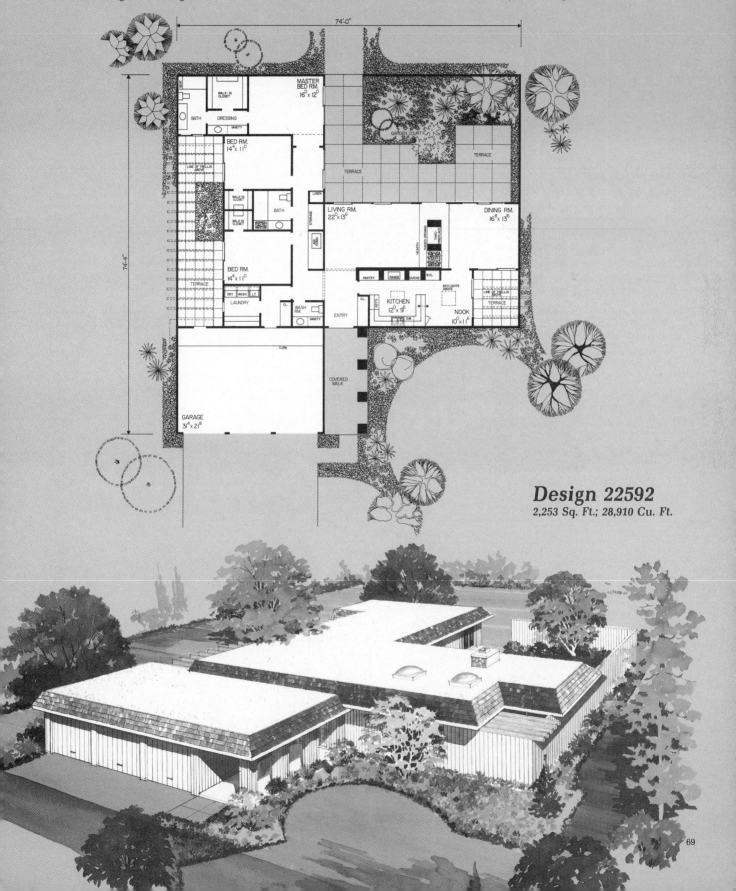

Design 22592
2,253 Sq. Ft.; 28,910 Cu. Ft.

Design 22523
2,055 Sq. Ft.; 43,702 Cu. Ft.

● You'll want the investment in your new home to be one of the soundest you'll ever make. And certainly the best way to do this is to make sure your new home has unexcelled exterior appeal and outstanding interior livability. For those who like refreshing contemporary lines, this design will rate at the top. The wide overhanging roof, the brick masses, the glass areas, the raised planters, and the covered front entrance highlight the facade. As for the interior, all the elements are present to assure fine living patterns. Consider the room relationships and how they function with one another. Note how they relate to the outdoors.

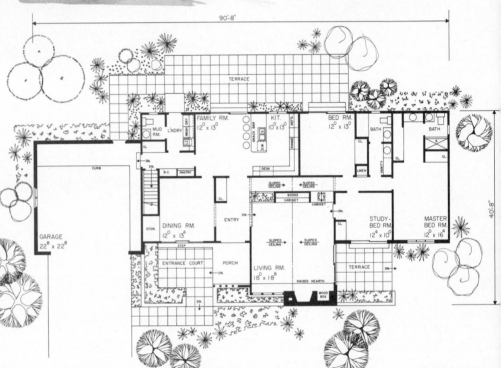

Design 21111
2,248 Sq. Ft.; 18,678 Cu. Ft.

● "Great", will be just the word to characterize the ownership of this home. The trim hip-roof with its wide overhang, the massiveness of the vertical brick piers, and the extension of the brick wall to form a front court are but a few of the features. Among the other features include the four bedrooms, two full baths and extra wash room, a spacious L-shaped living and dining area, a dramatic family room and a mud room.

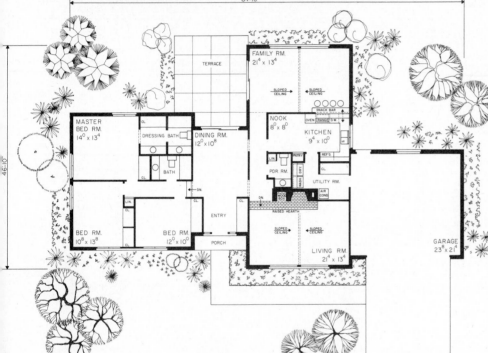

TERRACE

FAMILY RM.
21⁴ x 13⁴

SLOPED CEILING   SLOPED CEILING

MASTER BED RM.
14⁰ x 13⁴

DRESSING BATH

DINING RM.
12⁰ x 10⁸

NOOK
8⁰ x 8⁰

KITCHEN
9⁴ x 10⁰

SNACK BAR

OVEN | RANGE | D.W.

REF'G.

BATH

LIN.

POR. RM.

WASH | DRY

ENTRY

UTILITY RM.

BED RM.
10⁸ x 13⁸

LIN.

DN.

CL.

ENTRY

DN.

HEATER BOX

AIR COND.

RAISED HEARTH

BED RM.
12⁰ x 10⁰

PORCH

SLOPED CEILING   SLOPED CEILING

LIVING RM.
21⁴ x 13⁴

GARAGE
23⁸ x 21⁴

84'-10"

46'-10"

Design 22359
2,078 Sq. Ft.; 22,400 Cu. Ft.

● The low-pitched, wide-overhanging roof with its exposed beams, acts as a visor for the dramatic glass gable end of the projecting living room. This will be an exceedingly pleasant room with its sunken floor, sloped ceiling, large glass area, and raised hearth fireplace. At the rear of this living rectangle is the family room. This room also has a sloped ceiling and a glass gable end. In addition, there is the snack bar and sliding glass doors to the protected terrace. Between these two living areas is the efficient kitchen with its adjacent eating area. The utility room and its laundry equipment is nearby, as is the powder room. A separate dining room acts as the connecting link to the bedroom zone. Note the master bedroom with its dressing room, twin lavatories and two closets.

Design 22860
2,240 Sq. Ft.; 27,685 Cu. Ft.

● Here is truly a unique home to satisfy your family's desires for something appealing and refreshing. This three bedroom home is also, the very embodiment of what's new and efficient in planning and technology. This is an excellent example of outstanding coordination of house structure, site, interior livability and the sun. Orienting this earth sheltered house toward the south assures a warm, bright and cheerful interior. Major contributions to energy-efficiency result from the earth covered roof, the absence of northern wall exposure and the lack of windows on either end of the house. This means a retention of heat in the winter and cool air in the summer. An effective use of skylights provide the important extra measure of natural light to the interior. Sliding glass doors in the living and dining rooms also help bring the light to the indoors. This earth sheltered house makes no sacrifice of good planning and excellent, all 'round livability. The section is cut through the living room and the skylit hall looking toward the bedrooms.

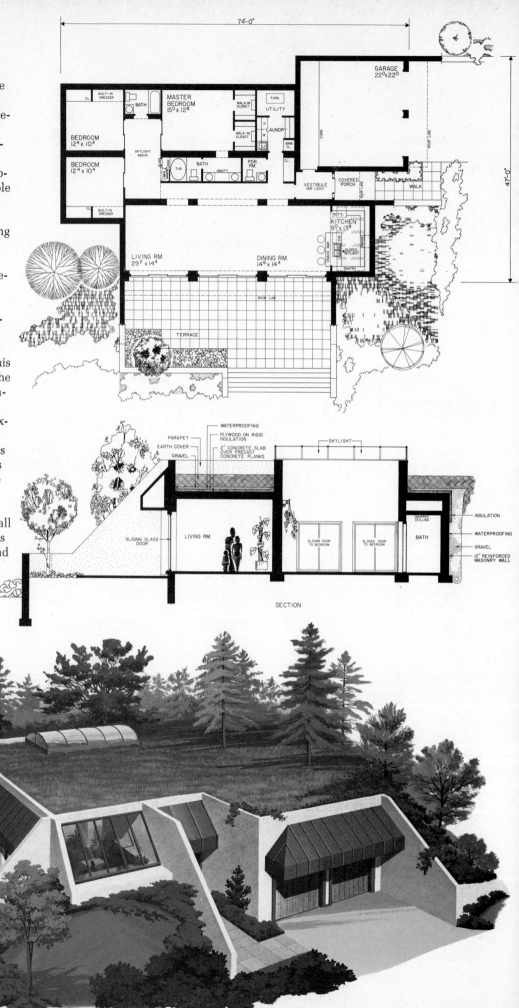

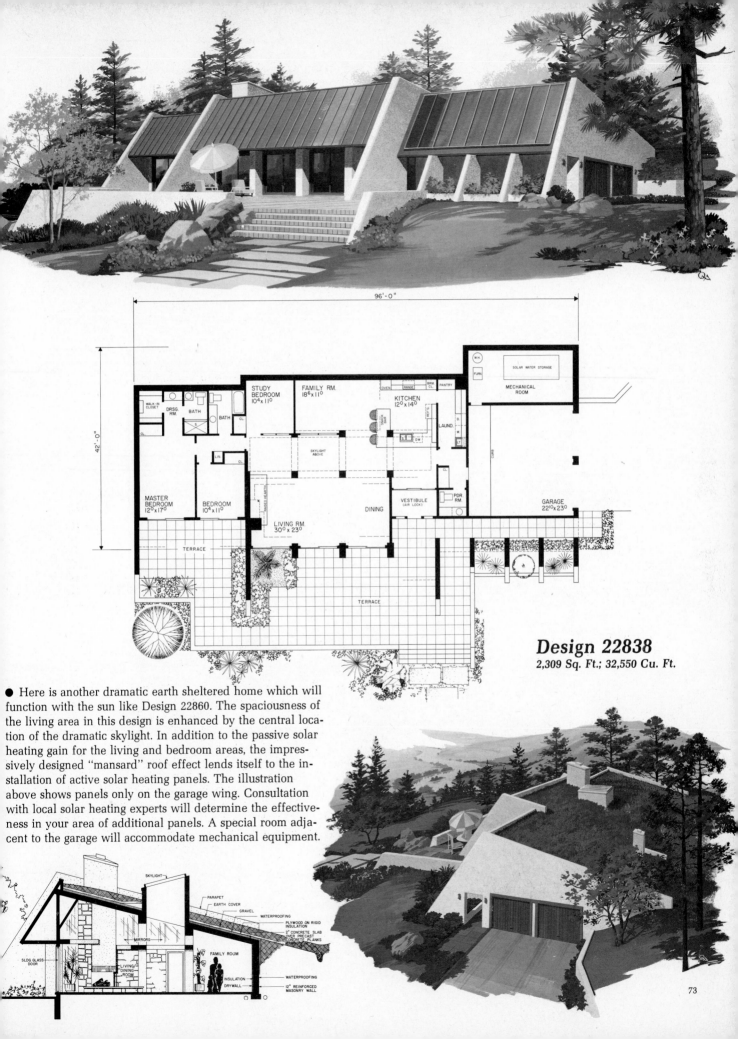

Design 22838
2,309 Sq. Ft.; 32,550 Cu. Ft.

● Here is another dramatic earth sheltered home which will function with the sun like Design 22860. The spaciousness of the living area in this design is enhanced by the central location of the dramatic skylight. In addition to the passive solar heating gain for the living and bedroom areas, the impressively designed "mansard" roof effect lends itself to the installation of active solar heating panels. The illustration above shows panels only on the garage wing. Consultation with local solar heating experts will determine the effectiveness in your area of additional panels. A special room adjacent to the garage will accommodate mechanical equipment.

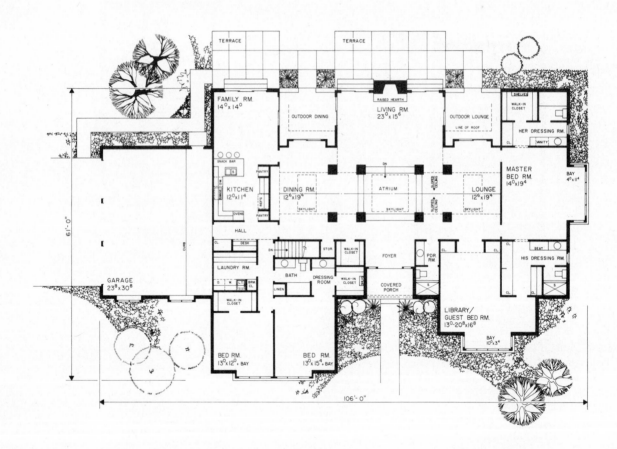

Design 22791 3,809 Sq. Ft.; 64,565 Cu. Ft.

● The use of vertical paned windows and the hipped roof highlight the exterior of this unique design. Upon entrance one will view a charming sunken atrium with skylight above plus a skylight in the dining room and one in the lounge. Formal living will be graciously accommodated in the living room. It features a raised hearth fireplace, two sets of sliding glass doors to the rear terrace plus two more sliding doors, one to an outdoor dining terrace and the other to an outdoor lounge. Informal living will be enjoyed in the family room with snack bar and in the large library. All will praise the fine planning of the master suite. It features a bay window, "his" and "her" dressing room with private baths and an abundance of closet space.

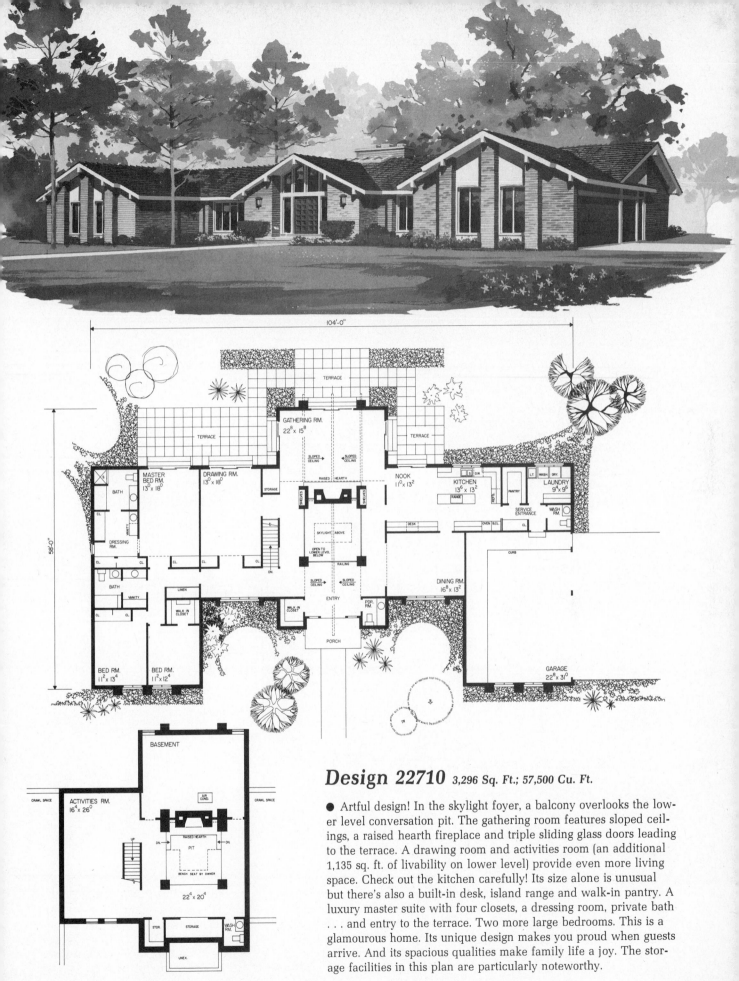

Design 22710 *3,296 Sq. Ft.; 57,500 Cu. Ft.*

● Artful design! In the skylight foyer, a balcony overlooks the lower level conversation pit. The gathering room features sloped ceilings, a raised hearth fireplace and triple sliding glass doors leading to the terrace. A drawing room and activities room (an additional 1,135 sq. ft. of livability on lower level) provide even more living space. Check out the kitchen carefully! Its size alone is unusual but there's also a built-in desk, island range and walk-in pantry. A luxury master suite with four closets, a dressing room, private bath . . . and entry to the terrace. Two more large bedrooms. This is a glamourous home. Its unique design makes you proud when guests arrive. And its spacious qualities make family life a joy. The storage facilities in this plan are particularly noteworthy.

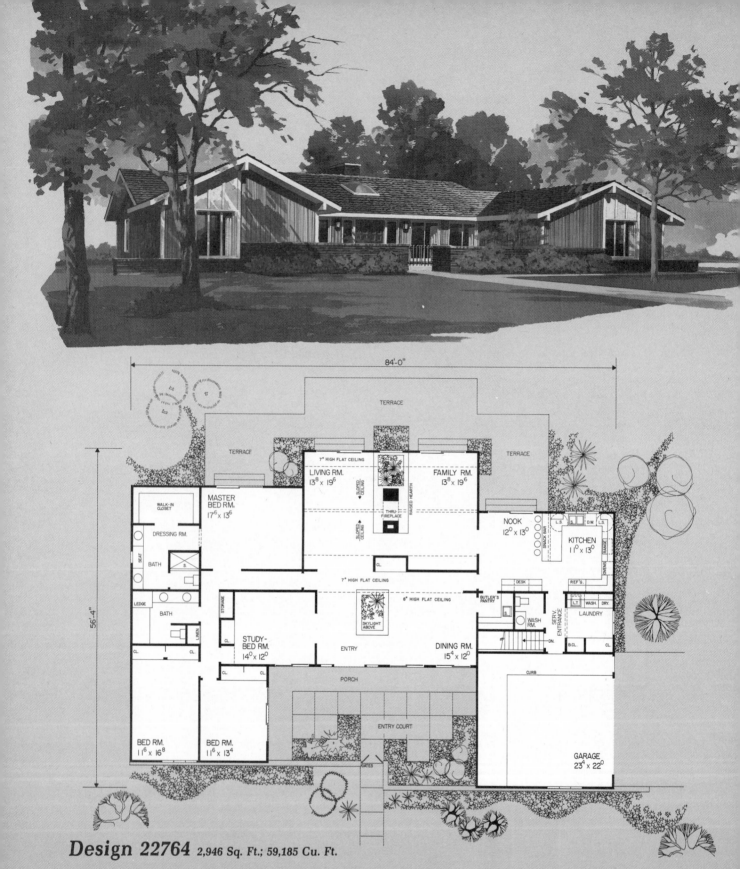

Design 22764 2,946 Sq. Ft.; 59,185 Cu. Ft.

● If uniqueness is what you're looking for in your new home then this three (optional four) bedroom design will be ideal. Notice the large gated-in entry court, vertical paned windows and contrasting exterior materials. All of these features compose an attractive design suitable for any location. Within but a second after entering this home one will be confronted with features galore. The entry/dining area has a focal point of a built-in planter with sky-light above. The living room and family room both have an attractive sloped ceiling. They share a raised hearth thru-fireplace and both have access to the large wrap-around terrace. The kitchen-nook area also has access to the terrace and has the features of a snack bar, built-in desk and large butler's pantry.

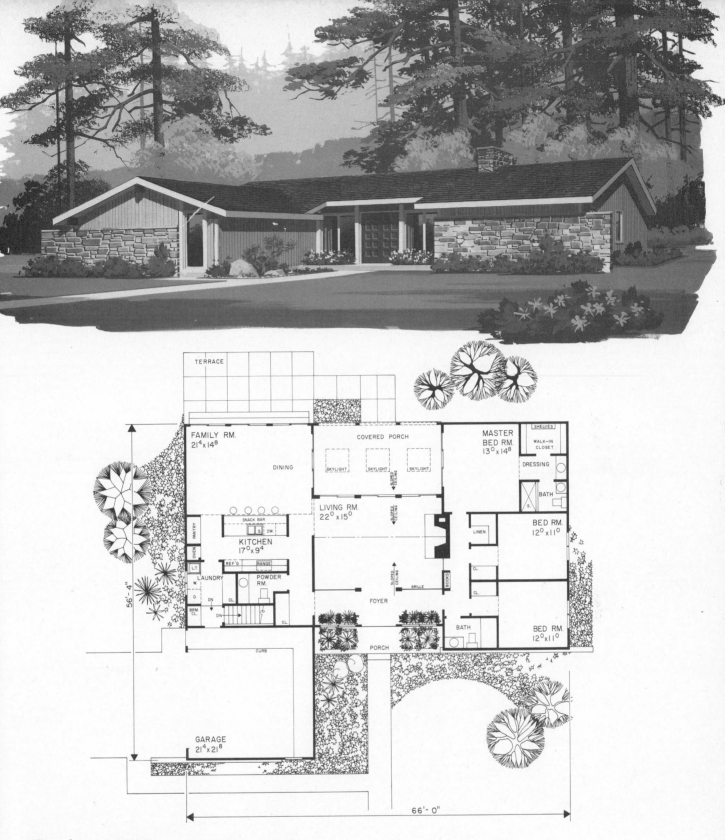

TERRACE

FAMILY RM.
21⁴ x 14⁸

DINING

COVERED PORCH

SKYLIGHT   SKYLIGHT   SKYLIGHT

SLOPED CEILING

MASTER
BED RM.
13⁰ x 14⁸

SHELVES

WALK-IN
CLOSET

DRESSING

BATH

SNACK BAR

KITCHEN
17⁰ x 9⁴

PANTRY

OVEN

LIVING RM.
22⁰ x 15⁰

SLOPED CEILING

LINEN

BED RM.
12⁰ x 11⁰

REF'G   RANGE

LT.

LAUNDRY

POWDER
RM.

W.
D.
BRM
CL.

CL.

DN
DN

CL.

SLOPED CEILING

GRILLE

BOOKS

CL.
CL.

FOYER

CURB

PORCH

BATH

BED RM.
12⁰ x 11⁰

GARAGE
21⁴ x 21⁸

56'- 4"

66'- 0"

Design 22790 2,075 Sq. Ft.; 45,630 Cu. Ft.

● Enter this contemporary hip-roofed home through the double front doors and immediately view the sloped ceilinged living room with fireplace. This room will be a sheer delight when it comes to formal entertaining. It has easy access to the kitchen and also a powder room nearby. The work area will be convenient. The kitchen has an island work center with snack bar. The laundry is adjacent to the service entrance and stairs leading to the basement. This area is planned to be a real "step saver". The sleeping wing consists of two family bedrooms, bath and master bedroom suite. Maybe the most attractive feature of this design is the rear covered porch with skylights above. It is accessible by way of sliding glass doors in the family/dining area, living room and master bedroom.

Design 22793 2,065 Sq. Ft.; 48,850 Cu. Ft.

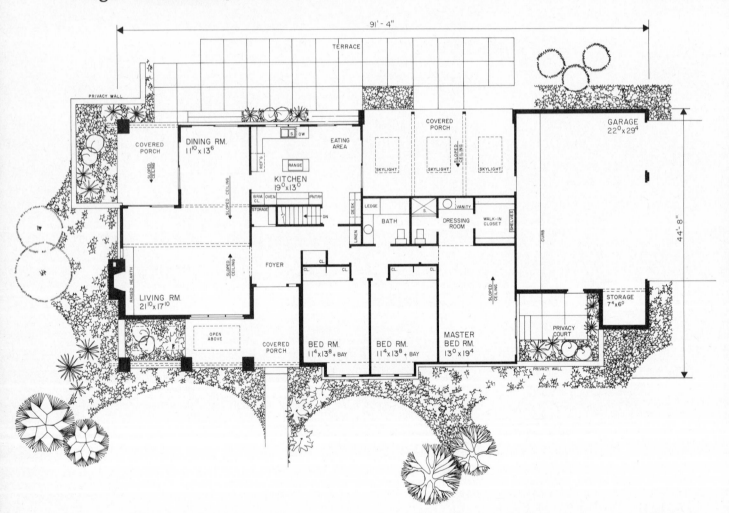

● Privacy will be enjoyed in this home both inside and out. The indoor-outdoor living relationships offered in this plan are outstanding. A covered porch at the entrance. A privacy court off the master bedroom divided from the front yard with a privacy wall. A covered porch serving both the living and dining rooms through sliding glass doors. Also utilizing a privacy wall. Another covered porch off the kitchen eating area. This one is the largest and has skylights above. Also a large rear terrace. The kitchen is efficient with eating space available, an island range and built-in desk. Storage space is abundant. Note storage area in the garage and its overall size. Three front bedrooms. Raised hearth fireplace in the living room.

Design 22765 3,365 Sq. Ft.; 59,820 Cu. Ft.

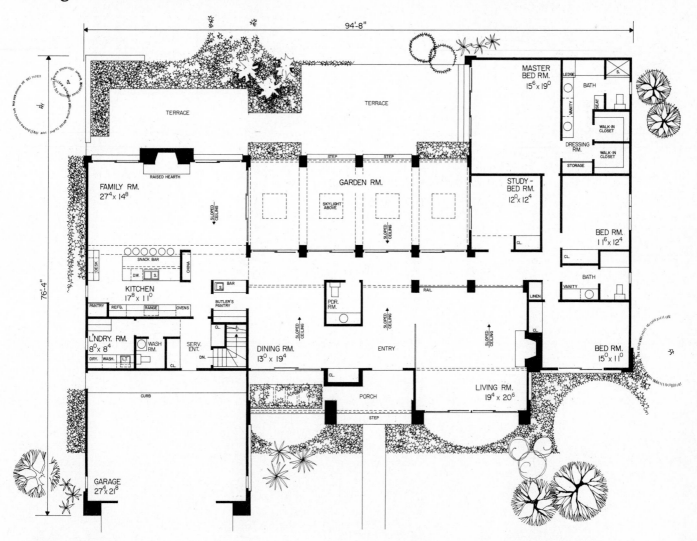

94'-8"

76'-4"

TERRACE

TERRACE

RAISED HEARTH

FAMILY RM.
27⁴ x 14⁸

GARDEN RM.

SKYLIGHT
ABOVE

SLOPED CEILING

MASTER BED RM.
15⁶ x 19⁰

LEDGE

S.

BATH

VANITY

SEAT

WALK-IN CLOSET

DRESSING RM.

WALK-IN CLOSET

STORAGE

STUDY - BED RM.
12⁰ x 12⁴

CL.

BED RM.
11⁶ x 12⁴

CL.

BATH

VANITY

SNACK BAR

CHINA

DESK

DW.

S.

KITCHEN
17⁸ x 11⁰

PANTRY

REFG.

RANGE

OVENS

BUTLER'S PANTRY

CL.

BAR

S.

PDR. RM.

SLOPED CEILING

SLOPED CEILING

RAIL

LINEN

CL.

SLOPED CEILING

L'NDRY. RM.
8⁰ x 8⁴

WASH RM.

SERV. ENT.

DRY.

WASH.

LT.

CL.

DINING RM.
13⁰ x 19⁴

DN.

ENTRY

CURB

CL.

PORCH

LIVING RM.
19⁴ x 20⁶

STEP

BED RM.
15⁰ x 11⁰

GARAGE
27⁴ x 21⁸

● This three (optional four) bedroom contemporary is a most appealing design. It offers living patterns that will add new dimensions to your everyday routine. The sloped ceilings in the family room, dining room and living room add much spaciousness to this home.

The efficient kitchen has many fine features including the island snack bar and work center, built-in desk, china cabinet and wet bar. Adjacent to the kitchen is a laundry room, wash room and stairs to the basement. Formal and informal living will each have its own

area. A raised hearth fireplace and sliding glass doors to the rear terrace in the informal family room. Another fireplace in the front formal living room. You will enjoy all that natural light in the garden room from the skylights in the sloped ceiling.

Design 22866 2,371 Sq. Ft.; 50,120 Cu. Ft.

● An extra living unit has been built into the design of this home. It would make an excellent "mother-in-law" suite. Should you choose not to develop this area as indicated, maybe you might use it as two more bedrooms, a guest suite or even as hobby and game rooms. Whatever its final use, it will compliment the rest of this home. The main house also deserves mention. The focal point will be the large gathering room. Its features include a skylight, sloped ceiling, centered fireplace flanked on both sides by sliding glass doors and adjacent is a dining room on one side, study on the other. The work center is clustered together. Three bedrooms and two baths make up the private area. Note the outdoor areas: court with privacy wall, two covered porches and a large terrace.

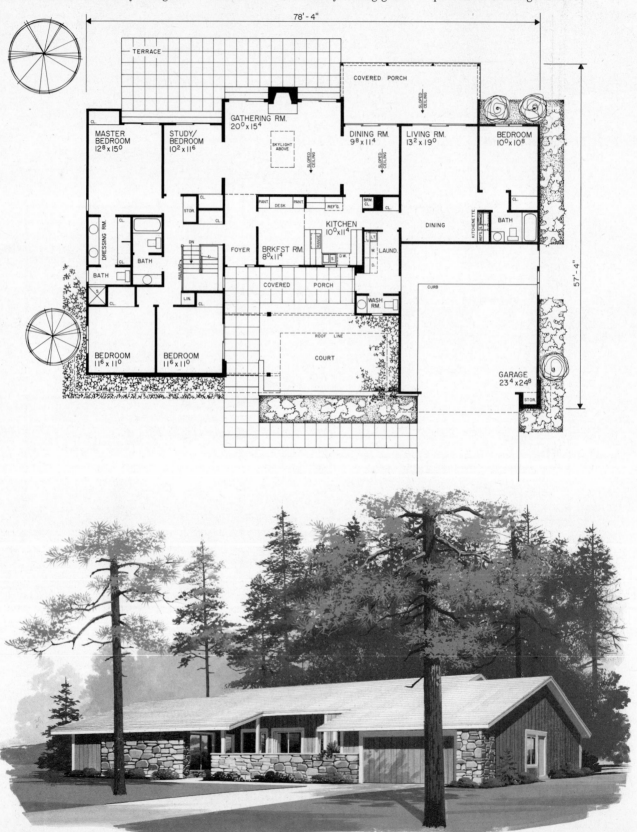

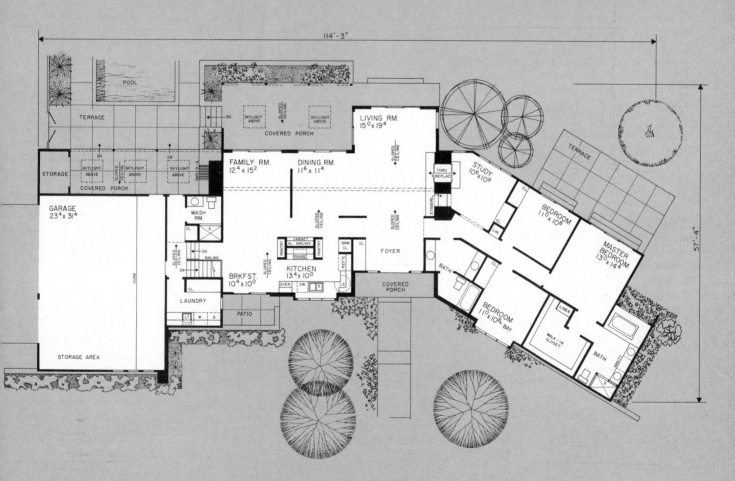

Design 22819 2,459 Sq. Ft.; 45,380 Cu. Ft.

● Indoor-outdoor living will be enjoyed to the fullest in this rambling one-story contemporary plan. Each of the rear rooms in this design, excluding the study, has access to a terrace or porch. Even the front breakfast room has access to a private dining patio. The covered porch off the living areas, family, dining and living rooms, has a sloped ceiling and skylights. A built-in barbecue unit and a storage room will be found on the second covered porch. Inside, the plan offers exceptional living patterns for various activities. Notice the thru-fireplace that the living room shares with the study. A built-in etagere is nearby. The three-car garage has an extra storage area.

Design 21026
2,506 Sq. Ft.; 26,313 Cu. Ft.

● When you move into this attractive home you'll find you and your family will begin to experience new dimensions in living. All areas will be forever conscious of the beauty of the out-of-doors. The front entry court provides both the quiet living room and the formal dining room with a delightful view. The functional terraces will expand the horizons of each of the other rooms. While the raised hearth fireplaces of the two living areas are major focal points, there are numerous convenient living features which will make everyday living a joy. Some of these features are the mud room, the pantry, the planning desk with china storage above, the snack bar and pass-thru. As noted in the illustration, an optional basement plan is included.

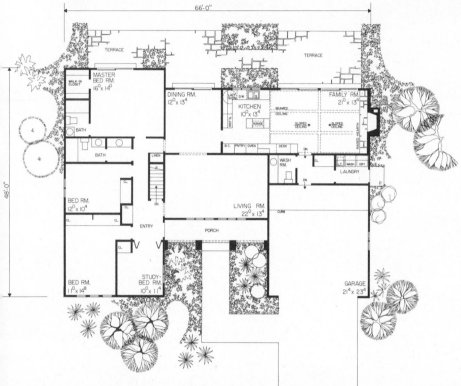

Design 22532
2,112 Sq. Ft.; 42,300 Cu. Ft.

● Here is a refreshing, modified U-shaped contemporary that is long on both looks and livability. The board and batten exterior creates simple lines which are complimented by the low-pitched roof with its wide overhang and exposed rafters. The appeal of the front court is enhanced by the massive stone columns at the edge of the covered porch. A study of the floor plan reveals interestingly different and practical living patterns. The location of the entry hall represents a fine conservation of space for the living areas. The L-shaped formal living-dining zone has access to both front and rear yards. The informal living area is a true family kitchen. Its open planning produces a spacious and cheerful area. Note sloping, beamed ceiling, raised hearth fireplace and sliding glass doors.

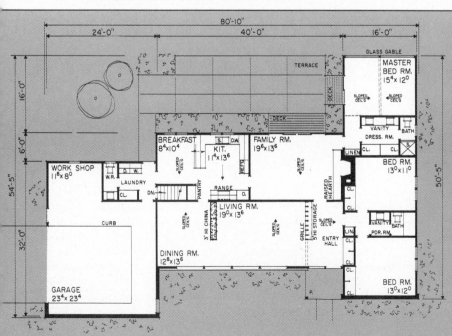

Design 21844
2,047 Sq. Ft.; 32,375 Cu. Ft.

● A sparkling contemporary with all the elements to help assure a lifetime of complete livability. This one-story home is essentially a frame dwelling with two dramatic areas of durable and colorful quarried stone. The low-pitched, wide-overhanging roof provides shelter for the front porch. In addition, it acts as a visor for the large glass areas. The plan is positively outstanding. The informal areas are to the rear of the plan and overlook the rear terrace. The formal, separate dining room and living room are strategically located to the front. The sleeping zone comprises a wing of its own with the master bedroom suite apart from the children's room. Don't miss the extra wash room, laundry and shop. Basement stairs are near this work area.

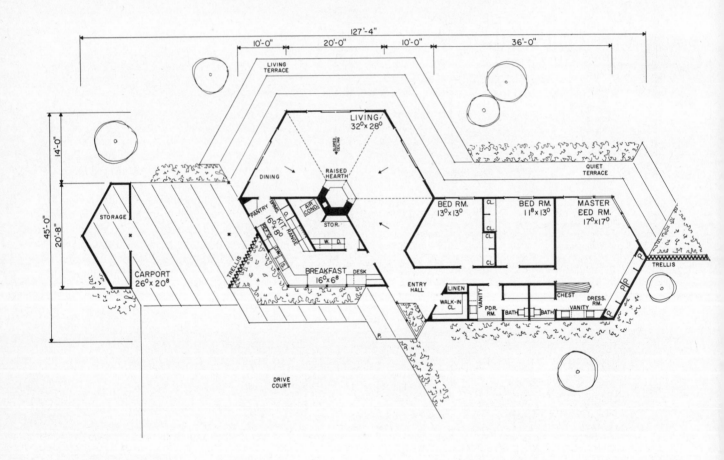

Design 21830 2,140 Sq. Ft.; 20,409 Cu. Ft.

● Interesting shapes make interesting plans and interesting plans frequently lead to new and exciting living patterns. This impressive facade houses a full measure of adventuresome living. And all of it practical and efficient.

The dramatic entry hall sets the stage. Its captivating angles are highlighted by the large glass panels which come to a point and help show-off the sunken planting area. The sleeping zone is outstanding. Each room features

sliding glass doors for access to the quiet terrace. The two baths are compartmented with the master bath highlighted by a vanity and twin lavatories. A wall of closets and built-in chest complete master bedroom.

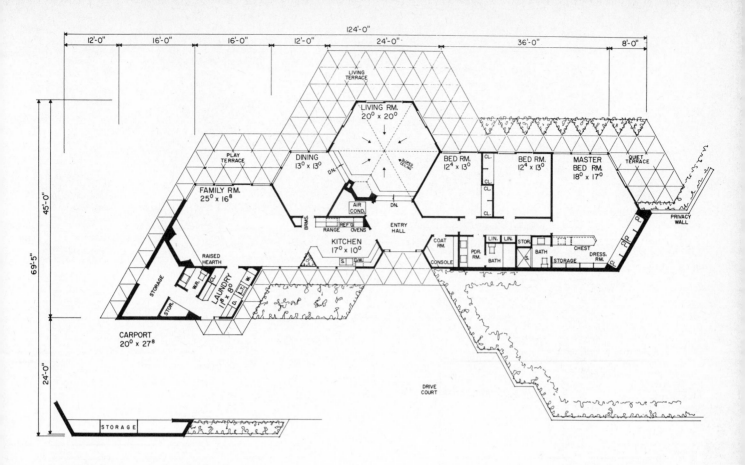

Design 21792 2,600 Sq. Ft.; 22,780 Cu. Ft.

● This plan will foster new dimensions in living. These will result from the dramatic interior and exterior wall angles and the delightful glass areas. The formal front exterior gives way to a rear exterior which permits a sweeping view of the outdoors from each of the major rooms. The kitchen, on the other hand, views the front yard and is but a step from the angular front entry hall. The rooms that are particularly noteworthy are the family room, the living room, and the master bedroom. All are spacious, have large glass areas, and function to the rear with their own outdoor terraces. Between the family room and carport is a fine, highly organized storage area.

Design 23157
2,296 Sq. Ft.; 23,534 Cu. Ft.

● Interesting? Indeed it is. And, practical, too! Projecting the glass gable end of this house with its wide overhanging roof toward the street creates a refreshing "new look". A roof covering the terrace attaches the two-car garage to the house. A masonry wall helps assure a fine degree of privacy to this family room terrace. The other side of the house also has a terrace. This quiet area is accessible from the formal living areas and master bedroom. The sleeping zone is highlighted by four bedrooms and two full baths. The living zone has both the formal and informal living areas. And the homemaker's center has an efficient U-shaped kitchen, a mud room area, a washer and dryer and a wash room.

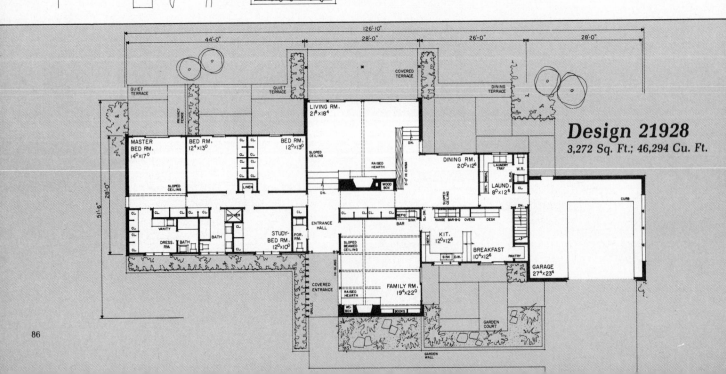

Design 21928
3,272 Sq. Ft.; 46,294 Cu. Ft.

Design 21937
2,052 Sq. Ft.; 36,931 Cu. Ft.

● A unique floor plan with an equally refreshing exterior. This modified L-shape home offers the active family excellent zoning. Here, the bedroom wing is off by itself with the big living room acting as a buffer from the informal activities of the family room. The location of the separate dining room is off the entrance hall, free of traffic, yet but a couple of steps from the wonderfully efficient U-shaped kitchen. The functioning of the informal areas — the kitchen and family room — is particularly noteworthy. They work well together without disturbing any other area of the house. The stairs to the basement are ideally located as are the two full baths. Observe how they serve various areas.

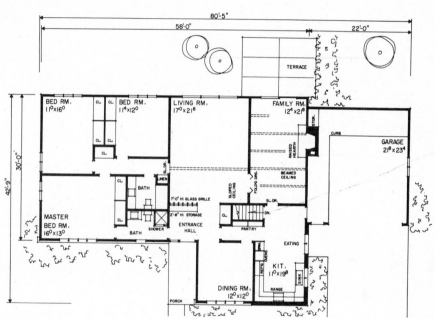

● If it is a house of distinction you are after you'll find that this contemporary home is worthy of your careful consideration. The dramatic exterior is a sure-fire stopper. Even the most casual passer-by will take that second look. The interesting roof surfaces, the massive brick chimney wall, the recessed front entrance, the raised planters, and the garden wall are among the features that spell design distinction. And yet, the exterior in only part of the story this home has to tell. Its interior is no less unique. Consider the sunken living room, the sloping beamed ceiling of the family room, the wonderful kitchen/laundry area, the fine sleeping area with all those closets, bath facilities, and sliding doors.

Design 22304

2,313 Sq. Ft.; 26,110 Cu. Ft.

● What an appealing home! And what a list of reasons why it is so eye-catching. First of all, there is the irregular shape and the low-pitched, wide-overhanging roof. Then, there is the interesting use of exterior materials, including vertical glass window treatment. Further, there are the raised planters flanking the proch of the recessed entrance. Inside, the traffic patterns are excellent. Among the focal points is the 33 foot, beam ceilinged living area. This will surely be fun to plan and furnish for the family's living and dining pursuits. Among other highlights is the layout of the laundry-kitchen-nook area. The extra wash room is strategically located. The sleeping wing has much to offer with its privacy, its convenient bath facilities, and its fine storage.

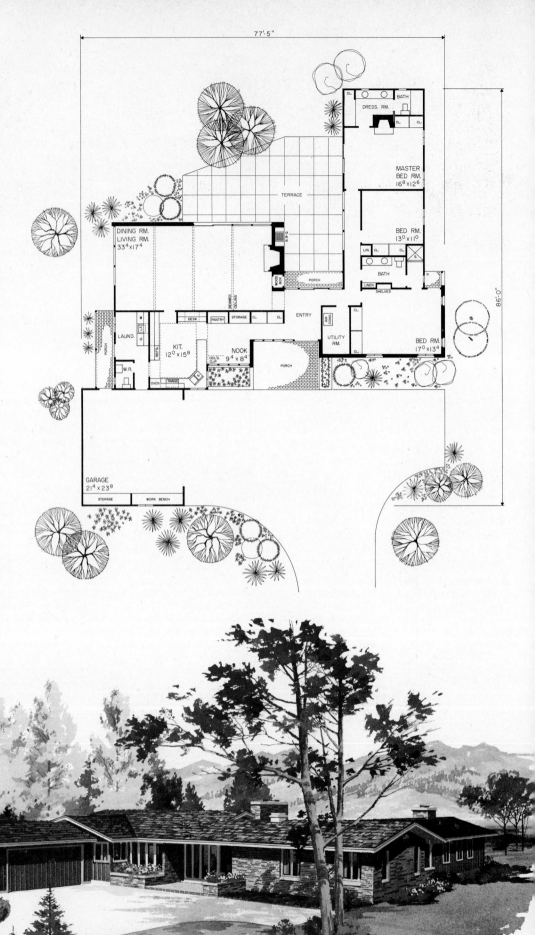

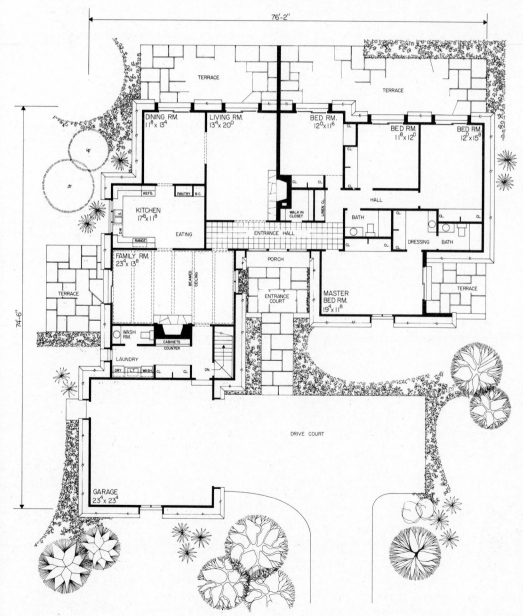

Design 22384
2,545 Sq. Ft.; 44,041 Cu. Ft.

● A dramatic Mansard roof with a contemporary adaption. The various overhanging and sloping roof planes give this L-shaped ranch home a unique appeal. Extended brick wing walls help create an entrance court leading to the attractively detailed front entry. The well-lighted entrance hall is spacious and effectively controls the traffic patterns to the major areas. Observe that each of the major rooms (kitchen excepted) enjoys direct access to outdoor living. The large master bedroom will have a full measure of privacy. On the other hand, the efficient kitchen is strategically located between dining and family rooms. A practical mud room area, adjacent to the entry from the garage, features wash room, laundry, closet and cabinet space. This home has a partial basement.

Design 21915 2,112 Sq. Ft.; 21,408 Cu. Ft.

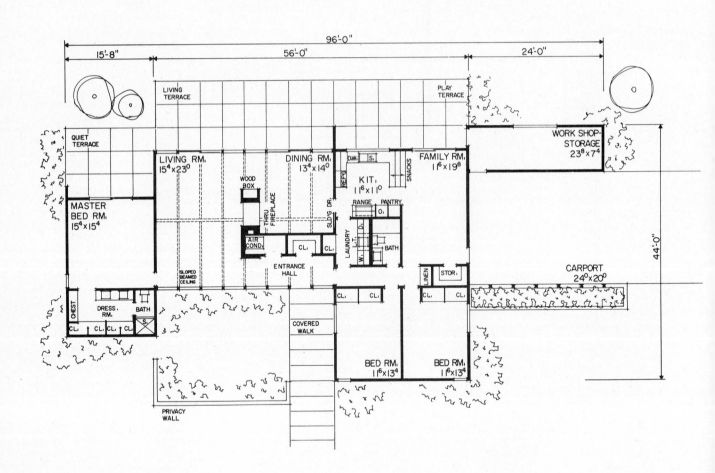

● This dramatic design offers new dimensions in living. If ever a floor plan made sense within the context of today's living patterns, this one does. Not only is this a plan for the children, it is one for the parents, as well. Notice how the dining room and kitchen are located near the center of the plan and function together ideally. To the left of this centralized area is the quiet, formal living room for adult relaxation and entertaining. Adjacent, to the adult formal area is the master bedroom with its own dressing room, bath, and quiet terrace. This whole area may properly be termed, "parent's territory". To the right of the front entrance is the children's area. This area is comprised of two bedrooms, bath, family room and play terrace.

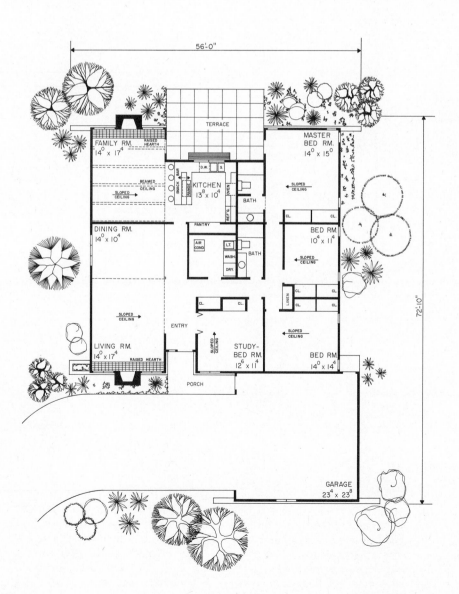

Design 22348
2,067 Sq. Ft.; 23,068 Cu. Ft.

● Contemporary design and planning can take many shapes. This house ably attests to what interesting shapes and fine living patterns can result. The varying roof planes and the brick masses help set the character. The recessed front door opens to the entry which leads straight to the kitchen at the rear of the plan. The living and dining rooms have sloped ceilings and are openly planned for a fine feeling of spaciousness. The sloping, beamed ceiling family room functions well with the efficient kitchen. There is a snack bar and access to the terrace. Each living area has a dramatic raised hearth fireplace. For sleeping facilities there are four bedrooms and two baths. Note how the terrace is accessible from the master bedroom. There is a serving counter on the terrace just below the kitchen window.

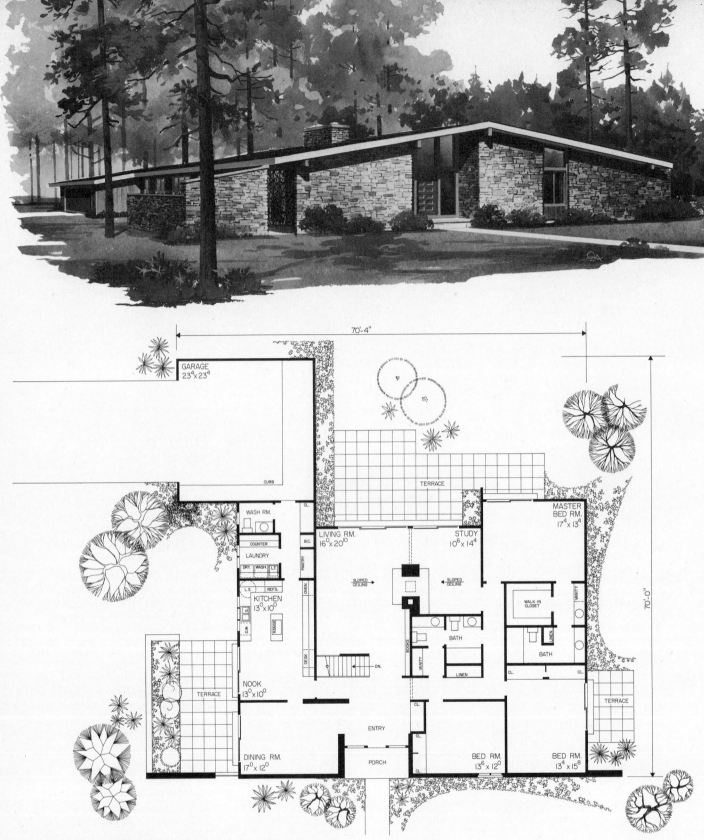

Design 22537 2,602 Sq. Ft.; 41,731 Cu. Ft.

● A low-pitched, wide overhanging roof and masses of quarried stone (make it some other material of your choice if you wish) set the character of this contemporary design. The recessed front entrance with its patterned door and glass panels is, indeed, dramatic.

An attractive wrought iron gate opens to the private, side eating terrace. Sloping ceilings and raised hearth through-fireplace highlight the living room/study area. Spaciousness is further enhanced by the open stairwell to the recreation area which may be devel-

oped below. The kitchen, with its island cooking range and plenty of counter and cupboard space will be a joy in which to function. The area between kitchen and garage is well-planned. The separate laundry has extra counter space.

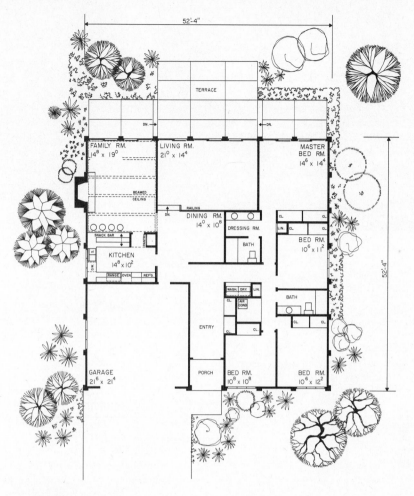

Design 22357
2,135 Sq. Ft.; 24,970 Cu. Ft.

● Palm trees on your site are not a prerequisite for the building of this distinctive home. If you and your family have a flair for things unique, the exterior, as well as the interior, of this attractive design will excite you. The low-pitched, wide overhanging hip roof has a slag surface. The equally spaced pillars and the spaces between the vertical boards are finished in stucco. This house is a perfect square measuring 52'-4''. The resulting plan is one that is practical and efficient. The kitchen will be a joy in which to work. A pass-thru provides the access to the snack bar of the beamed ceilinged family room. The formal dining area is but a couple steps away and overlooks the sunken living room. Four bedrooms and two baths make up the delightful sleeping zone.

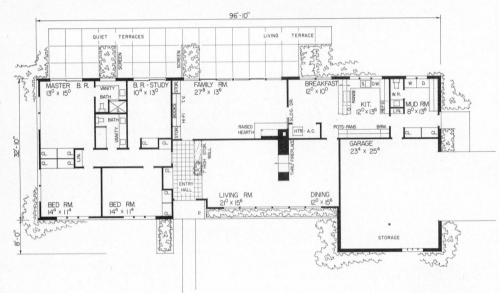

Design 21023
2,624 Sq. Ft.; 27,556 Cu. Ft.

● Features galore, and ones that will be sure to help guarantee years of convenient living. Starting with the sleeping zone, there are four bedrooms, two baths with built-in vanities, and plenty of closets. The delightfully large living areas occupy the center of the plan. Overlooking the front yard through a dramatic bank of windows is the formal area for living and dining. An attractive through fireplace acts as the practical room divider. To the rear, and functioning with the living terrace, is the 28 foot family room with its raised hearth fireplace and storage wall. The work center is highly efficient and well-located. Study the layouts and the manner in which the U-shaped kitchen will function.

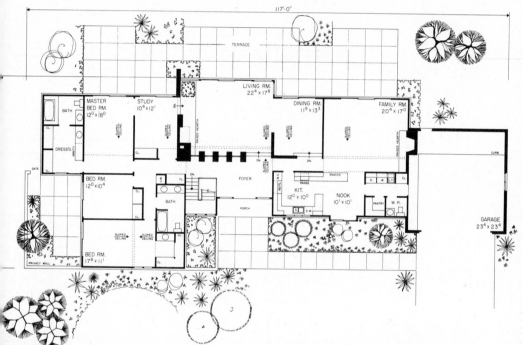

Design 22506
2,851 Sq. Ft.; 47,525 Cu. Ft.

● Here is a home that is sure to add an extra measure of fun to your family's living patterns. The exterior is extremely pleasing with the use of paned glass windows, the hipped roof and the double front doors. The initial impact of the interior begins dramatically in the large foyer. The ceiling is sloped, while straight ahead one views the sunken living room. Impressive are the masonry columns with a railing between each. The stairwell to the partial basement is open and has a view of the outdoor planter. The sleeping area consists of three bedrooms, baths and a study (or fourth bedroom if you perfer). Two raised hearth fireplaces, pantry, wash room and more. List your favorite features.

Design 21885
2,988 Sq. Ft.; 47,347 Cu. Ft.

● Here is a wonderfully arranged and delightfully packaged design to assure years of proud ownership. The pleasingly simple exterior is highlighted by wide overhanging roofs with interesting lines. Recessed double front doors open into a spacious floor plan featuring: Four bedrooms and two full baths in the sleeping area; a formal and informal living room, a separate dining room and two fireplaces in the living area and a convenient breakfast room.

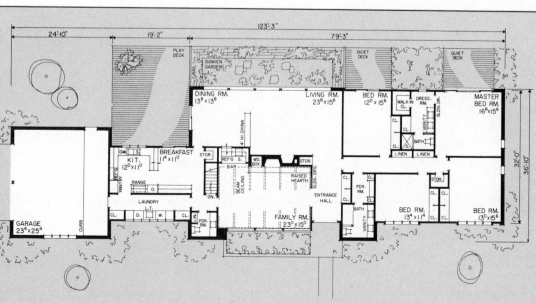

Design 22861
2,499 Sq. Ft.; 29,100 Cu. Ft.

● Berming the earth against the walls of a structure prove to be very energy efficient. The earth protects the interior from the cold of the winter and the heat of the summer. Interior lighting will come from the large skylight over the garden room. Every room will benefit from this exposed area. The garden room will function as a multi-purpose area for the entire family. The living/dining room will receive light from two areas, the garden room and the wall of sliding glass doors to the outside. Family living will be served by the efficient floor plan. Three bedrooms and two full baths are clustered together. The kitchen is adjacent to the air-locked vestibule where the laundry and utility rooms are housed. The section is cut through the dining, garden and master bedroom facing the kitchen.

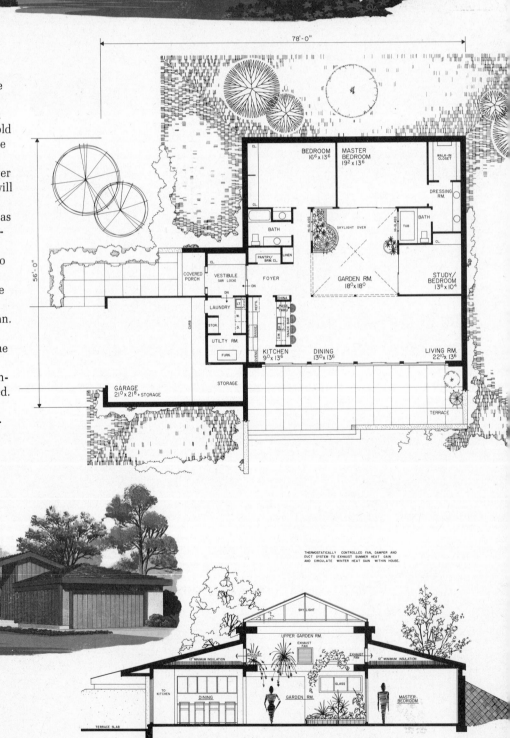

● Earth berms are banked against all four exterior walls of this design to effectively reduce heating and cooling demands. The berming is cost-efficient during both hot and cold seasons. In the winter, berming reduces heat loss through the exterior walls and shields the structure from cold winds. It helps keep warm air out during the summer. The two most dramatic interior highlights are the atrium and thru-fireplace. Topped with a large skylight, the atrium floods the interior with natural light. Shades are used to cover the atrium in the summer to prevent solar heat gain. Three bedrooms are featured in this plan and they each open via sliding glass doors to the atrium. This would eliminate any feeling of being closed in. An island with range and oven is featured in the kitchen. Informal dining will be enjoyed at the snack bar. The family/dining room can house those more formal dining occasions. The section at the right is cut through the study, atrium and rear bedroom looking toward master bedroom.

88'-0"

14'-8"

46'-0"

14'-8"

TERRACE

BEDROOM
11⁸ x 12⁸

DINING/ FAMILY RM.
18⁸ x 13⁰

BATH

CL.

BEDROOM
12⁸ x 11⁰

PASS THRU

LAUNDRY

CURB

REF G.

KITCHEN
12⁸ x 11⁸

CABINETS

FURN.

STORAGE

MASTER
BEDROOM
12⁸ x 14⁰

ATRIUM
17⁸ x 17⁸

SNACK BAR

RANGE

OVEN

PANTRY

CL.

PDR.
RM.

FOYER

GARAGE
26⁴ x 22⁰

DW

LEDGE ABOVE

WALK - IN
CLOSET

THRU
FIREPLACE

BATH

STUDY
10⁰ x 13⁰

LIVING RM.
17⁸ x 13⁰

TERRACE

PROPOSED PRIVACY WALL WHEN TERRACE FACES STREET

THERMOSTATICALLY CONTROLLED FAN, DAMPER AND DUCT SYSTEM TO EXHAUST SUMMER HEAT GAIN AND CIRCULATE WINTER HEAT GAIN WITHIN HOUSE.

SKYLIGHT

UPPER ATRIUM

EXHAUST
FAN

EXHAUST
FAN

12" MINIMUM INSULATION

12" MINIMUM INSULATION

STUDY

ATRIUM

BEDROOM

EARTH BERM

RETAINING WALL

FLAGSTONE

TERRACE SLAB

SECTION

Design 22833
2,386 Sq. Ft.; 27,735 Cu. Ft.

Design 21781

2,410 Sq. Ft.; 29,224 Cu. Ft.

● Looking for something different in exterior design and contemporary floor planning? If so, consider this design which might be characterized as Oriental Modern. Creating the visual appeal are such features as the hip-roof with its wide overhang, the masses of brick, the delightful planting area and the recessed front entrance with its double doors. The indoor-outdoor living relationships offered by this plan are outstanding. Observe the terraces and how they function with the various areas of the plan. The delightful dining terrace is particularly noteworthy. A study of the floor plan reveals excellent zoning. The sleeping zone is separated from the informal living zone and work center by the formal living and dining rooms and large center entrance hall. Don't miss the mud room area. Truly a great family house for all the members to enjoy!

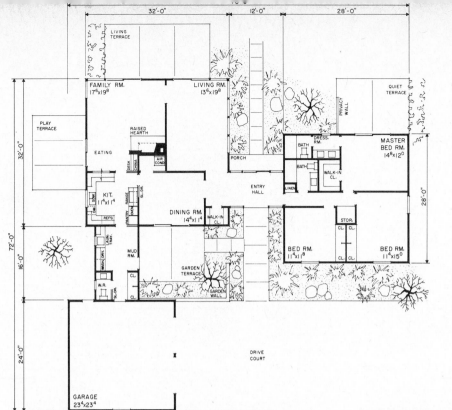

Design 21925
2,064 Sq. Ft.; 22,026 Cu. Ft.

● New and refreshing living patterns can take many forms. Here, living patterns are related in such a manner as to result in what appears to be three distinct units, attached by passageways to produce a "cluster". If ever you've wished that your sleeping area could enjoy complete privacy from the rest of the house, you should find this unique plan of interest. If ever you wished you could take only a couple of steps in one direction and be in the dining room, and a couple in another direction and be in the family room, this practical plan will appeal to you. And, if you ever wished you could really control the entry of dirt and mud you'll appreciate this plan.

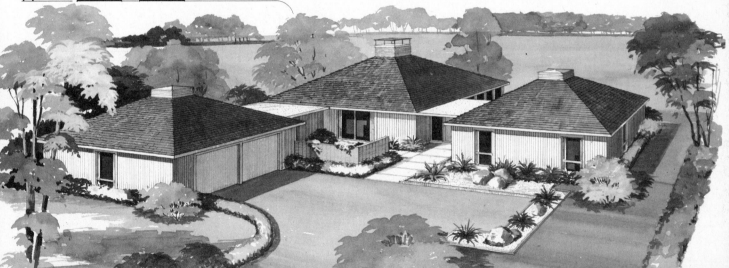

Design 21820
2,730 Sq. Ft.; 36,335 Cu. Ft.

● Whatever the location, snugly tucked in among the hills or impressively oriented on the flat-lands - this trim hip-roof ranch home will surely be fun to live in. Here is a gracious exterior whose floor plan has "everything". Traffic patterns are excellent. The zoning of the sleeping wing, as well as the formal and informal living areas, is outstanding. Indoor-outdoor living relationships are most practical and convenient.

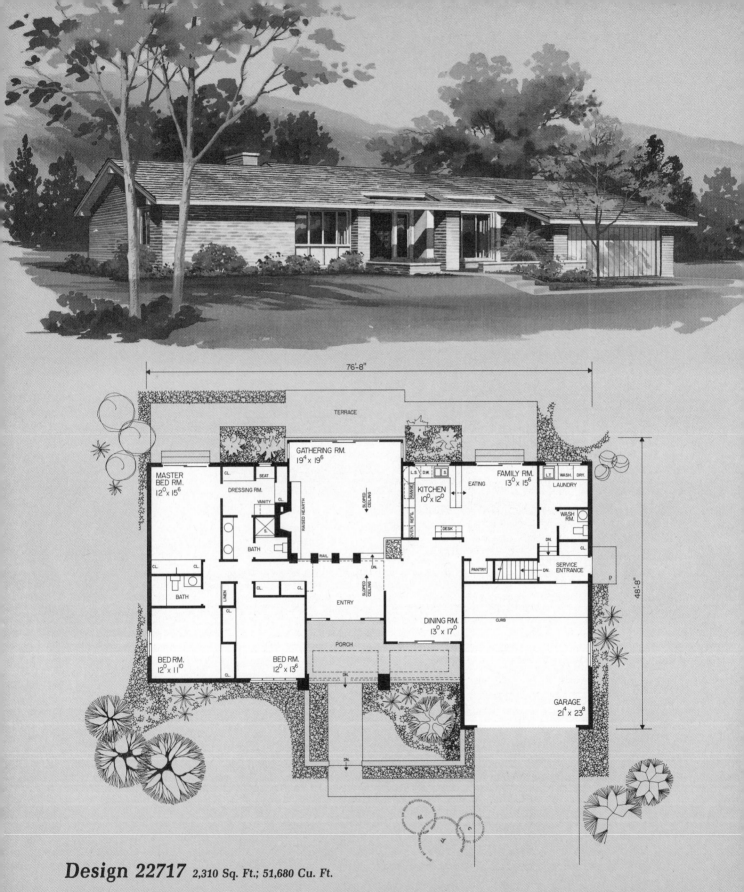

Design 22717 2,310 Sq. Ft.; 51,680 Cu. Ft.

● Great for family life! There's a spacious family room for casual activities. And a "work efficient" kitchen that features a built-in desk and appliances, a large pantry plus a pass-through to the family room for added conveni-ence. A first floor laundry, too, with adjacent wash room and stairs to the basement. Want glamour? There's a sloped ceiling in the entry hall plus a delightful "over the railing" view of the sunken gathering room. And the gathering room itself! More than 19' by 19' . . . with a sloped ceiling, raised hearth fireplace and sliding glass doors to the rear terrace. A 13' by 17' formal dining room, too. The curb area in garage is convenient.

Design 22789 2,732 Sq. Ft.; 54,935 Cu. Ft.

● An attached three car garage! What a fantastic feature of this three bedroom contemporary design. And there's more. As one walks up the steps to the covered porch and through the double front doors the charm of this design will be overwhelming. Inside, a large foyer greets all visitors and leads them to each of the three areas, each down a few steps. The living area has a large gathering room with fireplace and a study adjacent on one side and the formal dining room on the other. The work center has an efficient kitchen with island range, breakfast room, laundry and built-in desk and bar. Then there is the sleeping area. Note the raised tub with sloped ceiling.

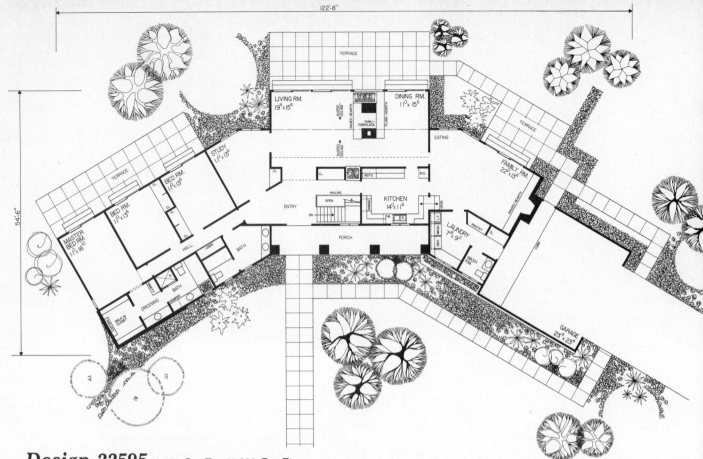

Design 22595 2,653 Sq. Ft.; 40,600 Cu. Ft.

● A winged design puts everything in the right place! At the center, formal living and dining rooms with sloped ceiling sharing one fireplace for added charm. Sliding glass doors in both rooms open onto the main terrace.

In the right wing, a spacious family room with another raised hearth fireplace, built-in desk, dining area and adjoining smaller terrace. Also, a first floor laundry with pantry and half bath. In the left wing, a study, the mas-

ter suite and family bedrooms (all bedrooms having access to a third terrace) plus baths . . . all well-located for quiet privacy. This home has a floor plan that helps you organize your life. Notice the open staircase to the basement.

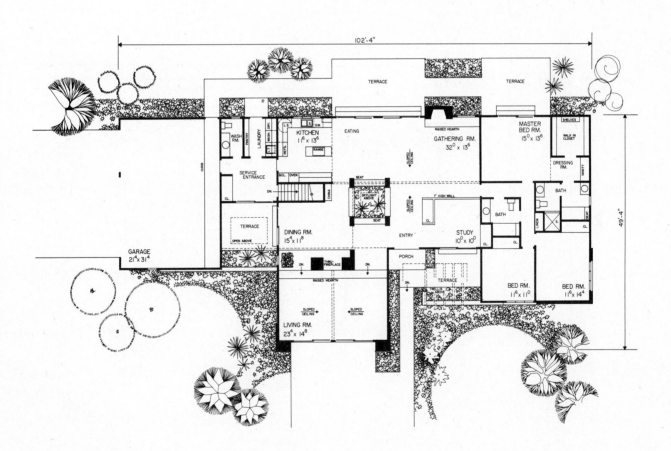

Design 22745 2,890 Sq. Ft.; 44,650 Cu. Ft.

● Just imagine the fun everyone will have living in this contemporary home with its frame exterior and accents of stone veneer (make it brick, if you prefer). The living areas revolve around the dramatic atrium-type planting area flooded with natural light from the skylight above. The formal living room is sunken and has a thru-fireplace to the dining room. Also a large gathering room with a second raised hearth fireplace, sloped ceiling, sliding glass doors to a rear terrace and informal eating area. Observe the sloping ceilings, the laundry with pantry, the wash room and the study. Master bedroom has a stall shower, a tub with seat, a vanity and two lavatories.

Design 22756 2,652 Sq. Ft.; 51,540 Cu. Ft.

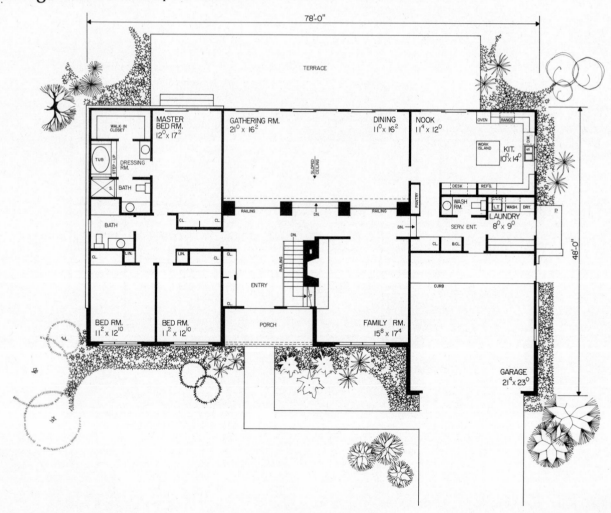

● This one-story contemporary is bound to serve your family well. With its many fine features it will assure the best in contemporary living. Notice the bath with tub and stall shower, dressing room and walk-in closet featured with the master bed-room. Two more family bedrooms. The sunken gathering room/dining room is highlighted by the sloped ceiling and sliding glass doors to the large rear terrace. This formal area is a full 32' x 16'. Imagine the great furniture placement that can be done in this area. In addition to the gathering room, there is an informal family room with fireplace. You will enjoy the efficient kitchen and get much use out of the work island, pantry and built-in desk. Note the service entrance with bath and laundry.

Design 22303 2,330 Sq. Ft.; 26,982 Cu. Ft.

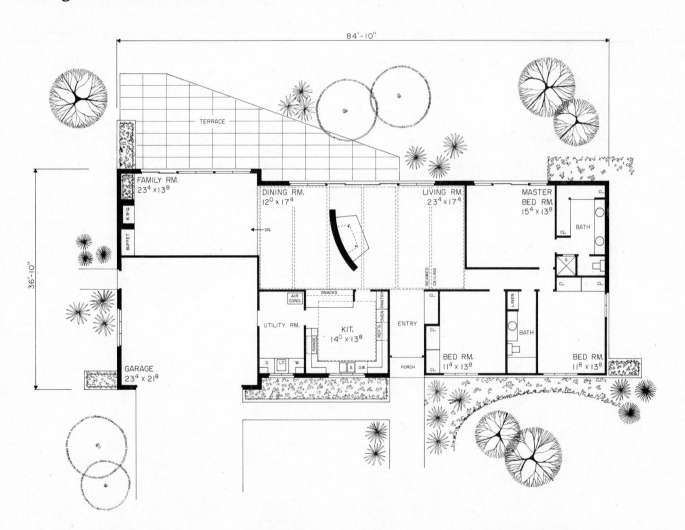

● This hip-roof ranch home has a basic floor plan that is the favorite of many. The reasons for its popularity are, of course, easy to detect. The simple rectangular shape means relatively economical construction. The living areas are large and are located to the rear to function through sliding glass doors with the terrace. The front kitchen is popular because of its view of approaching callers and its proximity to the front entry. The big utility room serves as a practical buffer between the garage and the kitchen.

Worthy of particular note is the efficiency of the kitchen, the stylish living room fireplace, the beamed ceiling, the sunken family room with its wall of built-ins (make that a music wall if you wish). Observe the snack bar and the fine master bath.

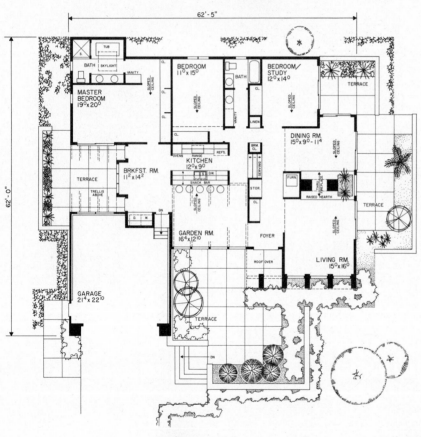

MASTER BEDROOM 19⁰ x 20⁰

BATH SKYLIGHT TUB

VANITY

BEDROOM 11⁰ x 15⁰

BEDROOM/ STUDY 12⁰ x 14⁰

BATH

LINEN

TERRACE

TERRACE

TRELLIS ABOVE

BRKFST. RM. 11² x 14²

OVENS RANGE REF'S

KITCHEN 12⁰ x 9⁰

SNACK BAR

DINING RM. 15⁰ x 9⁰-11⁴

BRM CL.

STOR.

FURN.

RAISED HEARTH

TERRACE

GARDEN RM. 16⁴ x 12¹⁰

FOYER

DN

GARAGE 21⁴ x 22¹⁰

ROOF OVER

LIVING RM. 15⁰ x 16⁰

TERRACE

DN

62'-5"

62'-0"

Design 22858
2,231 Sq. Ft.; 28,150 Cu. Ft.

● This sun oriented design was created to
face the south. By doing so, it has mini-
mal northern exposure. It has been designed primarily for the more temperate
U.S. latitudes using 2 x 6 wall construction. The morning sun will brighten the
living and dining rooms along with the
adjacent terrace. Sun enters the garden
room by way of the glass roof and walls.
In the winter, the solar heat gain from the
garden room should provide relief from
high energy bills. Solar shades allow you
to adjust the amount of light that you
want to enter in the warmer months. Interior planning deserves mention, too. The
work center is efficient. The kitchen has a
snack bar on the garden room side and a
serving counter to the dining room. The
breakfast room with laundry area is also
convenient to the kitchen. Three bedrooms are on the northern wall. The master bedroom has a large tub and a separate shower with a four foot square skylight above. When this design is oriented
toward the sun, it should prove to be energy efficient and a joy to live in.

Tudor & English Versions
With a Special Appeal

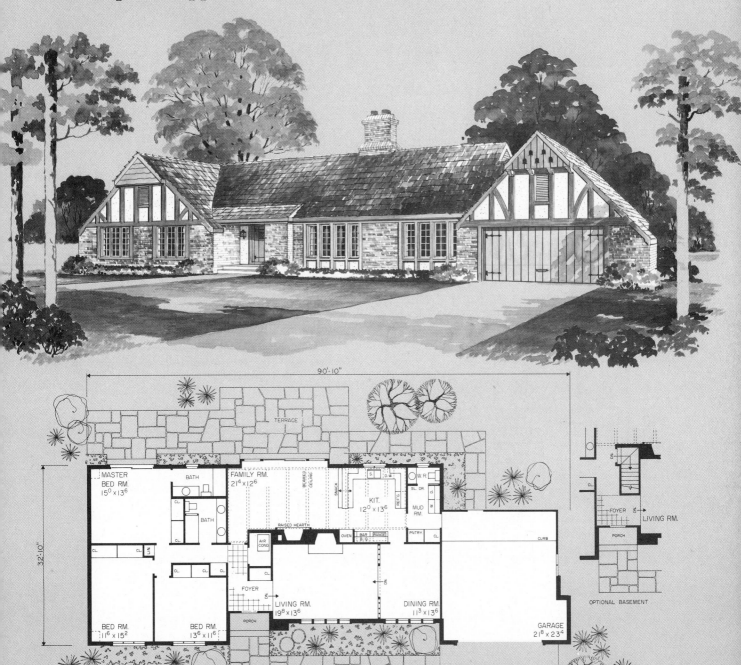

Design 22318 2,029 Sq. Ft.; 31,021 Cu. Ft.

● Warmth and charm are characteristics of the Tudor adaptations. This modest sized home, with its twin front-facing gabled roofs, represents a great investment. While it will be an exciting and refreshing addition to any neighborhood, its appeal will never grow old. The covered front entrance opens to the center foyer. Traffic patterns flow in an orderly and efficient manner to the three main zones — the formal dining zone, the sleeping zone and the informal living zone. The sunken living room with its fireplace is separated from the dining room by an attractive trellis divider. A second fireplace along with beamed ceiling and sliding glass doors highlight the family room. Note snack bar, mud room, cooking facilities, two full baths and optional basement.

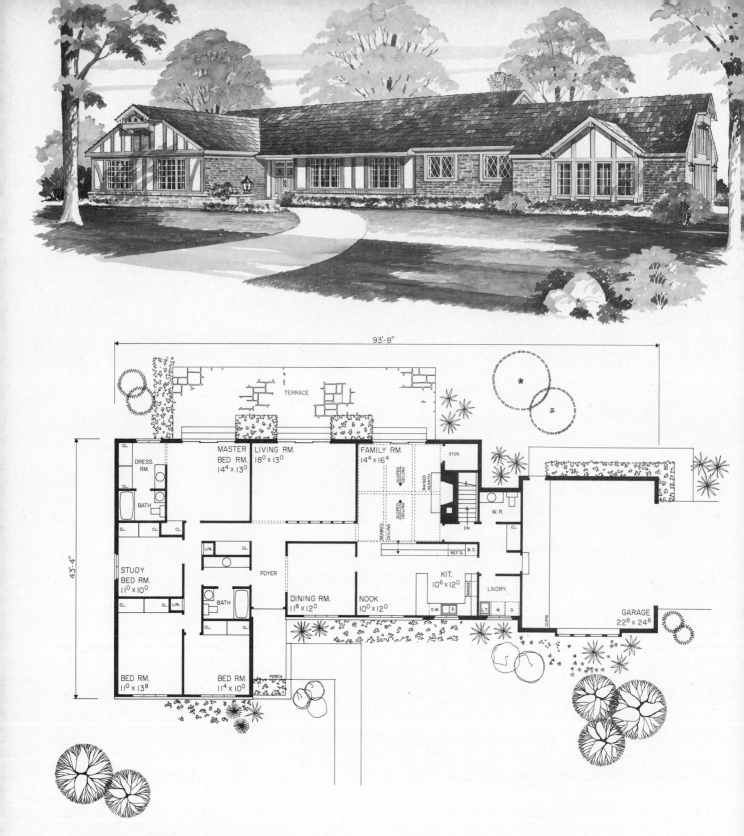

Design 22515 2,363 Sq. Ft.; 46,676 Cu. Ft.

● Another Tudor adaptation with all the appeal that is inherent in this design style. The brick veneer exterior is effectively complimented by the beam work, the stucco, and the window treatment. The carriage lamp perched on the planter wall adds a delightful touch as do the dovecotes of the bedroom wing and over the garage door. The livability of the interior is just great. The kitchen, nook, and dining room overlook the front yard. Around the corner from the kitchen is the laundry with an extra wash room not far away. Sloping, beamed ceiling and raised hearth fireplace are highlights of the family room. Like the living room and master bedroom it functions with rear terrace. Note vanity outside main bath. Stolid wood posts on 3 foot wall separate living room and hall.

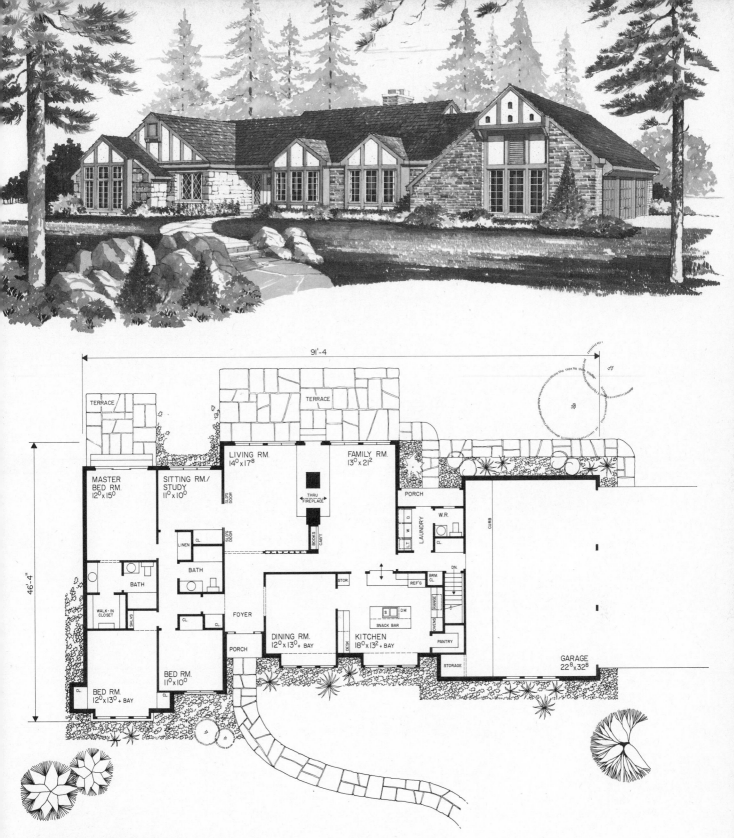

TERRACE

TERRACE

LIVING RM.
14⁰ x 17⁸

FAMILY RM.
13⁰ x 21²

MASTER
BED RM.
12⁰ x 15⁰

SITTING RM./
STUDY
11⁰ x 10⁰

SLDG
DOOR

THRU
FIREPLACE

SLDG
DOOR

PORCH

W.R.

LINEN

CL.

BOOKS

CABT.

LT. W D

LAUNDRY

CL.

BATH

BATH

STOR.

REF'G

DN.

BRM.
CL.

CURB

WALK-IN
CLOSET

SHLVS

CL.

CL.

FOYER

DINING RM.
12⁰ x 13⁰ + BAY

DESK

RANGE

OVENS

SNACK BAR

KITCHEN
18⁰ x 13² + BAY

PANTRY

BED RM.
11⁰ x 10⁰

PORCH

S   D.W.

STORAGE

GARAGE
22⁸ x 32⁸

BED RM.
12⁰ x 13⁰ + BAY

CL.

CL.

91'-4

46'-4"

Design 22785 2,375 Sq. Ft.; 47,805 Cu. Ft.

● Exceptional Tudor design! Passersby will surely take a second glance at this fine home wherever it may be located. And the interior is just as pleasing. As one enters the foyer and looks around, the plan will speak for itself in the areas of convenience and efficiency. Cross room traffic will be avoided. There is a hall leading to each of the three bedrooms and study of the sleeping wing and another leading to the living room, family room, kitchen and laundry with wash room. The formal dining room can be entered from both the foyer and the kitchen. Efficiency will surely be the by-word when describing the kitchen. Note the fine features: a built-in desk, pantry, island snack bar with sink and pass-thru to the family room. The fireplace will be enjoyed in the living and family rooms.

Design 21989

2,282 Sq. Ft.; 41,831 Cu. Ft.

● High style with a plan as contemporary as today and tomorrow. There is, indeed, a feeling of coziness that emanates from the ground-hugging qualities of this picturesque home. Inside, there is livability galore. There's the sunken living room and the separate dining room to function as the family's formal living area. Then, overlooking the rear yard, there's the informal living area with its beamed ceiling family room, kitchen and adjacent breakfast room.

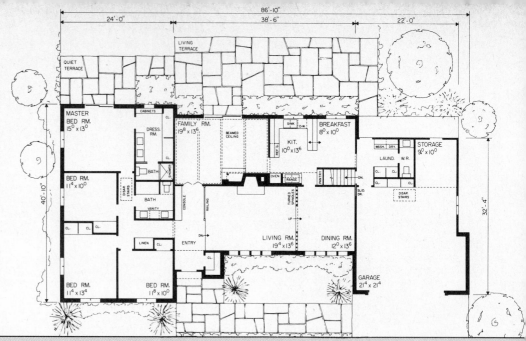

Design 22378

2,580 Sq. Ft.; 49,792 Cu. Ft.

● If yours is a preference for an exterior that exudes both warmth and formality, the styling of English Tudor may suit your fancy. A host of architectural features blend together to produce this delightfully appealing exterior. Notice the interesting use of contrasting exterior materials. Don't overlook the two stylish chimneys. The manner in which the interior functions to provide the fine living patterns is outstanding. Each of four main rooms — look out on the rear terrace.

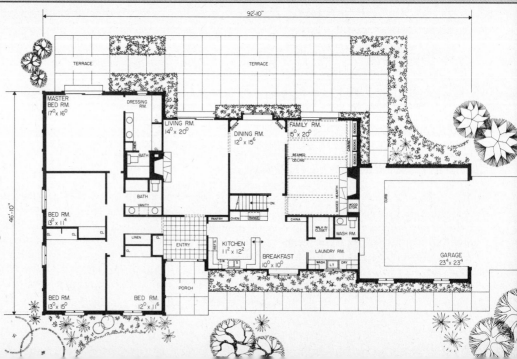

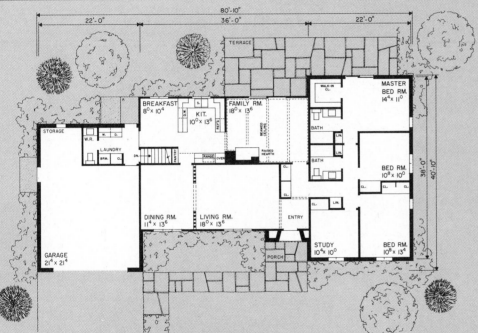

Design 22129
2,057 Sq. Ft.; 36,970 Cu. Ft.

● This four bedroom home is zoned for convenient living. The sleeping area, with its two full baths and plenty of closets, will have a lot of privacy. The formal living and dining rooms function together and may be completely by-passed when desired. The informal living areas are grouped together and overlook the rear yard. The family room with its beamed ceiling is but a step from the kitchen. The U-shaped kitchen is handy to both the breakfast and dining rooms.

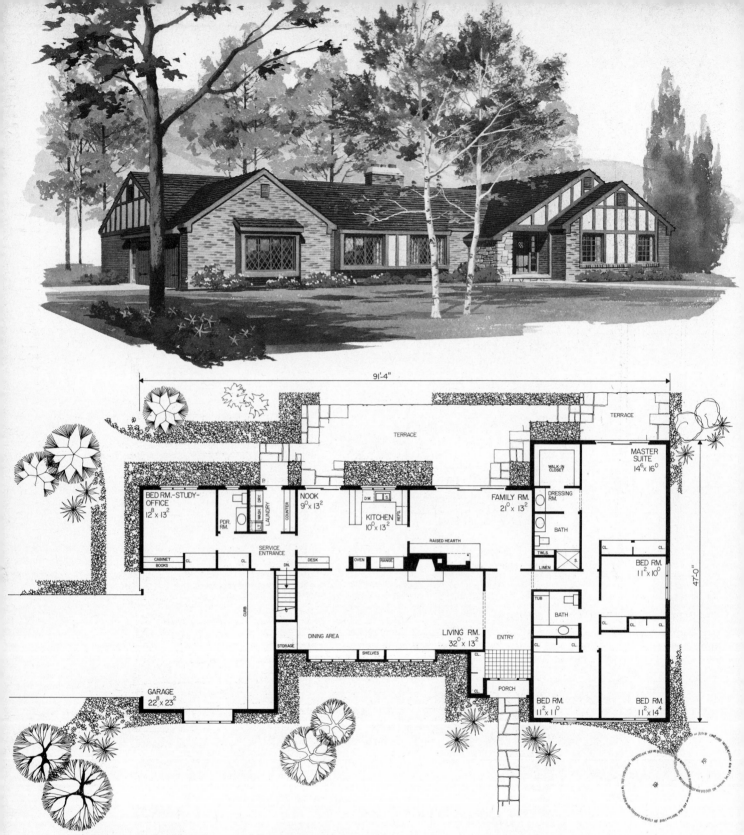

Design 22573 2,747 Sq. Ft.; 48,755 Cu. Ft.

● A Tudor ranch! Combining brick and wood for an elegant look. With a living/dining room measuring 32' by 13' (large indeed) fully appointed with a traditional fireplace and built-in shelves flanked by diagonally paned windows. There's much more! A

family room with a raised hearth fireplace and sliding glass doors that open onto the terrace. A U-shaped kitchen with lots of built-ins . . . a range, an oven, a desk. Plus a separate breakfast nook. The sleeping facilities consist of three family bed-

rooms plus an elegant master bedroom suite. A conveniently located laundry with a folding counter is in the service entrance. Adjacent to the laundry is a wash room and in the corner of the plan is a study or make it a fifth bedroom if you prefer.

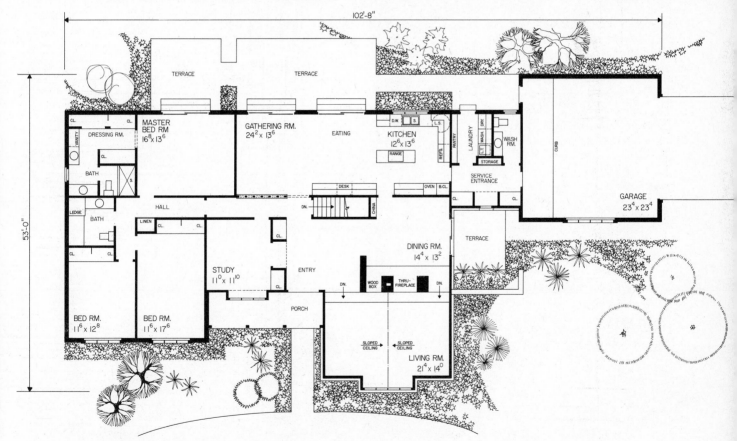

Design 22746 *2,790 Sq. Ft.; 57,590 Cu. Ft.*

● This impressive one-story will surely be the talk-of-the-town. And not surprisingly, either. It embodies all the elements to assure a sound investment and years of happy family livability. The projecting living room with its stucco, simulated wood beams, and effective window treatment add a dramatic note. Sunken by two steps, this room will enjoy much privacy. The massive double front doors are sheltered by the covered porch and lead to the spacious entry hall. The interior is particularly well-zoned. The large rear gathering room will cater to the family's gregarious instincts. Outdoor enjoyment can be obtained on the three terraces. Also a study for those extra quiet moments. Be sure to observe the plan closely for all of the other fine features.

Design 22620
2,048 Sq. Ft.; 42,000 Cu. Ft.

● An enclosed courtyard! That sets this home apart right from the start. There are more unusual features inside. Like the 21' by 15' keeping room . . . complete with a wet bar, built-in bookcase, fireplace/woodbox combination. Plus sliding glass doors leading to the terrace. That's the kind of space you need for family life as well as entertaining! There's a formal dining room, too! And a well-designed kitchen. U-shaped for efficiency, with a built-in oven and range. Plus a separate breakfast room. Around the corner, the first floor laundry. That puts all the work areas together, saving you time and energy. Four large bedrooms grouped together for privacy. Ideal planning throughout.

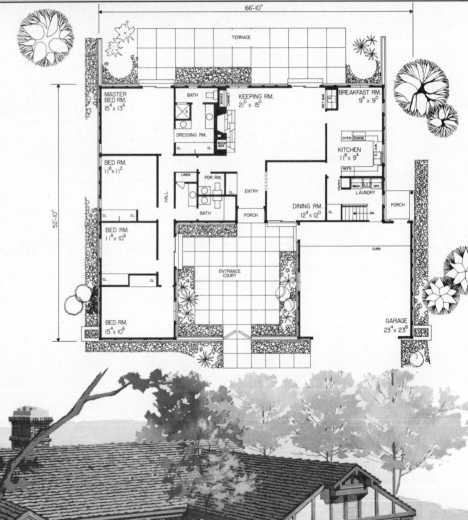

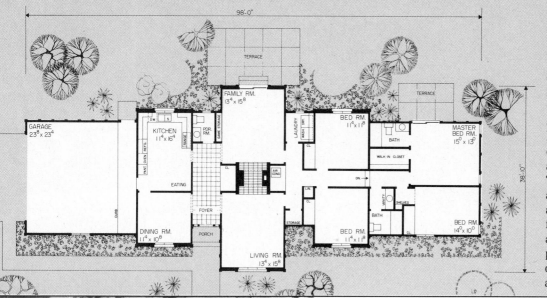

Design 22385
2,100 Sq. Ft.; 27,205 Cu. Ft.

● The charm of Tudor styled exterior adaptations is difficult to beat. Here is a hip-roof version which highlights the effective use of stucco, patterned brick and exposed beam work. The varying roof planes and the massive chimney, along with the recessed front entrance enhance the appeal. A study of the floor plan is most revealing. Excellent zoning is readily apparent.

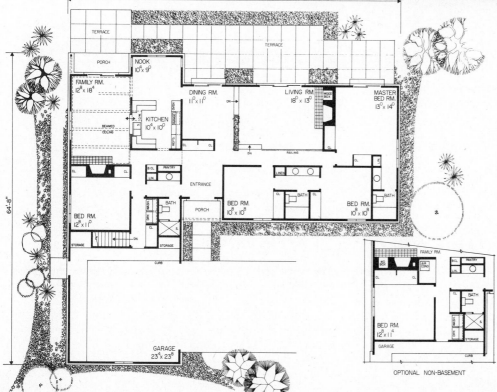

Design 22613
2,132 Sq. Ft.; 38,328 Cu. Ft.

● A classic Tudor! With prominent wood and stucco styling. And unique features throughout. Start with the sunken living room where an attractive railing has replaced the anticipated hallway wall. For more good looks, a traditional fireplace with an attached woodbox and sliding glass doors that open onto the terrace. There's a formal dining room, too, also with access onto the terrace. Together these rooms form a gracious center for entertaining! For casual times, a family room with a beamed ceiling, fireplace and summer porch. And a work-efficient kitchen plus a roomy breakfast nook.

OPTIONAL NON-BASEMENT

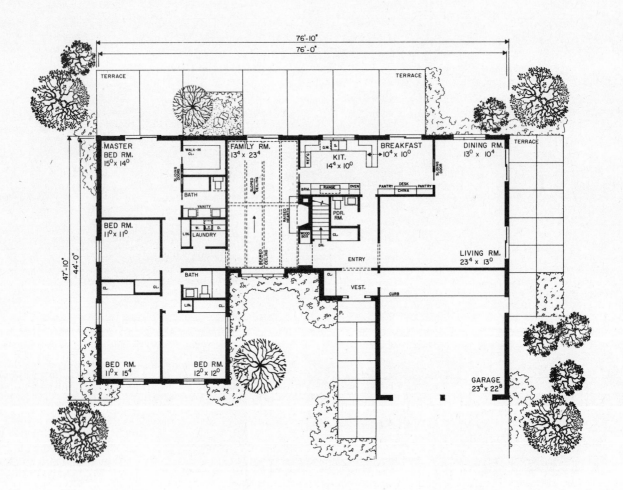

Design 22142 2,450 Sq. Ft.; 43,418 Cu. Ft.

● Adaptations of Old England have become increasingly popular in today's building scene. And little wonder; for many of these homes when well-designed have a very distinctive charm. Here is certainly a home which will be like no other in its neighborhood. Its very shape adds an extra measure of uniqueness. And inside, there is all the livability the exterior seems to fortell. The sleeping wing has four bedrooms, two full baths and the laundry room — just where the soiled linen originates. The location of the family room is an excellent one. It is convenient for children because their traffic usually flows between family room and bedrooms. The spacious formal living and dining area will enjoy its privacy and be great fun to furnish.

Design 22317 3,161 Sq. Ft.; 57,900 Cu. Ft.

● Here's a rambling English manor with its full measure of individuality. Its fine proportions and irregular shape offer even the most casual of passers-by delightful views of fine architecture. The exterior boasts an interesting use of varying materials. In addition to the brick work, there is vertical siding, wavy-edged horizontal siding and stucco. Three massive chimneys provide each of the three major wings with a fireplace. The overhanging roof provides the cover for the long front porch. Note the access to both the foyer as well as the service hall. The formal living room, with its sloping beamed ceiling, and fireplace flanked by book shelves and cabinets, will be cozy, indeed. Study rest of plan. It's outstanding. Don't miss the three fireplaces and three full baths.

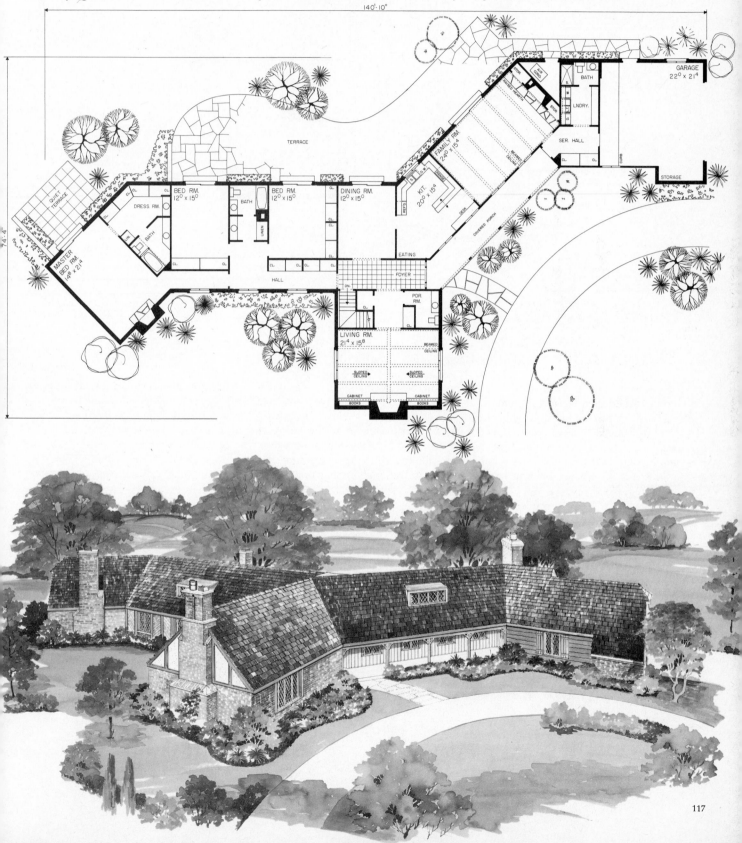

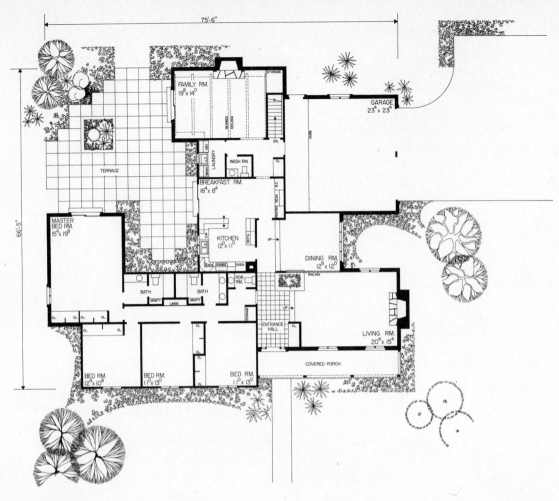

Design 22387 2,744 Sq. Ft.; 41,682 Cu. Ft.

● This rambling Tudor design will not fail to excite even the most casual of visitors. Its inviting facade is enhanced by its distinctive configuration. But such an appealing exterior is only a prelude to what the interior has to offer. Zoned for privacy, the four bedroom, 2½ bath sleeping area is outstanding. To the right of the entrance hall is the sunken living room which has a most commanding fireplace. The efficient kitchen effectively services the sunken dining room and the spacious breakfast room. Far removed from the sleeping and formal living areas is the beamed ceiling family room. Indoor-outdoor living relationships are delightfully maintained with utilization of those sliding glass doors to the strategically located terrace. Observe laundry, washroom and basement.

Design 22350 3,044 Sq. Ft. — Excluding Atrium; 60,900 Cu. Ft.

● This commanding Tudor adaptation has a distinctive character all its own. The interesting roof design, the contrasting brick and stucco, the diamond lite windows, the recessed double front doors, the carriage lamps, and massive chimneys are features which contribute to the charm of this impressive facade. And the extraordinary appeal of this design carries right on inside. The atrium is strategically located for full enjoyment from all living areas. A recessed terrace is directly accessible from the wonderful master suite as well as from the family room and breakfast nook. High ceilings add to the dramatic spaciousness of the formal living area. Note that the living room is sunken, has a raised hearth fireplace. The library is isolated and has its own fireplace.

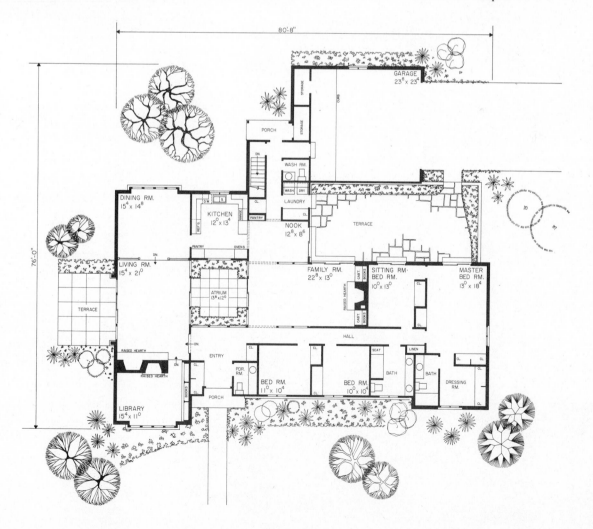

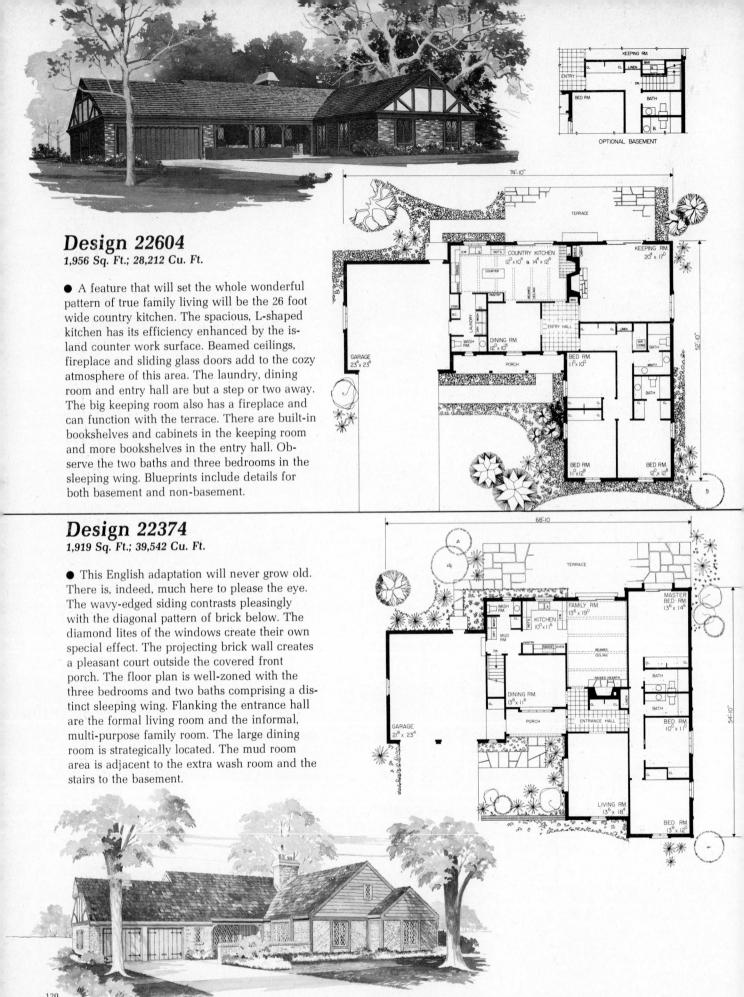

Design 22604
1,956 Sq. Ft.; 28,212 Cu. Ft.

● A feature that will set the whole wonderful pattern of true family living will be the 26 foot wide country kitchen. The spacious, L-shaped kitchen has its efficiency enhanced by the island counter work surface. Beamed ceilings, fireplace and sliding glass doors add to the cozy atmosphere of this area. The laundry, dining room and entry hall are but a step or two away. The big keeping room also has a fireplace and can function with the terrace. There are built-in bookshelves and cabinets in the keeping room and more bookshelves in the entry hall. Observe the two baths and three bedrooms in the sleeping wing. Blueprints include details for both basement and non-basement.

Design 22374
1,919 Sq. Ft.; 39,542 Cu. Ft.

● This English adaptation will never grow old. There is, indeed, much here to please the eye. The wavy-edged siding contrasts pleasingly with the diagonal pattern of brick below. The diamond lites of the windows create their own special effect. The projecting brick wall creates a pleasant court outside the covered front porch. The floor plan is well-zoned with the three bedrooms and two baths comprising a distinct sleeping wing. Flanking the entrance hall are the formal living room and the informal, multi-purpose family room. The large dining room is strategically located. The mud room area is adjacent to the extra wash room and the stairs to the basement.

Formal French Facades
For Gracious Living

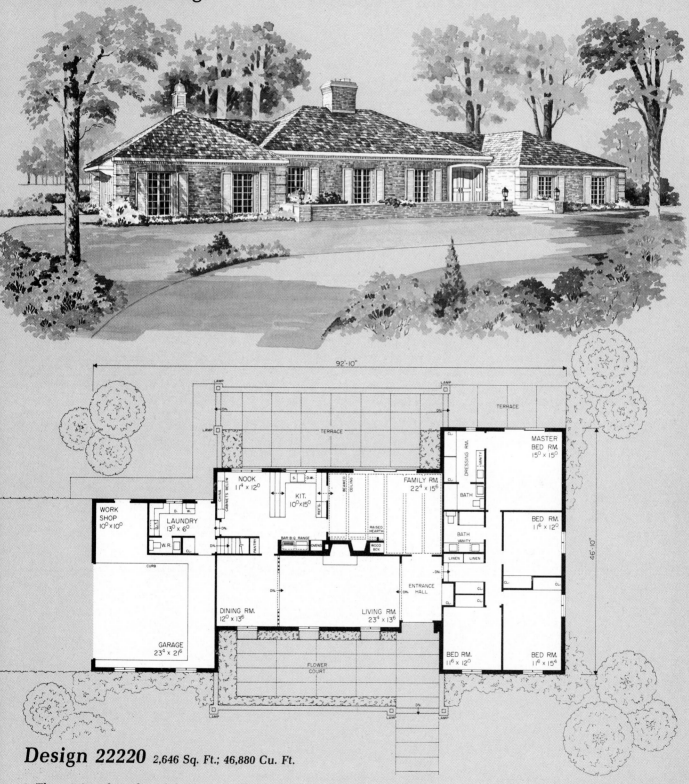

Design 22220 2,646 Sq. Ft.; 46,880 Cu. Ft.

● The gracious formality of this home is reminiscent of a popularly accepted French styling. The hip-roof, the brick quoins, the cornice details, the arched window heads, the distinctive shutters, the recessed double front doors, the massive center chimney, and the delightful flower court are all features which set the dramatic appeal of this home. This floor plan is a favorite of many. The four bedroom, two bath sleeping wing is a zone by itself. Further, the formal living and dining rooms are ideally located. For entertaining they function well together and look out upon the pleasant flower court. Overlooking the raised living terrace at the rear are the family and breakfast rooms and work center. Don't miss the laundry, extra wash room and work shop in garage.

● You'll want life's biggest investment — the purchase of a home — to be a source of everlasting enjoyment. To assure such a rewarding dividend, make every effort to match your family's desired living patterns with a workable plan. Of course, you'll want your plan enveloped by a stunning exterior. Consider both the interior and exterior of this design. Each is impressive. The sleeping zone comprises a separate wing and is accessible from both living and kitchen areas. There are four bedrooms, two full baths and plenty of closets. The 32 foot wide living and dining area will be just great fun to decorate. Then, there is the large family room with its raised hearth fireplace and sliding glass doors to the terrace. Note the fine laundry with wash room nearby. The extra curb area in the garage is great for storing small garden equipment.

● This French design is surely impressive. The exterior appearance will brighten any area with its French roof, paned-glass windows, masonry brick privacy wall and double front doors. The inside is just as appealing. Note the unique placement of rooms and features. The entry hall is large and leads to each of the areas in this plan. The formal dining room is outstanding and guests can enter through the entry hall. While serving one can enter by way of the butler's pantry (notice it's size and that it has a sink). To the right of the entry is a sizable parlor. Then there is the gathering room with fireplace, sliding glass doors and adjacent study. The work center is also outstanding. There is the U-shaped kitchen, island range, snack bar, breakfast nook, pantry plus wash room and large laundry near service entrance. Basement stairs are also nearby.

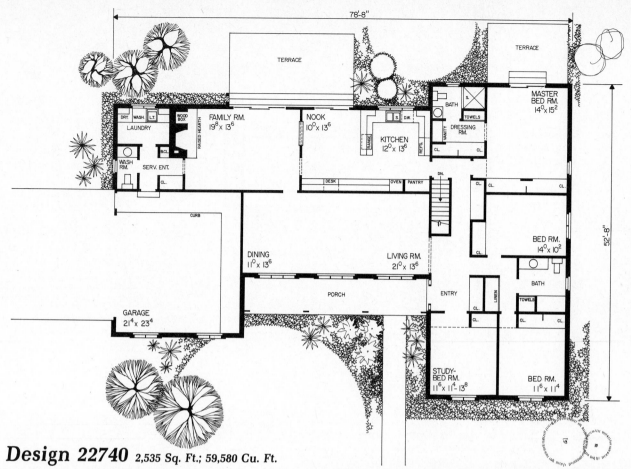

Design 22740 2,535 Sq. Ft.; 59,580 Cu. Ft.

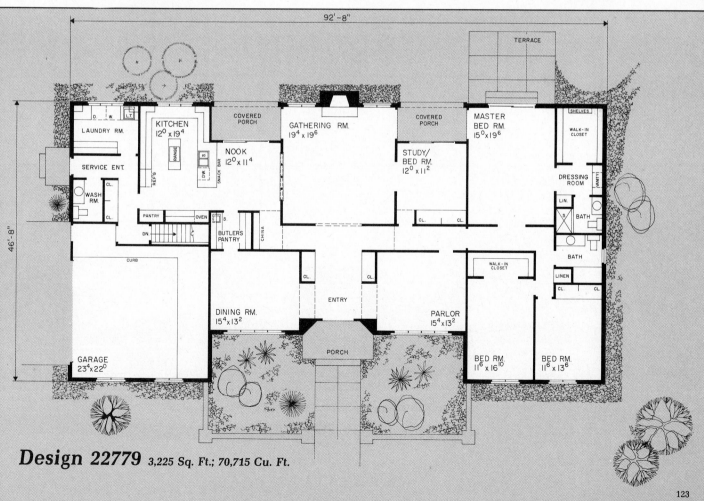

Design 22779 3,225 Sq. Ft.; 70,715 Cu. Ft.

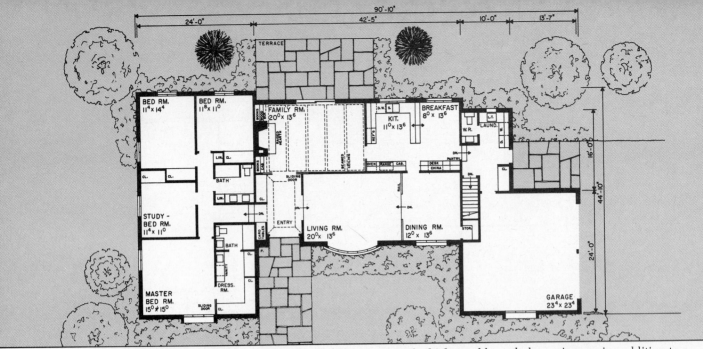

● Here are three delightful French Provincial adaptations, any one of which would surely be an impressive addition to a neighborhood. Each design features a sleeping wing of four bedrooms, two full baths, and plenty of closets. Further, each design has a separate first floor laundry with an adjacent wash room. Observe the sunken living room . . .

Design 21345
2,026 Sq. Ft.; 18,743 Cu. Ft.

Design 22134 2,530 Sq. Ft.; 44,458 Cu. Ft.

. . . and the beamed ceiling family room of Design 22134 above. Don't miss its big dressing room or raised hearth fire-place. Design 21345 has both its family and living rooms located to the rear and functioning with the terrace. Design 21054 has an efficient work area and a large formal dining room.

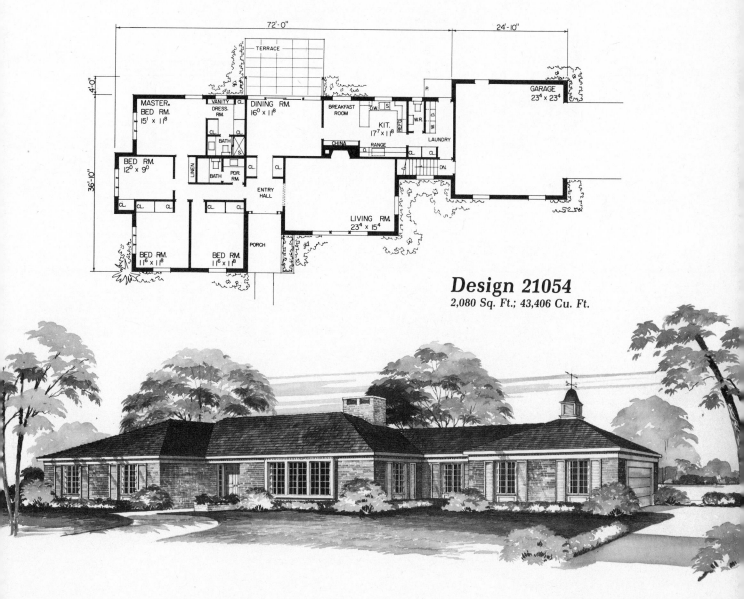

Design 21054
2,080 Sq. Ft.; 43,406 Cu. Ft.

73'-0"

67'-10"

TERRACE

BED RM.
12⁰ x 14⁰

FAMILY RM.
14⁰ x 18⁴

WOOD BOX

LIVING RM.
24⁸ x 18⁴

DINING RM.
15⁰ x 12⁰

SLOPED CEILING

BEAMED CEILING

DN.

CL.

ENTRY

DN.

AIR COND.

SERVING

PANTRY

REFG.

RANGE

OVENS

CL. CL.

BATH

LINEN

CL.

AIR COND.

KIT.
10⁰ x 14⁶

FOUNTAIN

BREAKFAST
10⁰ x 8⁸

BED RM.
12⁰ x 14⁴

BRM.

D.

W.

SLIDING DOOR

PANTRY

W.H.

W.R.

GATE

BED RM.
12⁰ x 13⁸

BOOKS

CL.

GARAGE
25⁰ x 21⁰

BATH

DRESS. RM.

SLDG. DOOR

MASTER BED RM.
12⁸ x 18⁸

ENTRANCE COURT

CL. CL. CL. CL. CL. CL.

Design 22177 2,802 Sq. Ft.; 34,133 Cu. Ft.

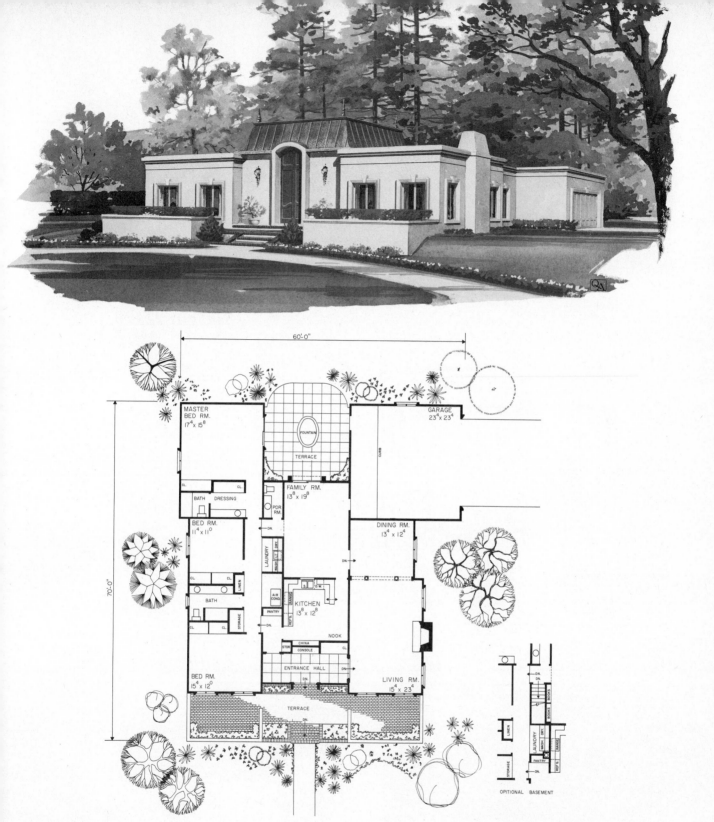

Design 22347 *2,322 Sq. Ft.; 26,572 Cu. Ft.*

● The regal character of this distinctive home is most inviting. The symmetry of the front exterior is enhanced by the raised terrace. The recessed front entrance shelters panelled double doors which open to the formal hall. Traffic may pass to the right directly into the sunken living room. To the left is the sunken three bedroom, two-bath sleeping area. The center of the plan features the efficient kitchen with nook space and the family room. The rear terrace, enclosed on three sides to assure privacy, is accessible from master bedroom, as well as family room, through sliding glass doors. Separating the formal living and dining rooms are finely proportioned, round wood columns. Don't overlook the first floor laundry. Blueprints include details for optional partial basement.

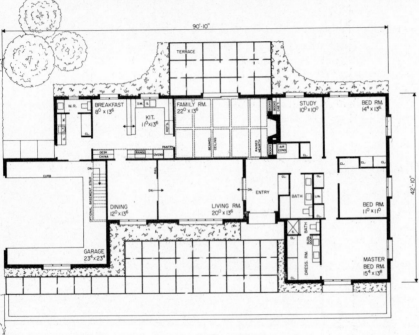

Design 22179
2,439 Sq. Ft.; 33,043 Cu. Ft.

● The formality of this French adaptation is a pleasing picture to behold. Wherever you may choose to build it, this one-story will most assuredly receive the accolades of passers-by. It is the outstanding proportion and the fine detail that make this a home of distinction. What's inside is every bit as delightful as what is outside. Your family will enjoy its three sizable bedrooms. The study will be a favorite haven for those who wish a period of peace and quiet. The sunken living room and the informal family room offer two large areas for family living. For eating there is the breakfast and separate dining room. Two baths and extra wash room serve the family well.

Design 22851
2,739 Sq. Ft.; 55,810 Cu. Ft.

● This spacious one-story has a classic Country French hip roof. The front entrance creates a charming entry. Beyond the covered porch is an octagonal foyer. A closet, shelves and powder room are contained in the foyer. All of the living areas overlook the rear yard. Sliding glass doors open each of these areas to the rear terrace. Their features include a fireplace in the living room, skylight in the dining room and a second set of sliding glass doors in the family room leading to a side covered porch. An island range and other built-ins are featured in the spacious, front kitchen.

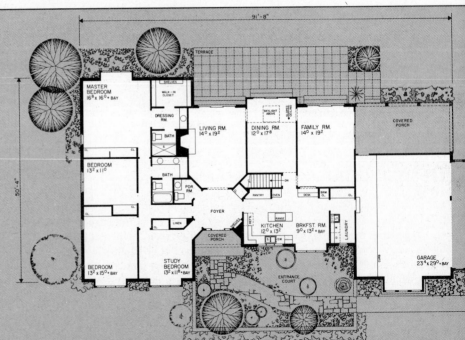

Design 21892
2,036 Sq. Ft.; 26,575 Cu. Ft.

● The romance of French Provincial is captured here by the hip-roof masses, the charm of the window detailing, the brick quoins at the corners, the delicate dentil work at the cornices, the massive centered chimney, and the recessed double front doors. The slightly raised entry court completes the picture. The basic floor plan is a favorite of many. And little wonder, for all areas work well together, while still maintaining a fine degree of separation of functions. The highlight of the interior, perhaps, will be the sunken living room. The family room, with its beamed ceiling, will not be far behind in its popularity. The separate dining room, mud room, efficient kitchen, complete the livability.

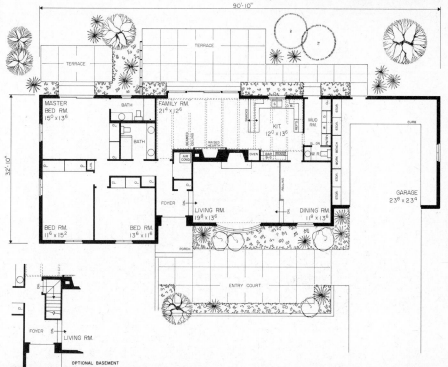

Design 21363

2,078 Sq. Ft.; 23,637 Cu. Ft.

● Picture this impressive L-shaped home with its French detailing sitting on your site just waiting for you and your family to move in. It will certainly be a glorious day. However, before the first shovel full of ground is turned you will have fun deciding upon the options this designs offers. As shown by the illustrations, you have your choice of building with or without a basement. Further, you may want to decide to have a fireplace flanked by bookshelves located in the living room. This family oriented design has four bedrooms. The master bedroom has its own private bath, while the three children's bedrooms are served by the main bath.

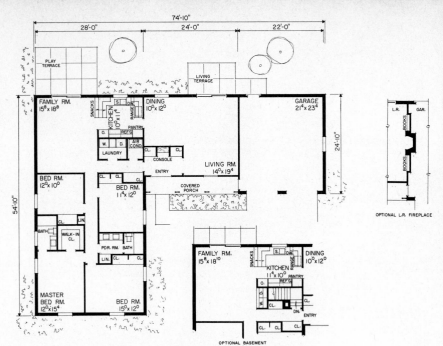

Design 21874

2,307 Sq. Ft.; 39,922 Cu. Ft.

● Certainly the exterior of this French adaptation with its hip-roof, wrought iron, attractive windows, brick quoins at the corners, and cupola, doesn't look familiar. Here is truly good design — in high style. Nor is the interior likely to look very familiar, either. Have you ever seen quite the livability this one-story has to offer? There are five bedrooms, 2½ baths, separate dining room, informal family room, efficient kitchen, convenient laundry, and an attached two-car garage. The storage is outstanding. There are plenty of wardrobe closets, linen storage, china cabinet, kitchen cupboard, and laundry cabinets. There is even a storage unit on the covered front porch.

Design 21881

2,472 Sq. Ft.; 44,434 Cu. Ft.

● Whether you park your car in the garage as the owner of this attractive home, or in the area reserved for guests, you'll be sure to appreciate all that this design has to offer. Its appealing exterior is one which will forever serve the family ideally. Once inside, you are but a few steps from the family and living rooms. The kitchen is but a couple of steps beyond the laundry and wash room with the informal family room just around the corner. Whether enjoyed to the front or the rear of this home, outdoor living will be gracious, indeed. Note the covered porch and the terraces in the rear. There are three of them!

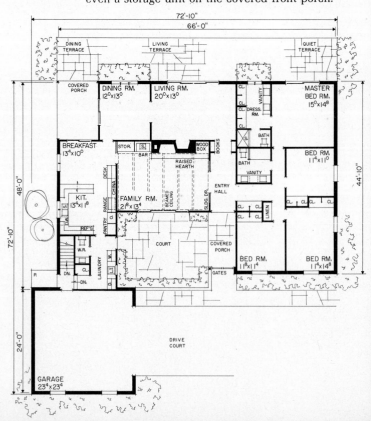

Design 21228 2,583 Sq. Ft. — First Floor; 697 Sq. Ft. — Second Floor; 51,429 Cu. Ft.

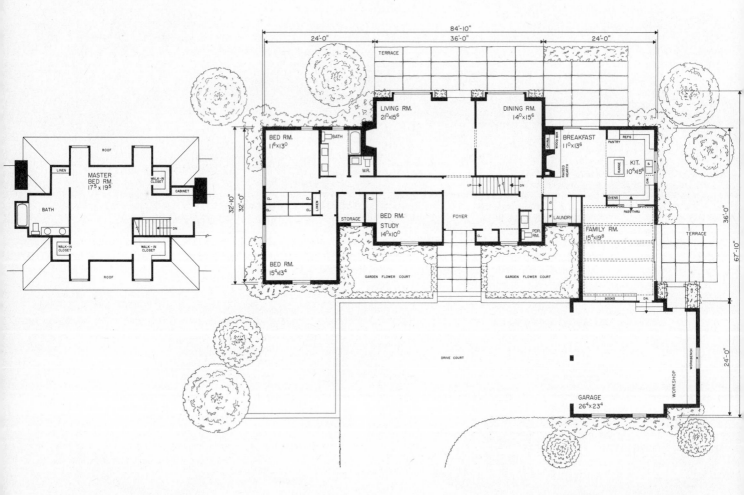

● This beautiful house has a wealth of detail taken from the rich traditions of French Regency design. The roof itself is a study in pleasant dormers and the hips and valleys of a big flowing area. A close examination of the plan shows the careful arrangement of space for privacy as well as good circulation of traffic. The spacious formal entrance hall sets the stage for good zoning. The informal living area is highlighted by the updated version of the old country kitchen. Observe the fireplace, and the barbecue. While there is a half-story devoted to the master bedroom suite, this home functions more as a one-story country estate design than as a 1½ story.

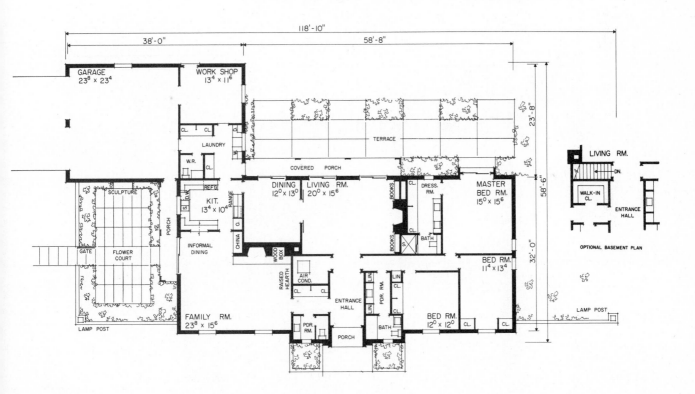

Design 21784 *2,686 Sq. Ft.; 32,515 Cu. Ft.*

● Truly impressive, and surely a home of which dreams are made. Yet, its basic rectangular shape, its economical use of space, its tremendous livability and its outstanding design make it a worthy lifetime investment. Consider the features which will serve you so well and make you such a proud home-owner for so many years to come. The pleasant formality of the front entrance invites one through the double front doors to a spacious interior. Study the zoning. The formal living and dining rooms will enjoy their deserved privacy and function with their own rear outdoor living facilities. The family room and kitchen function together and have an enclosed court.

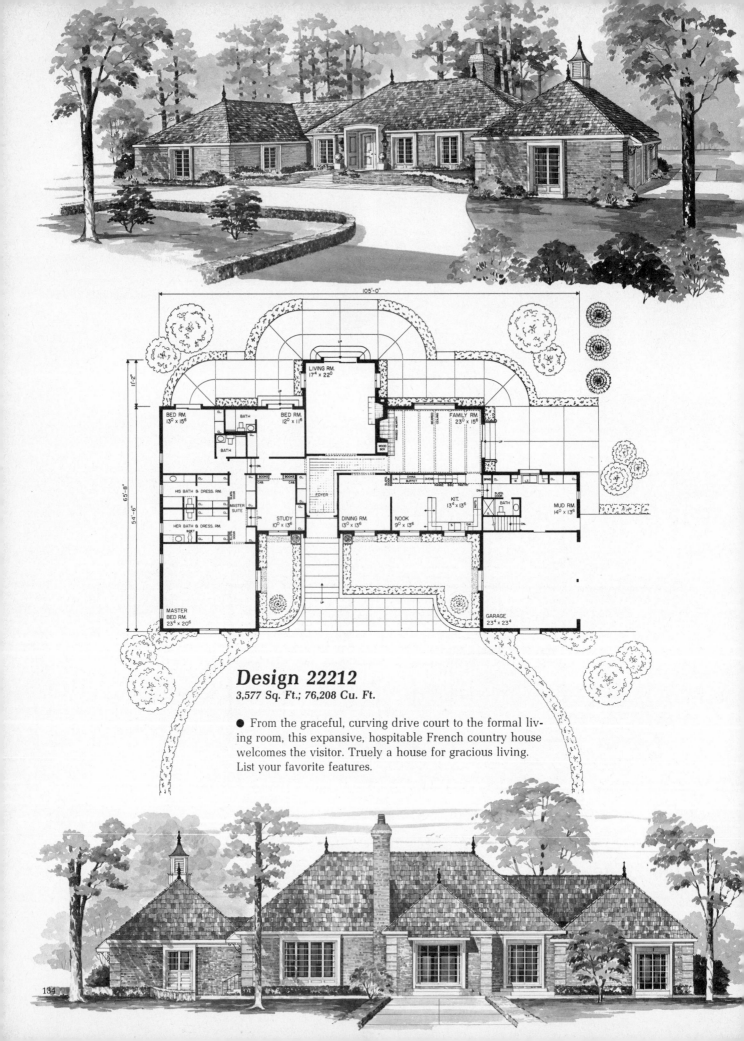

Design 22212
3,577 Sq. Ft.; 76,208 Cu. Ft.

● From the graceful, curving drive court to the formal living room, this expansive, hospitable French country house welcomes the visitor. Truely a house for gracious living. List your favorite features.

Spanish & Western Variations
For Active Families

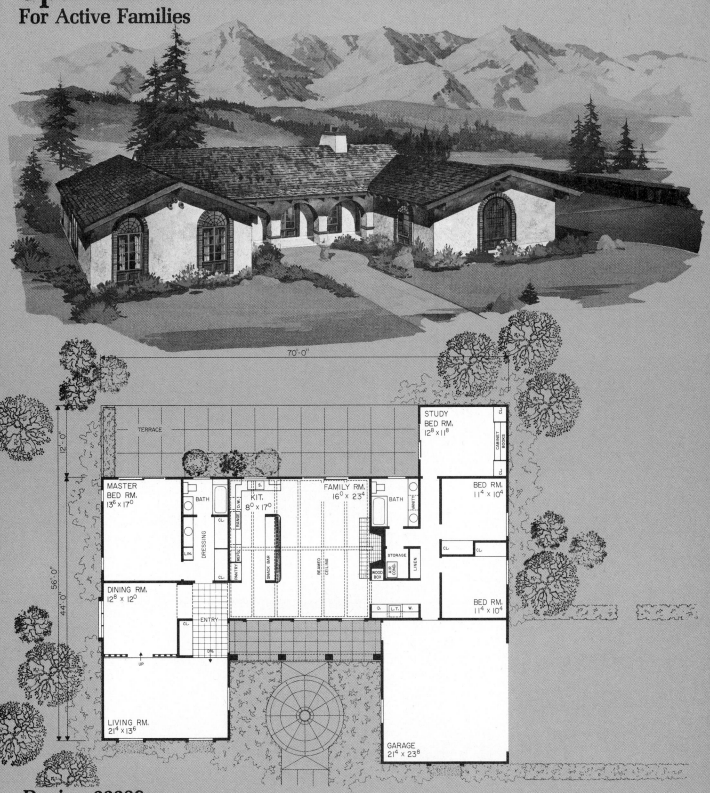

Design 22236 2,307 Sq. Ft.; 28,800 Cu. Ft.

● Living in this Spanish adaptation will truly be fun for the whole family. It will matter very little whether the backdrop matches the mountains above, becomes the endless prairie, turns out to be the rolling farmland, or is the backdrop of a suburban area. A family's flair for distinction will be satisfied by this picturesque exterior, while its requirements for everyday living will be gloriously catered to. The hub of the plan will be the kitchen-family room area. The beamed ceiling and raised hearth fireplace will contribute to the cozy, informal atmosphere. The separate dining room and the sunken living room function together formally. The master bedroom will enjoy its privacy from the three children's rooms located at the opposite end of the plan.

Design 22820 2,261 Sq. Ft.; 46,830 Cu. Ft.

● A privacy wall around the courtyard with pool and trellised planter area is a gracious area by which to enter this one-story design. The Spanish flavor is accented by the grillework and the tiled roof. Interior livability has a great deal to offer. The front living room has slid- ing glass doors which open to the en- trance court; the adjacent dining room features a bay window. Informal activ- ities will be enjoyed in the rear family room. Its many features include a slop- ed, beamed ceiling, raised hearth fire- place, sliding glass doors to the terrace and a snack bar for those very infor- mal meals. A laundry and powder room are adjacent to the U-shaped kitchen. The sleeping wing can remain quiet away from the plan's activity centers. Notice the three-car garage with an extra storage area.

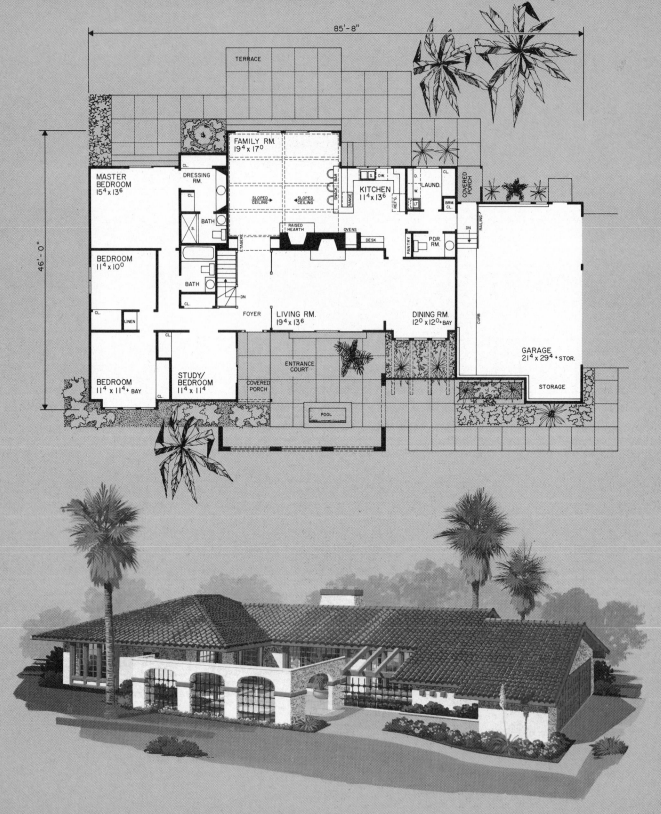

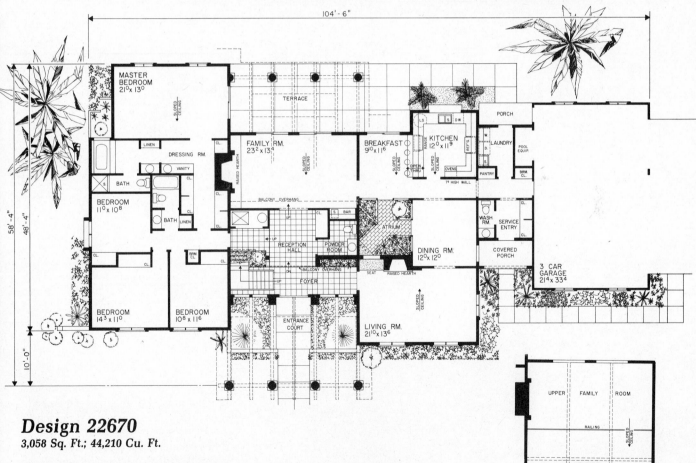

Design 22670
3,058 Sq. Ft.; 44,210 Cu. Ft.

● A centrally located interior atrium is one of the most interesting features of this Spanish design. The atrium has a built-in seat and will bring light to its adjacent rooms; living, dining and breakfast. Beyond the foyer, sunken one step, is a tiled reception hall that includes a powder room. This area leads to the sleeping wing and up one step to the family room. Overlooking the family room is a railed lounge, 279 square feet, which can be used for various activities. The work center area will be convenient to work in.

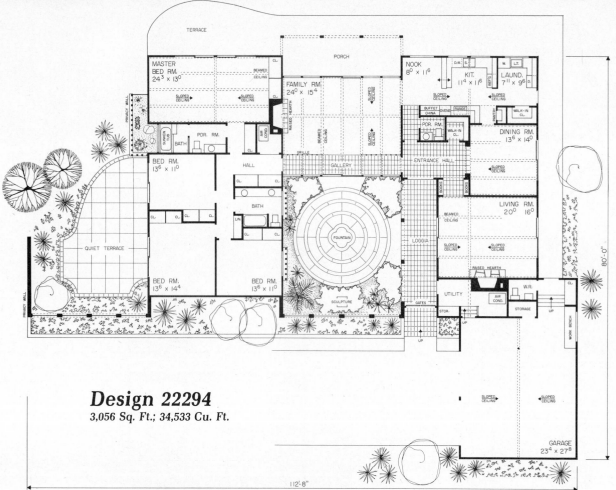

Design 22294
3,056 Sq. Ft.; 34,533 Cu. Ft.

Floor plan labels:

TERRACE · MASTER BED RM. 24³ x 13⁰ · BEAMED CEILING · SLOPED CEILING · PORCH · FAMILY RM. 24⁰ x 15⁴ · NOOK 8⁰ x 11⁶ · D.W. · KIT. 11⁴ x 11⁶ · LAUND. 7¹¹ x 9⁶ · W. LT. · REF'G · RANGE · WALK-IN CL. · BUFFET CHINA · OVENS · PDR. RM. · WALK-IN CL. · DINING RM. 13⁶ x 14⁰ · SLOPED CEILING · BATH · SUNKEN TUB · PDR. RM. · AIR COND. · RAISED HEARTH · GRILLE · GALLERY · ENTRANCE HALL · BOOKS · LIVING RM. 20⁰ x 16⁰ · BEAMED CEILING · SLOPED CEILING · PRIVACY WALL · BED RM. 13⁶ x 11⁰ · HALL · CL. · BATH · LIN. · FOUNTAIN · LOGGIA · SLOPED CEILING · QUIET TERRACE · CL. · CL. · CL. · BED RM. 13⁶ x 14⁴ · BED RM. 13⁶ x 11⁰ · SCULPTURE · GATES · STOR. · UTILITY · RAISED HEARTH · AIR COND. · W.R. · STORAGE · CL. · UP · WORK BENCH · SLOPED CEILING · SLOPED CEILING · GARAGE 23⁴ x 27⁸ · PRIVACY WALL

112'-8" · 80'-0"

● Here is a western ranch with an authentic Spanish flavor. Striking a note of distinction, the arched privacy walls provide a fine backdrop for the long, raised planter. The low-pitched roof features tile and has a wide overhang with exposed rafter tails. The interior is wonderfully zoned. The all-purpose family room is flanked by the sleeping wing and the living wing. Study each area carefully for the planning is excellent and the features are many. Indoor-outdoor integration is outstanding. At left — the spacious interior court. The covered passage to the double front doors is dramatic, indeed.

Design 22335 2,674 Sq. Ft.; 41,957 Cu. Ft.

● Surely a winner for those who have a liking for the architecture of the Far West. With or without the enclosure of the front court, this home with its stucco exterior, brightly colored roof tiles, and exposed rafter tails will be impressive, indeed. The floor plan reflects a wonderfully zoned interior. This results in a fine separation of functions which helps assure convenient living. The traffic patterns which flow from the spacious foyer are most efficient. Study them. While the sleeping wing is angled to the front line of the house, the sunken living room projects, at an angle, from the rear. Worthy of particular notice are such highlights as the two covered porches, the raised hearth fireplaces, the first floor laundry, the partial basement and the oversized garage with storage space.

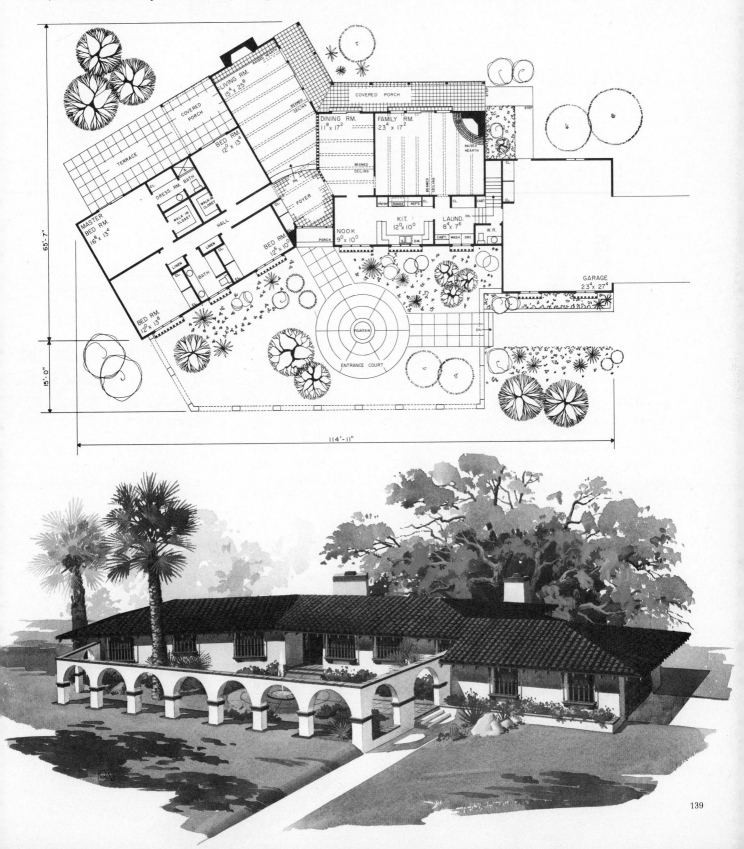

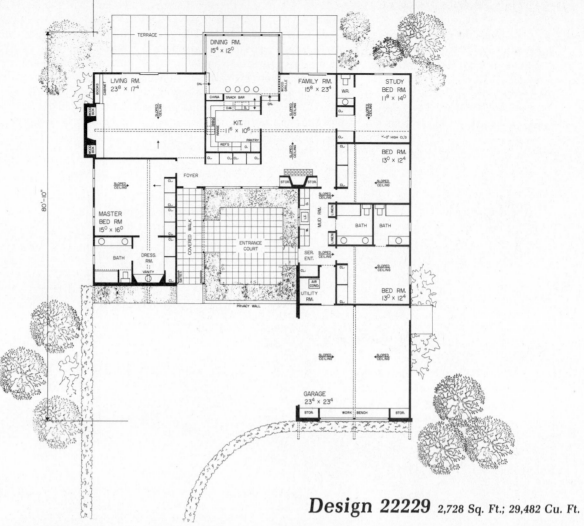

Design 22229 2,728 Sq. Ft.; 29,482 Cu. Ft.

● Rustic in character, this ranch home offers all the amenities that carefree living should be heir to. The irregular shape results in an enclosed front entrance court. Twin gates open to the coverd walk which looks out upon the delightful private court on its way to the front door. Traffic patterns are interesting. This house is zoned so as to provide maximum privacy to the living room and master bedroom. At the other end of the house are the children's rooms and the informal, multi-purpose family room. The kitchen is strategically located. The projecting dining room with its abundance of glass will permit the fullest enjoyment of the outdoors at mealtime. Don't miss the sloped ceilings and two fireplaces. Convenient living at its best will be enjoyed by all in this one-story design.

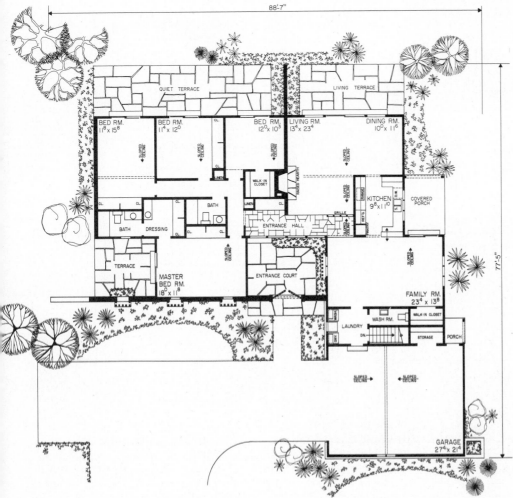

Design 22370
2,232 Sq. Ft.; 35,848 Cu. Ft.

● Whatever the setting - near mountains of the Far West, or in a subdivision of the Mid West - this L-shaped ranch home will deliver a lifetime of excellent livability. Behind the twin gates, opening from the drive court, is a delightful entrance court with massive beam-work above. A somewhat similar area provides the master bedroom with its own privacy terrace. Three additional bedrooms, each functioning through sliding glass doors with rear terrace. The open planning of the living and dining rooms provide a spacious and formal living zone. It, too, has its outdoor living area. A covered porch is adjacent to the family room and provides an excellent view of the kitchen.

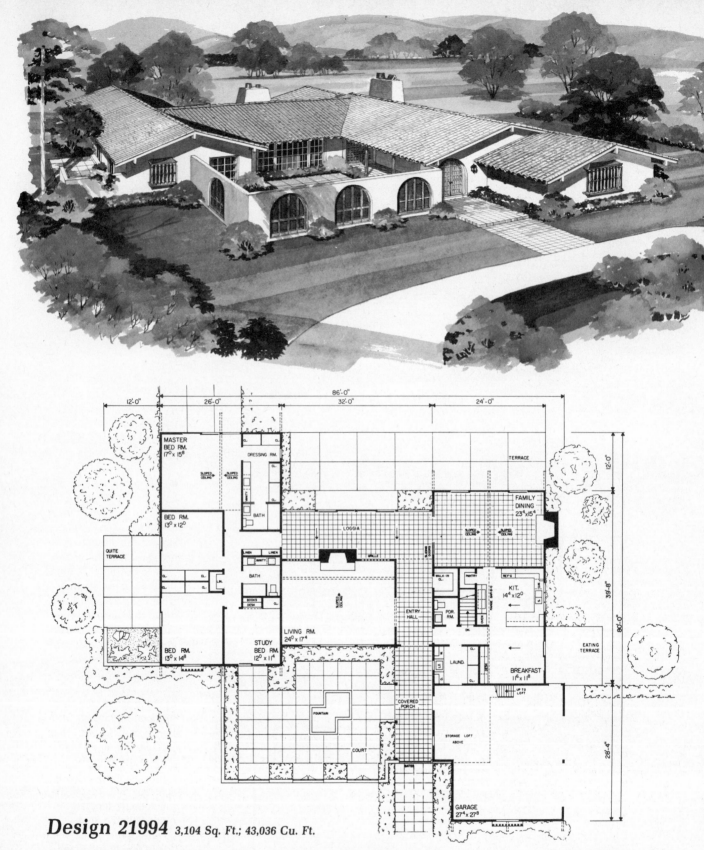

Design 21994 3,104 Sq. Ft.; 43,036 Cu. Ft.

● The Spanish flavor of the old Southwest is delightfully captured by this sprawling ranch house. Its L-shape and high privacy wall go together to form a wide open interior court. This will be a great place to hold those formal and/or informal garden parties. The plan itself is wonderfully zoned. The center portion of the house is comprised of the big, private living room with sloped ceiling. Traffic patterns will noiselessly skirt this formal area. The two wings—the sleeping and informal living—are connected by the well-lighted and spacious loggia. In the sleeping wing, observe the size of the various rooms and the fine storage. In the informal living wing, note the big family room and breakfast room that family members will enjoy.

● Echoing design themes of old Spain, this history house distills the essence of country houses built by rancheros in Early California. Yet its floor plan provides all the comfort and convenience essential to our contemporary living.

Among its charming features is a secluded court, or patio; a greenhouse tucked in behind the garage; a covered rear porch; a low-pitched wide overhanging roof with exposed rafter tails; sloping beamed ceilings. Contri-

buting to the authenticity of the design are the two sets of panelled doors. The covered walk to the front doors provides a sheltered area adjacent to the court. Once inside, the feeling of space continues to impress.

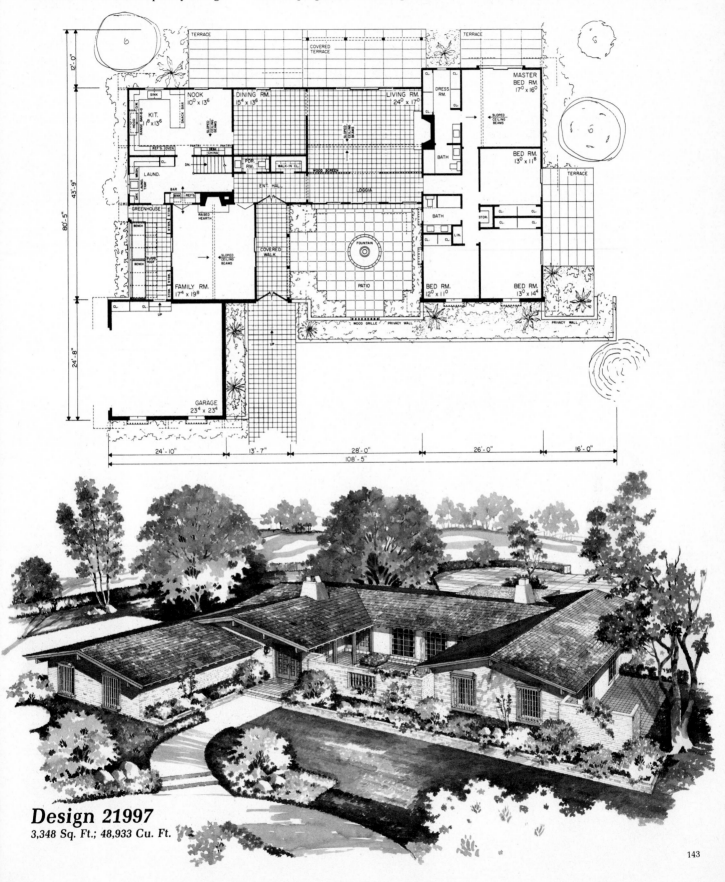

Design 21997
3,348 Sq. Ft.; 48,933 Cu. Ft.

● A spectacular foyer! Fully 21' long, it offers double entry to the heart of this home . . . a 21' by 21' gathering room, complete with sloped ceiling, raised hearth fireplace and sliding glass doors onto the terrace. There's a formal dining room, too. Plus a well-located study . . . insuring space for solitude or undisturbed work. The kitchen features a snack bar and a breakfast nook with sliding doors onto the terrace . . . an arrangement that's sure to make every meal easy and pleasant. For more convenience, a pantry and first-floor laundry. In the master suite, a dressing room with entry to the bath, four closets . . . and sliding doors onto the terrace! Two more bedrooms if you wish to convert the study . . . or one easily large enough for two children, with a dressing area and private entry to the second bath.

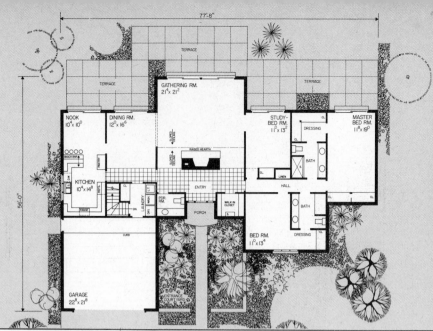

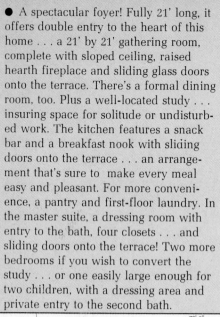

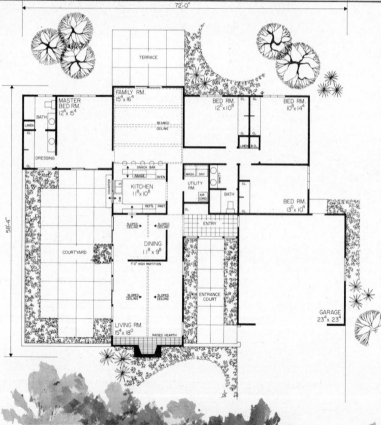

Design 22386
1,994 Sq. Ft.; 22,160 Cu. Ft.

● This distinctive home may look like the Far West, but don't let that inhibit you from enjoying the great livability it has to offer. Wherever built, you will surely experience a satisfying pride of ownership. Imagine, entrance court in addition to a large side courtyard! A central core is made up of the living, dining, and family rooms, plus the kitchen. Each functions with an outdoor living area. The younger generation has its sleeping zone divorced from the master bedroom. The location of the attractive attached garage provides direct access to the front entry. Don't miss the vanity, the utility room with laundry equipment, the snack bar, and the raised hearth fireplace. Note three pass-throughs from the kitchen. Observe the beamed and sloping ceilings of the living areas.

Design 22594 2,294 Sq. Ft.; 42,120 Cu. Ft.

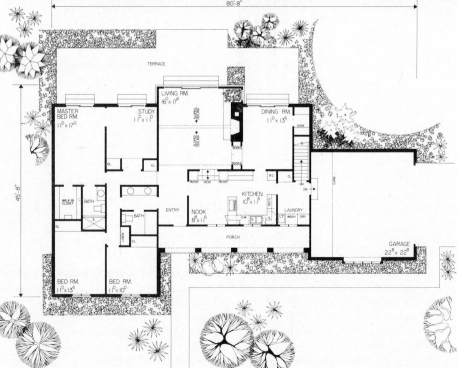

Design 22557
1,955 Sq. Ft.; 43,509 Cu. Ft.

● This eye-catching design with a flavor of the Spanish Southwest will be as interesting to live in as it will be to look at. The character of the exterior is set by the wide overhanging roof with its exposed beams; the massive arched pillars; the arching of the brick over the windows; the panelled door and the horizontal siding that contrasts with the brick. The elegantly large master bedroom/study suite is a focal point of the interior. However, if necessary, the study could become the fourth bedroom. The living and dining rooms are large and are separated by a massive raised hearth fireplace.

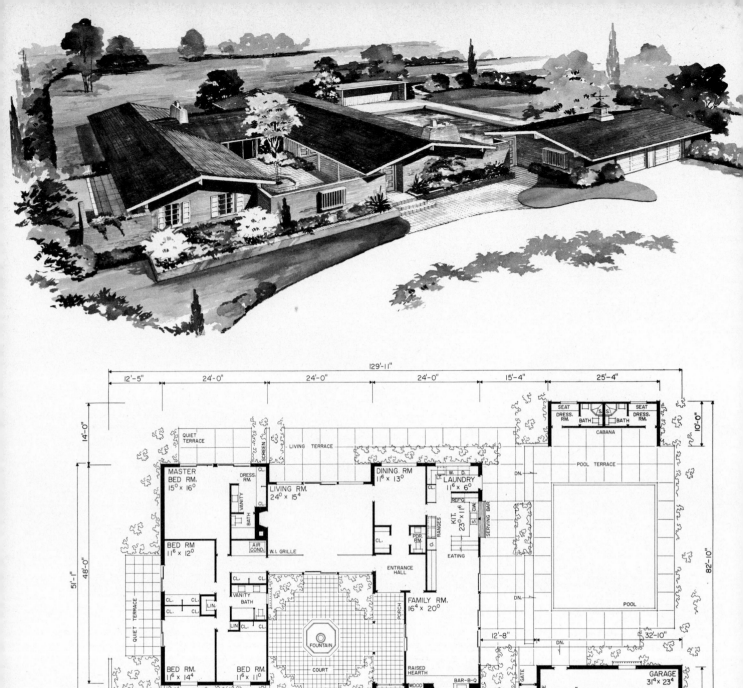

Design 21756 *2,736 Sq. Ft.; 29,139 Cu. Ft.*

● Reminiscent of the West and impressive, indeed. If you are after something that is luxurious in both its appearance and its livability this design should receive your consideration. This rambling ranch house, which encloses a spacious and dramatic flower court, is designed for comfort and privacy indoors and out. Study the outdoor areas. Notice the seclusion each of them provides. Three bedrooms, plus a master suite with dressing room and bath form a private bedroom wing. Formal and informal living areas serve ideally for various types of entertaining. There is excellent circulation of traffic throughout the house. The kitchen is handy to the formal dining room and the informal family room. Don't miss raised hearth fireplace.

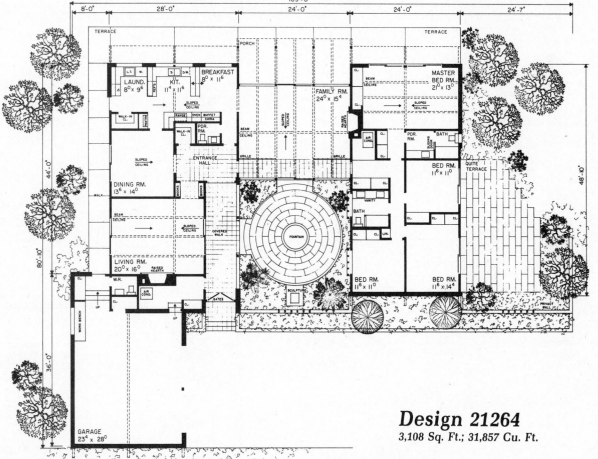

Design 21264
3,108 Sq. Ft.; 31,857 Cu. Ft.

● A romantic adaptation from the Spanish Southwest. This design is truly distinctive, both in its exterior styling and in its gracious floor plan. Its exterior beauty is characterized by the series of low-pitched, overhanging roofs, the extended rafter ends, the blank masonry wall masses and the paneled double front gates. Behind the front privacy wall is the unique, enclosed court. The stroll up the covered walk to the entrance hall will be a delightful experience, indeed. The entrance hall routes traffic to the formal dining and living rooms, the efficient work center and to the passageway between the family room and court to the four bedroom sleeping wing. Study the many other features. You will be able to make a long list.

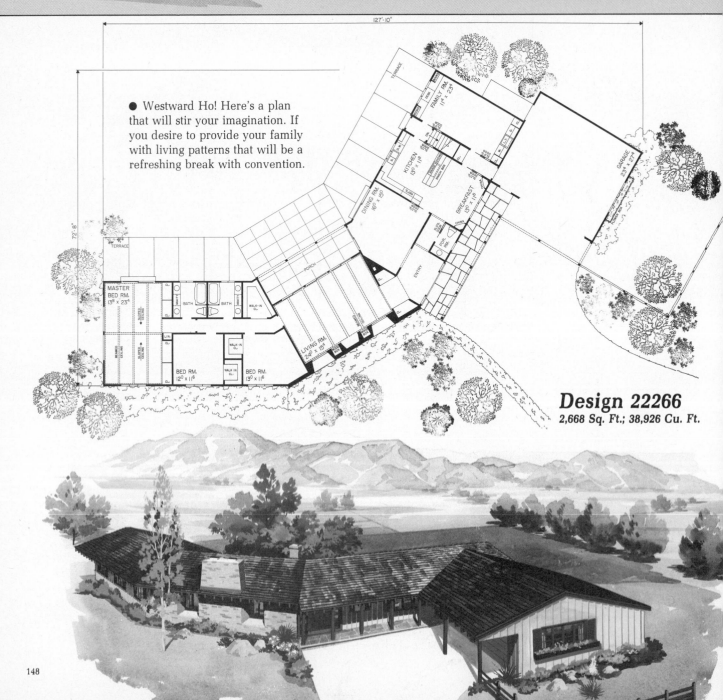

● Westward Ho! Here's a plan that will stir your imagination. If you desire to provide your family with living patterns that will be a refreshing break with convention.

Design 22266
2,668 Sq. Ft.; 38,926 Cu. Ft.

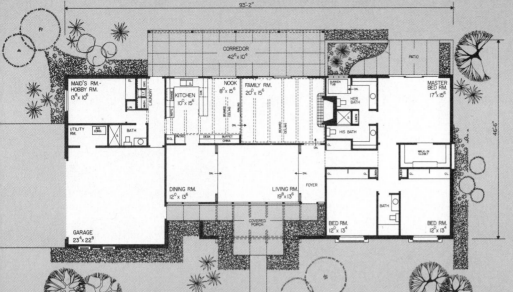

Design 22231
2,740 Sq. Ft.; 31,670 Cu. Ft.

● The features that will appeal to you about this flat-roofed Spanish hacienda are almost endless. Of course, the captivating qualities of the exterior speak for themselves. The extension of the front bedroom wall to form the inviting arch is distinctive. Once inside, any list of features will continue to grow rapidly. Both the family and living rooms are sunken. Private patio adjacent to the master suite.

Design 22258 2,504 Sq. Ft.; 26,292 Cu. Ft.

● Here's a real Western Ranch House with all the appeal of its forebears. As for the livability offered by this angular design, the old days of the rugged west never had anything like this.

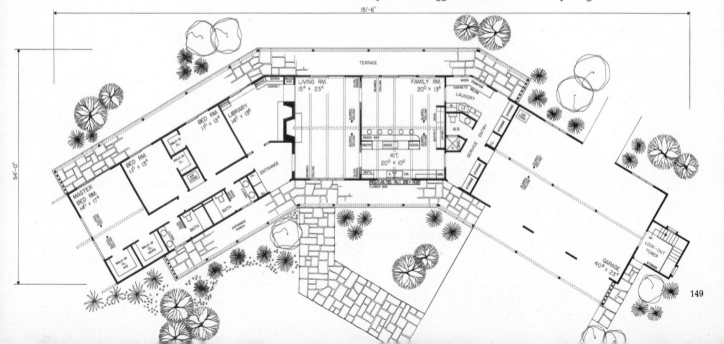

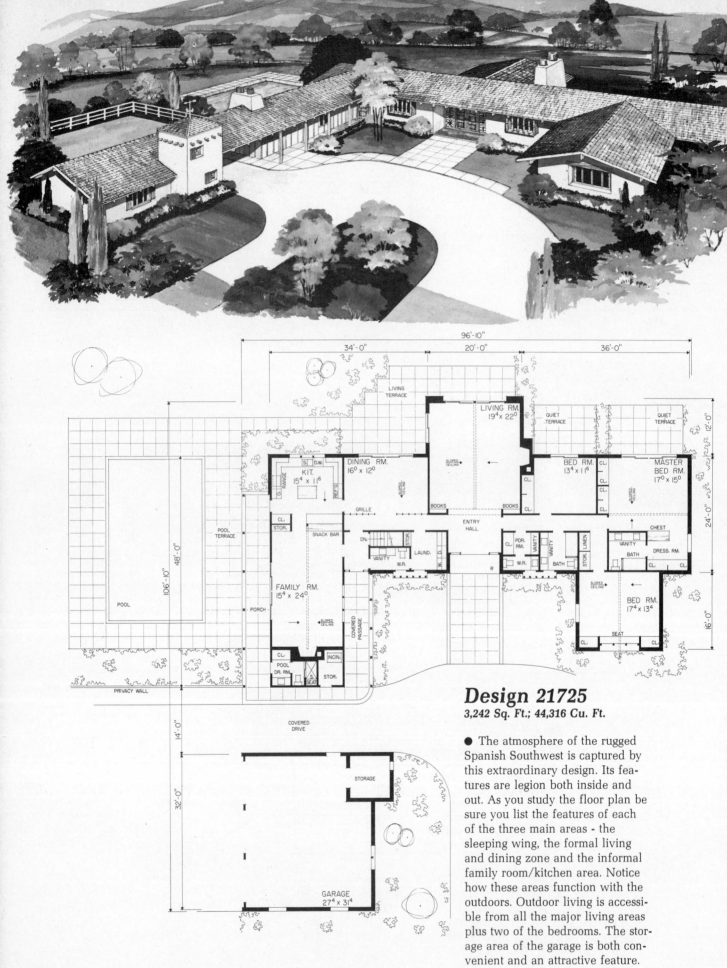

Design 21725
3,242 Sq. Ft.; 44,316 Cu. Ft.

● The atmosphere of the rugged Spanish Southwest is captured by this extraordinary design. Its features are legion both inside and out. As you study the floor plan be sure you list the features of each of the three main areas - the sleeping wing, the formal living and dining zone and the informal family room/kitchen area. Notice how these areas function with the outdoors. Outdoor living is accessible from all the major living areas plus two of the bedrooms. The storage area of the garage is both convenient and an attractive feature.

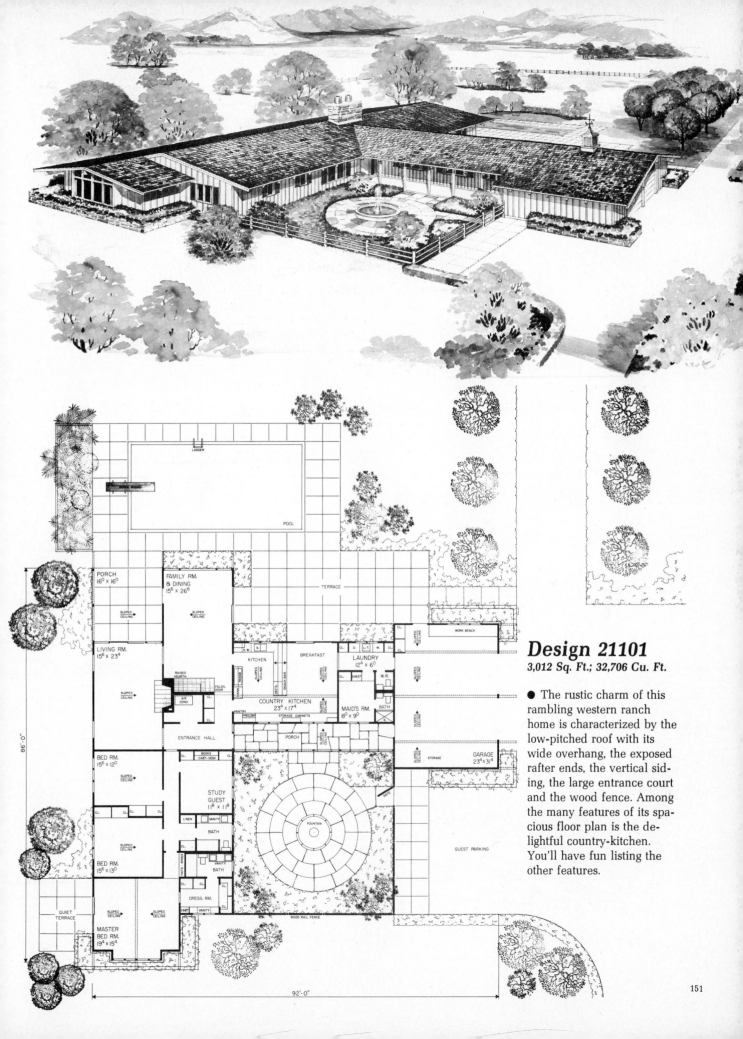

Design 21101
3,012 Sq. Ft.; 32,706 Cu. Ft.

● The rustic charm of this rambling western ranch home is characterized by the low-pitched roof with its wide overhang, the exposed rafter ends, the vertical siding, the large entrance court and the wood fence. Among the many features of its spacious floor plan is the delightful country-kitchen. You'll have fun listing the other features.

151

Design 21825
2,170 Sq. Ft.; 21,417 Cu. Ft.

● Five wonderful out-
door living areas headed
by the front private court
are highlights of this impressive U-shaped, four
bedroom home. The low-
pitched, wide overhang-
ing roof, the exposed rafters, the grille work and
the attractive gate are all
features which remind
one of the Spanish South-
west.

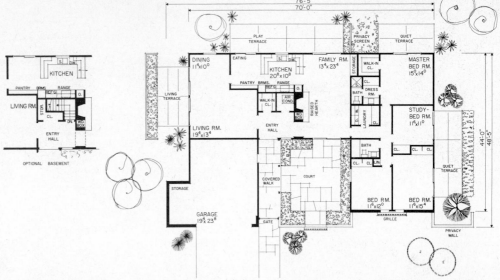

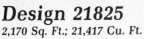

Design 22590
2,380 Sq. Ft.; 26,680 Cu. Ft.

● A large enclosed garden courtyard.
A rear terrace. Formal living and dining rooms, plus a family room with a
raised hearth fireplace. Three large
bedrooms, including a master suite
with a dressing room and private bath.
These are just some of the outstanding
features of this design. This home is
designed for easy living, whether
you're entertaining with a summer barbecue or a formal dinner party. And
it's got the extras you want to help en-
sure life-long convenience . . . an island range and built-in desk in the
kitchen, a first-floor laundry, lots of
convenient storage. You will like the
strategically placed walk-in closet adjacent to the kitchen.

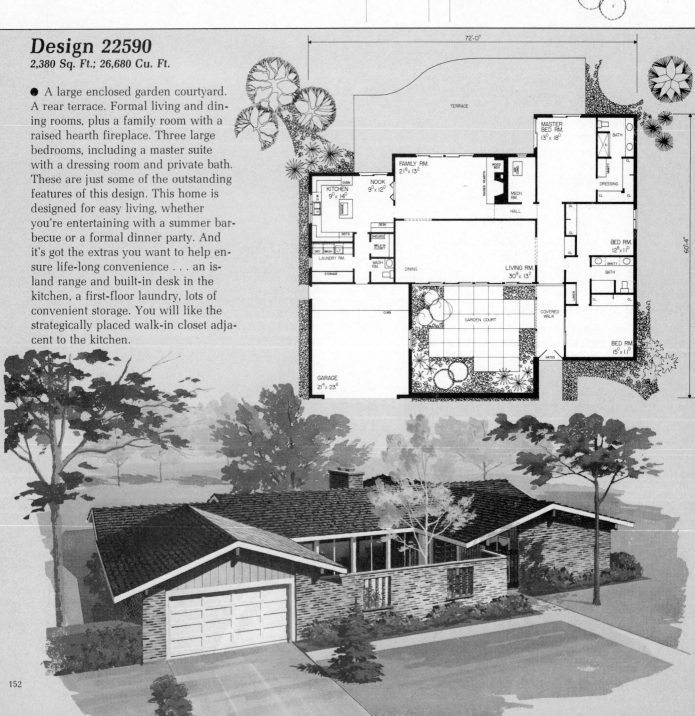

152

Design 21754
2,080 Sq. Ft.; 21,426 Cu. Ft.

● Boasting a traditional Western flavor, this rugged U-shaped ranch home has all the features to assure grand living. The low-pitched, wide-overhanging roof with exposed rafters, the masses of brick, and the panelled doors with their carriage lamps above are among the exterior highlights which create this design's unique character. The private front flower court, inside the high brick wall, fosters a delightfully dramatic atmosphere which carries inside. The floor plan is positively unique and exceptionally livable. Wonderfully zoned, the three bedrooms enjoy their full measure of privacy. Observe the dressing room, walk-in closet and linen storage. The formal living and dining rooms function together in a most pleasing fashion. An attractive open railing separates the dining room from the sunken living room.

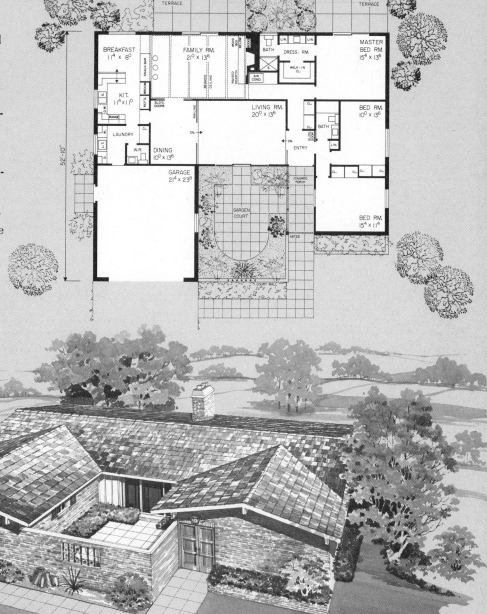

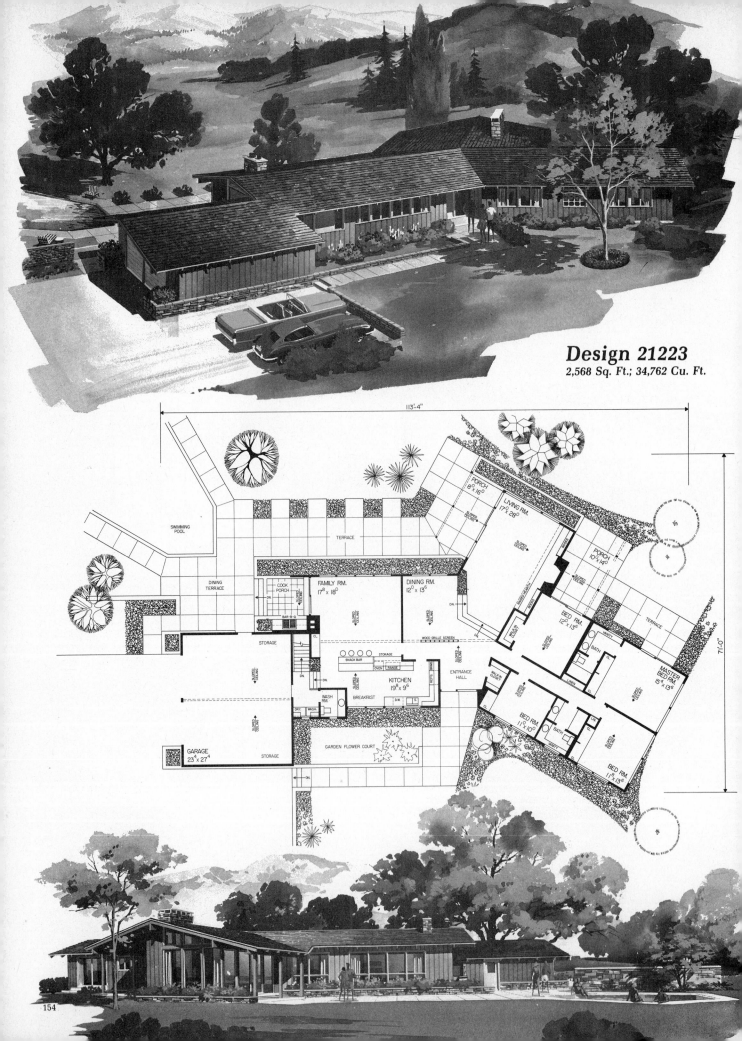

Design 21223
2,568 Sq. Ft.; 34,762 Cu. Ft.

113'-4"

71'-0"

SWIMMING POOL

TERRACE

DINING TERRACE

PORCH
8⁰ x 16⁰

LIVING RM.
17⁹ x 28⁰

PORCH
10⁰ x 14⁰

TERRACE

FAMILY RM.
17⁸ x 18⁰

COOK PORCH

DINING RM.
12⁰ x 13⁶

BED RM.
12⁰ x 13⁶

BATH

VANITY

MASTER BED RM.
15⁴ x 13⁶

STORAGE

SNACK BAR

STORAGE

OVEN RANGE

WOOD GRILLE SCREEN

ENTRANCE HALL

WALK-IN CLOSET

LINEN

KITCHEN
19⁸ x 9⁶

BREAKFAST

WASH RM.

DRY. WASH.

D.W.

BED RM.
11⁹ x 10⁰

BATH

LIN.

VANITY

GARAGE
23⁴ x 27⁴

STORAGE

GARDEN FLOWER COURT

BED RM.
11⁸ x 13⁶

Atriums & Courtyards
Bring the Outdoors In

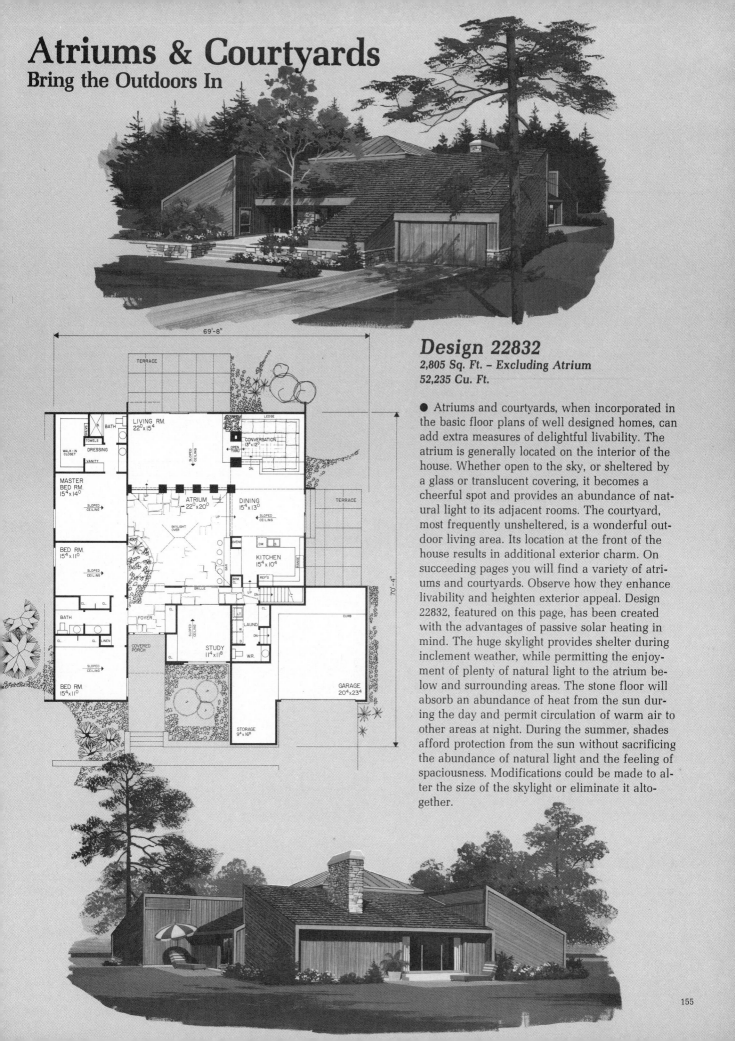

Design 22832
2,805 Sq. Ft. – Excluding Atrium
52,235 Cu. Ft.

● Atriums and courtyards, when incorporated in the basic floor plans of well designed homes, can add extra measures of delightful livability. The atrium is generally located on the interior of the house. Whether open to the sky, or sheltered by a glass or translucent covering, it becomes a cheerful spot and provides an abundance of natural light to its adjacent rooms. The courtyard, most frequently unsheltered, is a wonderful outdoor living area. Its location at the front of the house results in additional exterior charm. On succeeding pages you will find a variety of atriums and courtyards. Observe how they enhance livability and heighten exterior appeal. Design 22832, featured on this page, has been created with the advantages of passive solar heating in mind. The huge skylight provides shelter during inclement weather, while permitting the enjoyment of plenty of natural light to the atrium below and surrounding areas. The stone floor will absorb an abundance of heat from the sun during the day and permit circulation of warm air to other areas at night. During the summer, shades afford protection from the sun without sacrificing the abundance of natural light and the feeling of spaciousness. Modifications could be made to alter the size of the skylight or eliminate it altogether.

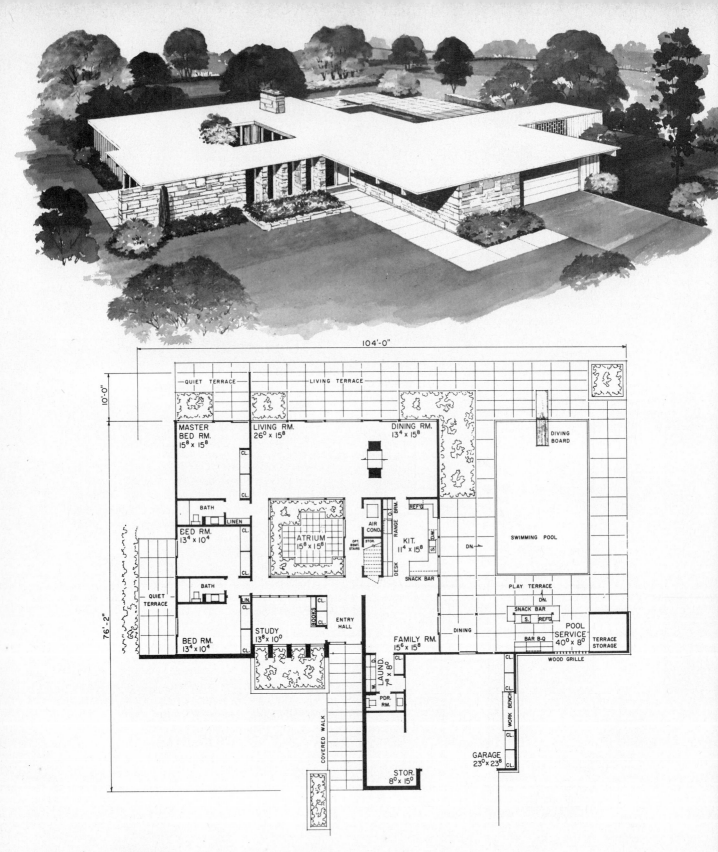

Design 21224 2,569 Sq. Ft. — Excluding Atrium; 23,634 Cu. Ft.

● For complete privacy while experiencing the delights of the outdoors try this atrium house. Occupying a commanding position, the interior court is approximately 15 feet square. It creates a unique atmosphere. The major traffic patterns around this dramatic glass enclosed atrium will be delightful. The living room with its own glass walls could hardly be more bright, cheerful, and spacious. A two-way fireplace can be enjoyed equally from the living and dining rooms. With few changes, this flat-roof contemporary, could function as a four bedroom home. There are two full baths plus an extra powder room. Note laundry, garage storage facilities, and covered dining terrace. Don't overlook the other unique outdoor features in this area.

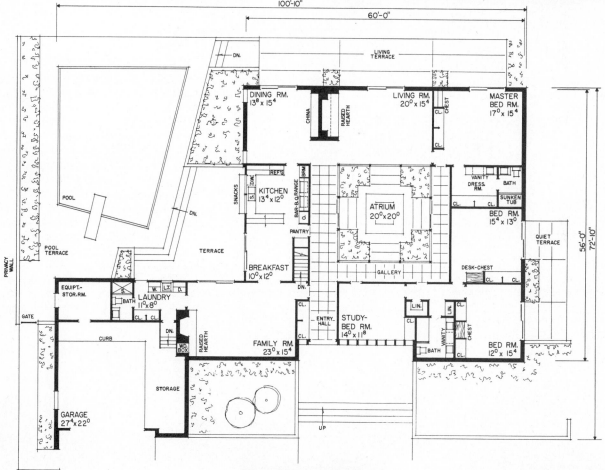

Design 21836 *3,374 Sq. Ft. — Excluding Atrium; 39,095 Cu. Ft.*

● Impressive, indeed! This flat-roofed, atrium home has all the features for luxurious living. What could be more dramatic than the wide steps leading up to the recessed front entrance? This expanse of walkway flanked by effective planting merely sets the stage for a delightful experience in living upon passing through the double front doors. The 400 square foot atrium is the hub around which the various activities of the family revolve. Whatever the season, the daily routine will surely be enriched by the experience of such an awareness of the outdoors while indoors. Study the zoning of this exciting home. It is most practical. Of particular interest, is the terrace overlooking the swimming pool. See storage room in the garage.

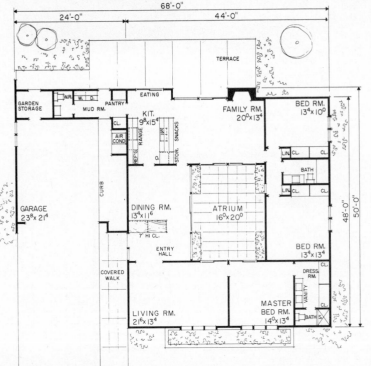

Design 21841
**1,920 Sq. Ft. — Excluding Atrium
19,806 Cu. Ft.**

● Atrium living is wonderfully illustrated by this attractive design. You forever will be aware of its delightful presence and it will offer pleasingly different patterns of living to your family. It may be in constant use since the skylight provides protection during inclement weather. Clever planning results in excellent zoning of the basic area of the plan. The formal living room and master bedroom are located to the front and enjoy plenty of peace and quiet. The children's rooms are by themselves and are but a few steps from the informal family room. The efficient kitchen has eating space and functions ideally with the dining and family rooms. A mud room is accessible from the garage and the rear terrace.

Design 21837 2,016 Sq. Ft. — Excluding Atrium; 27,280 Cu. Ft.

Design 21867

1,692 Sq. Ft. — Excluding Atrium
21,383 Cu. Ft.

● Looking for a new house involves a number of varied considerations. One that is most basic involves what you would like your family's living patterns to be. If you would like to introduce your family to something that is different and is sure to be fun for all, consider this dramatic atrium house. Parents and children alike will be thrilled by the experience and the environment engendered by this outdoor living area indoors. A skylight provides for the protection during inclement weather without restricting the flood of natural light. Notice how this atrium functions with the various areas. Observe relationships between children's rooms and family room between master bedroom and the quiet living room.

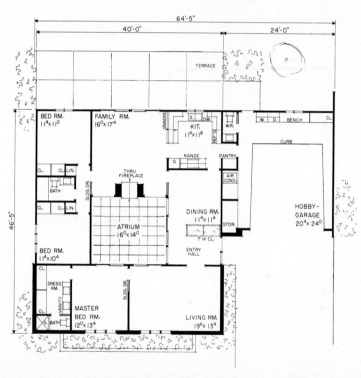

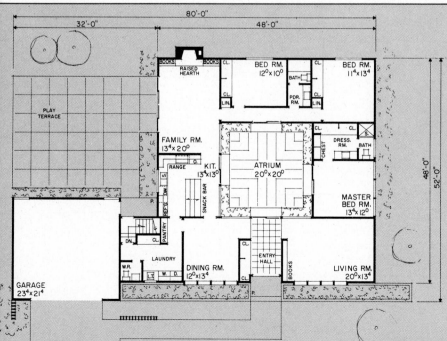

● Picture yourself and your family enjoying this new home. Sheltered from the weather, whatever the season, the atrium will be favorite spot for eating, reading, playing games or just plain sitting. Amidst all that natural light and those attractive planting areas, you'll enjoy the informality of outdoor living under controlled conditions. Four pairs of sliding glass doors make the atrium accessible from all areas of the house. Observe how the formal living room is located from the informal family room. Note kitchen snack bar and the separate dining room. Don't miss the laundry, pantry and extra wash room. The family room will also be a favorite spot. Its focal point is the raised hearth fireplace.

New Living Dimensions - Inside And Out

● Here is an impressive application of the Mansard type roof. Its wide overhang effectively compliments the simplicity of the brick masses. The curving driveway court strikes an appealing note. The entrance, flanked by planting areas, highlights double front doors. To each side, is an attractive glass panel. The breadth of the house is increased by the extension of the front wall. This, in turn, provides privacy for the side living terrace. To the rear, free standing brick walls provide further privacy as well as decorative appeal. The gently sloping roof has plastic domes which permit the interior to enjoy an added measure of natural light. Notice the indoor-outdoor living relationships available from every room in this design. For the active, growing family they are truly outstanding.

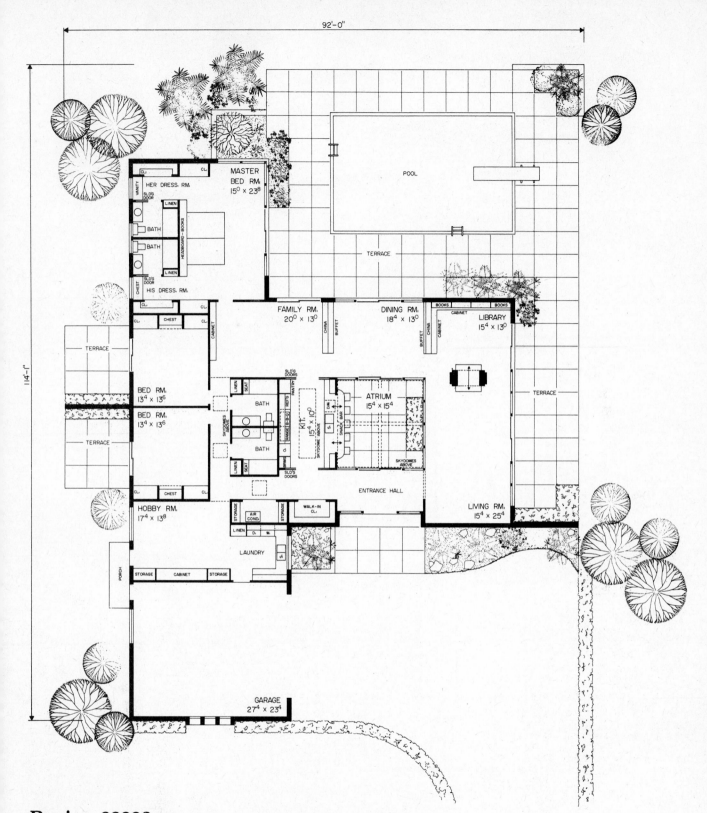

92'-0"

114'-1"

CL.
HER DRESS. RM.
CL.
VANITY
SLD'G DOOR
MASTER BED RM.
15⁰ x 23⁸
LINEN
BATH
BATH
HEADBOARD - BOOKS
LINEN
CHEST
SLD'G DOOR
HIS DRESS. RM.
POOL
TERRACE

TERRACE
CL.
CL.
CHEST
CL.
CABINET
FAMILY RM.
20⁰ x 13⁰
CHINA
BUFFET
DINING RM.
18⁴ x 13⁰
BUFFET
CHINA
CABINET
BOOKS
CABINET
BOOKS
LIBRARY
15⁴ x 13⁰

TERRACE
BED RM.
13⁴ x 13⁶
BED RM.
13⁴ x 13⁶
TERRACE
LINEN
SEAT
PANTRY
SLD'G DOORS
BATH
RANGE B-C
TRAYS
REF'S.
SKYDOMES ABOVE
BATH
LINEN
SEAT
SLD'G DOORS
BRMS
KIT.
15⁴ x 10⁰
SKYDOME ABOVE
D.W.
S.
SNACK BAR
ATRIUM
15⁴ x 15⁴
SKYDOMES ABOVE

TERRACE

CL.
CHEST
CL.
HOBBY RM.
17⁴ x 13⁸
STORAGE
AIR COND.
STORAGE
WALK-IN CL.
ENTRANCE HALL
LIVING RM.
15⁴ x 25⁴
LINEN
D.
W.
LAUNDRY
S.
PORCH
STORAGE
CABINET
STORAGE

GARAGE
27⁴ x 23⁴

Design 22226 *3,340 Sq. Ft. — Excluding Atrium; 41,290 Cu. Ft.*

● If anything has been left out of this home it would certainly be difficult to determine just what it is that is missing. Containing over 3,300 square feet, space for living is abundant, indeed. Each of the various rooms is large. Further, each major room has access to the outdoors. The efficient inside kitchen is strategically located in relation to the family and dining rooms. Observe how it functions with the enclosed atrium to provide a snack bar. Functional room dividers separate various areas. Study closely the living area. A two-way fireplace divides the spacious living room and the cozy library highlighted by built-in cabinets and bookshelves. A hobby room with laundry adjacent will be a favorite family activities spot. This home surely has numerous, impressive qualities to recommend it.

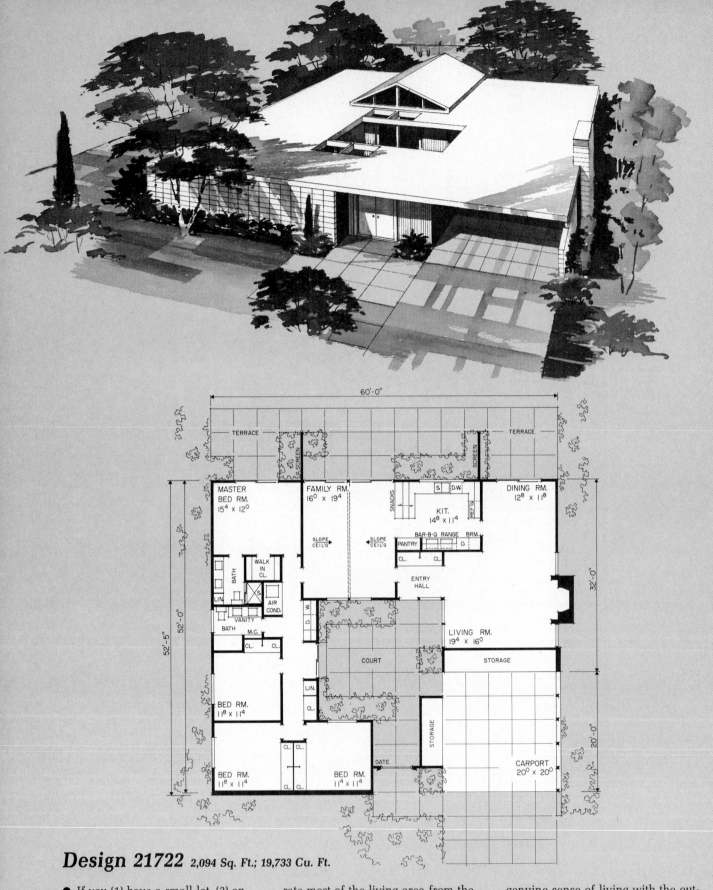

Floor plan labels:

TERRACE   TERRACE

60'-0"

MASTER BED RM. 15⁴ x 12⁰

FAMILY RM. 16⁰ x 19⁴

DINING RM. 12⁸ x 11⁸

SNACKS

KIT. 14⁸ x 11⁴

S   D.W.

REF'G.

SLOPE CEIL'G   SLOPE CEIL'G

BAR-B-Q   RANGE   BRM.

PANTRY   O.

CL.   CL.

BATH   WALK IN CL.

LIN   S.

AIR COND.

VANITY

BATH   M.C.

CL.   CL.

ENTRY HALL

D. W.

LIVING RM. 19⁴ x 16⁰

STORAGE

COURT

LIN.

CL.

BED RM. 11⁸ x 11⁴

STORAGE

BED RM. 11⁸ x 11⁴   CL. CL.   BED RM. 11⁴ x 11⁴   CL. CL.

GATE

CARPORT 20⁰ x 20⁰

52'-5"   52'-0"   32'-0"   20'-0"

Design 21722 2,094 Sq. Ft.; 19,733 Cu. Ft.

● If you (1) have a small lot, (2) an unquenchable desire for indoor-outdoor living, coupled with (3) a passion for privacy, this plan could be a solution for you. Start with a garden and wrap the house around it. Separate most of the living area from the courtyard by floor-to-ceiling panels of glass. Now raise the roof over the family room and install clerestory windows in each gable end. The result is complete privacy mixed with a genuine sense of living with the out-of-doors minus the heat of summer or the cold of winter. This arrangement also effectively zones living and sleeping areas. Don't overlook the four bedrooms and two baths.

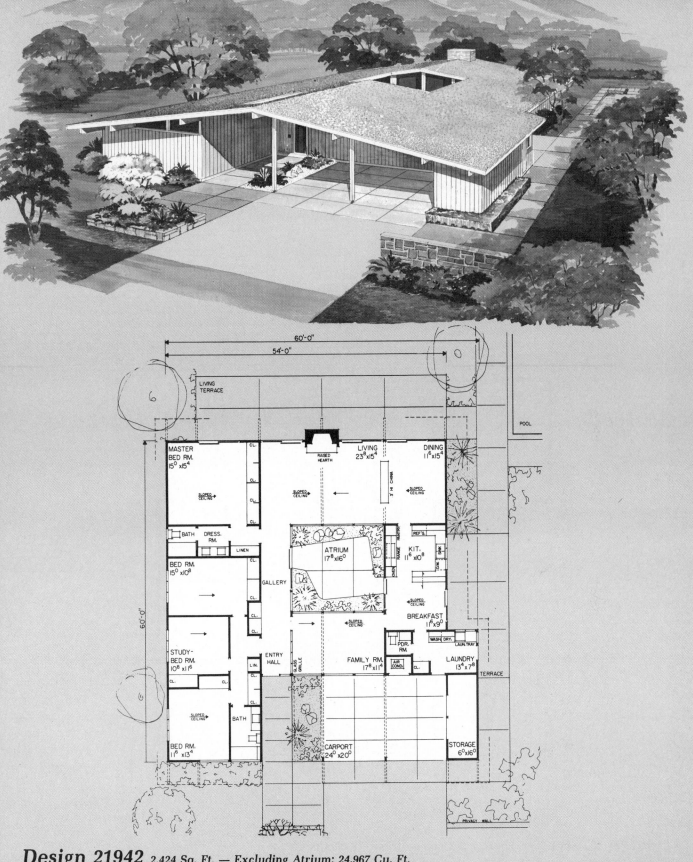

Design 21942 2,424 Sq. Ft. — Excluding Atrium; 24,967 Cu. Ft.

● If you happen to be among the many who would be receptive to a new dimension in livability, then this forward-looking contemporary might be just the home for you and your family. This sparkling design has a story to tell that is like no other. To begin with, the exterior is pleasingly dramatic. The low-pitched, wide overhanging roof cleverly covers both the walk to the front entry and the two-car carport. Inside, the prospect of living in this house becomes most exciting. Traffic patterns flow around the glass-walled atrium. This, is virtually an outdoor area indoors. Open to the sky, the atrium provides the spacious living and family rooms with unique backdrops.

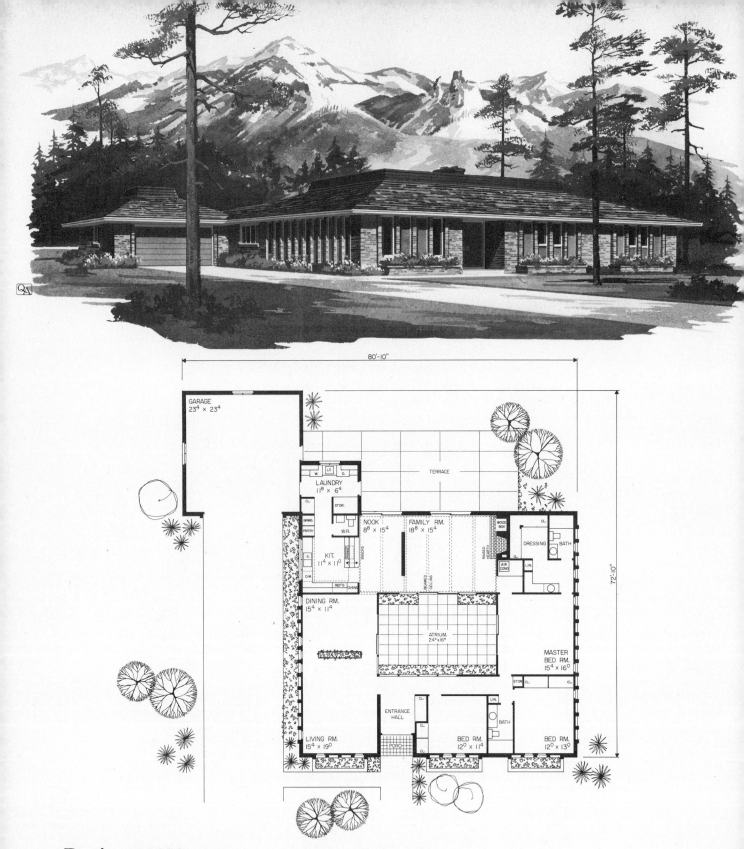

GARAGE
23⁴ x 23⁴

80'-10"

TERRACE

LAUNDRY
11⁸ x 6⁴

NOOK
8⁸ x 15⁴

FAMILY RM.
18⁸ x 15⁴

WOOD BOX

DRESSING

BATH

CL.

AIR COND

LIN

KIT.
11⁴ x 11⁰

RAISED HEARTH

DINING RM.
15⁴ x 11⁴

BEAMED CEILING

ATRIUM
24⁰ x 16⁶

MASTER BED RM.
15⁴ x 16⁰

STOR.

CL.

CL.

72'-10"

ENTRANCE HALL

LIN

BATH

LIVING RM.
15⁴ x 19⁰

PORCH

BED RM.
12⁰ x 11⁴

BED RM.
12⁰ x 13⁰

Design 22298 *2,489 Sq. Ft. – Excluding Atrium; 27,700 Cu. Ft.*

● If you've ever wanted to enjoy outdoor living indoors, this distinctive and refreshing design comes close to providing that opportunity. All the tremendous livability offered the basic rectangular plan is wrapped around a breathtaking 24 x 16 foot atrium which is open to the sky. Sliding glass doors provide direct access to this unique area from the family room, the dining room and the master bedroom. Also noteworthy is the functioning of other areas such as: the living and dining rooms; the kitchen and laundry; the master bedroom and its dressing/bath area. The two front bedrooms are serviced by a second full bath. That's a four foot, six inch high planter with storage below separating the living and dining rooms. This will be just a great area for formal entertaining.

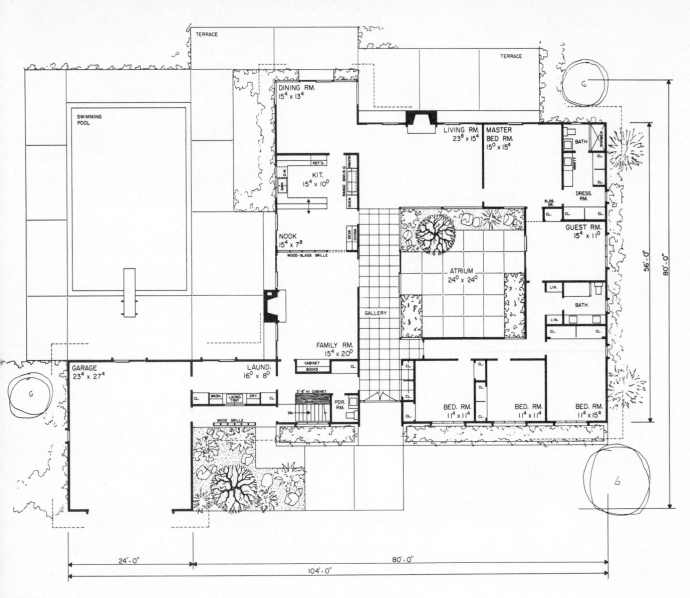

Design 21960 *3,274 Sq. Ft. — Excluding Atrium; 47,930 Cu. Ft.*

● Just think of the nature of your family's living patterns in this atrium house! They will be something new, and even exciting. There are four bedrooms, plus a guest room (make it the fifth bedroom, if you prefer). There's a big family room and a big-

ger living room. The kitchen is but a step from both the breakfast nook and the dining room. A laundry and powder room are strategically located between the family room and garage. The indoor-outdoor relationships are excellent. Sliding glass door units

open onto the outdoor terrace from the garage, the laundry, the nook, the dining, living and family rooms. The atrium is open to the sky and will provide enjoyment the year 'round. There is a partial basement extending below the family-dining room area.

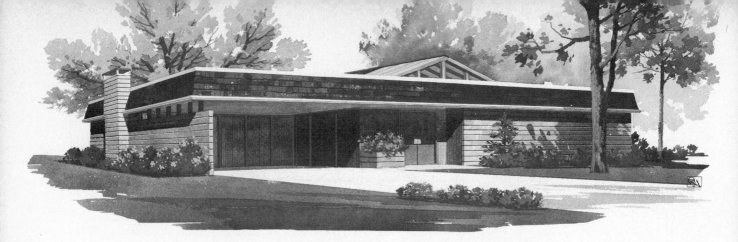

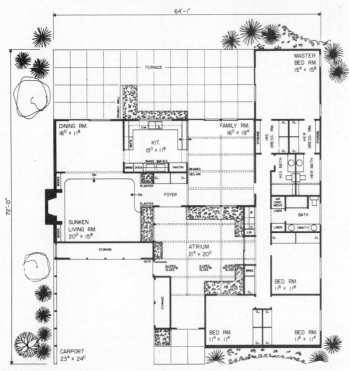

Design 22228
2,457 Sq. Ft. — Excluding Atrium; 28,218 Cu. Ft.

● For new living excitement the atrium will be a feature to assure unique day-to-day patterns of living. Completely enclosed, this delightful area will provide a full measure of privacy. Family living will be great fun in this contemporary home.

Design 22287
2,394 Sq. Ft.; 26,933 Cu. Ft.

● Here is a flat roof contemporary designed to be in harmony with the surroundings of the Far West. Yet, its fine proportions and sleek appearance would be a credit wherever built. Here, again, the covered court fosters a peaceful, welcoming atmosphere on the way to the front door. The center entrance hall routes traffic efficiently to the main areas. The kitchen is strategically located — handy to the front door, only a step from the two eating areas and just around the corner from the laundry and entrance from the garage. The formal living room functions well with the dining room. The family room is ideally located, too. It is close to the kitchen and directly accessible to the outdoors. Study the sleeping area.

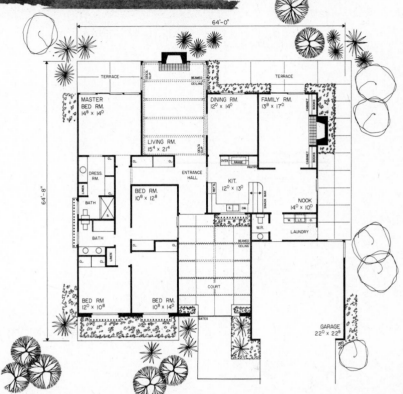

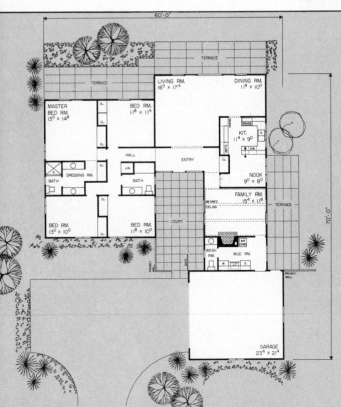

Design 22293
2,010 Sq. Ft.; 23,014 Cu. Ft.

● An L-shaped court design which gives the interesting appearance of a group of cluster units. The various hipped-roof planes have a wide overhang and an appealing raised cap. The sleeping area is a unit by itself and contains four bedrooms and two full baths. The living and dining rooms represent a delightfully spacious area with plenty of glass looking out on the rear terrace. Functioning through sliding glass doors with both the court and the side terrace, is the beamed ceiling family room. The garage appears to be a unit by itself, yet it is attached to the mud room with the extra wash room nearby.

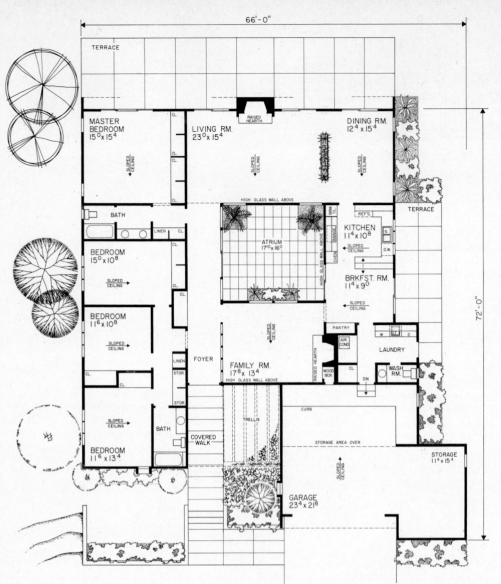

TERRACE

MASTER BEDROOM 15⁰ x 15⁴

SLOPED CEILING

BATH

LINEN CL.

BEDROOM 15⁰ x 10⁸

SLOPED CEILING

BEDROOM 11⁶ x 10⁸

SLOPED CEILING

LINEN STOR.

STOR.

FOYER

BATH

BEDROOM 11⁶ x 13⁴

SLOPED CEILING

COVERED WALK

66'-0"

LIVING RM. 23⁰ x 15⁴

SLOPED CEILING

RAISED HEARTH

HIGH GLASS WALL ABOVE

ATRIUM 17¹⁰ x 16⁰

SLOPED CEILING

FAMILY RM. 17⁸ x 13⁴

HIGH GLASS WALL ABOVE

TRELLIS

CURB

STORAGE AREA OVER

SLOPED CEILING

GARAGE 23⁴ x 21⁸

DINING RM. 12⁴ x 15⁴

SLOPED CEILING

TERRACE

KITCHEN 11⁴ x 10⁸

SLOPED CEILING

REF'G.

OVEN RANGE

D.W.

BRKFST. RM. 11⁴ x 9⁰

SLOPED CEILING

PANTRY

AIR COND.

RAISED HEARTH

WOOD BOX

CL.

DN

LAUNDRY

W D

WASH RM.

STORAGE 11⁴ x 15⁴

72'-0"

Design 22135

2,495 Sq. Ft. - Excluding Atrium
28,928 Cu. Ft.

● For those seeking a new experience in home ownership. The proud occupants of the contemporary home will forever be thrilled at their choice of such a distinguished exterior and such a practical and exciting floor plan. The variety of shed roof planes contrast dramatically with the simplicity of the vertical siding. Inside there is a feeling of spaciousness resulting from the sloping ceilings. The uniqueness of this design is further enhanced by the atrium. Open to the sky, this outdoor area, indoors, can be enjoyed from all parts of the house. The sleeping zone has four bedrooms, two baths and plenty of closets. The informal living zone has a fine kitchen and breakfast room. The formal zone consists of a large living-dining area with fireplace.

BRKFST. RM.

FAM. RM.

PANTRY

WOOD BOX

DN

LAUNDRY

W D

W.R.

DN

GARAGE

CURB

OPTIONAL PARTIAL BASEMENT

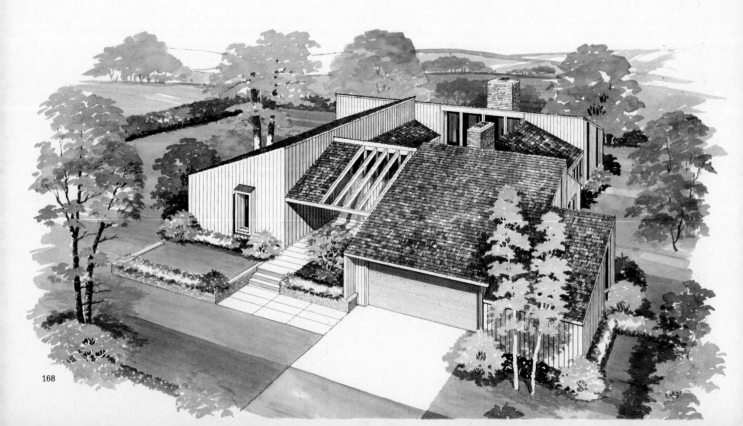

Design 21283 1,904 Sq. Ft. — Excluding Atrium; 18,659 Cu. Ft.

● Here is a unique home whose livable area is basically a perfect square. Completely adaptable to a narrow building site, the presence of the interior atrium permits the enjoyment of private outdoor living "indoors". Glass sliding doors open onto this delightful area with its attractive planting areas. In colder climates the atrium may be adapted to function as the formal living room, thus permitting the present living room to function as a study/guest room. In addition to the formal dining room, there is the informal snack bar in the family room accessible from the kitchen via the pass-thru. Three bedrooms, two baths, a fireplace and excellent storage facilities also are highlights of this plan. Don't miss the planting areas.

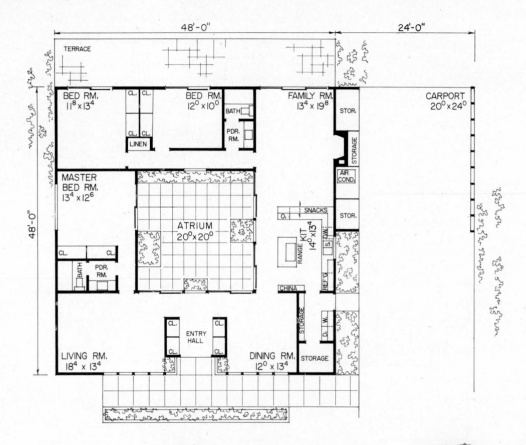

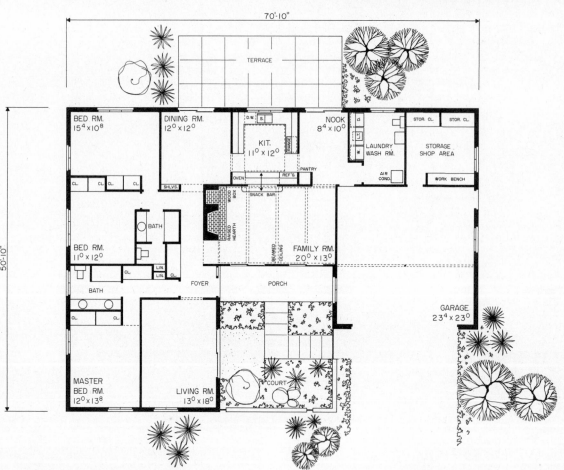

Design 22311 *2,205 Sq. Ft.; 19,880 Cu. Ft.*

● You could really have fun if you were to ask the various members of your family what they liked best about this contemporary design. Somebody, of course, would say the entrance court and how it functioned through sliding glass doors with the beamed ceilinged family room. Another, perhaps, would say the efficient rear kitchen flanked by the dining room and breakfast nook and overlooking the terrace. Others would chime in with the privacy of the front living room, the laundry/ wash room, all those closets and the large shop room behind the garage. Naturally, sooner or later, the list of favorite features would include the raised hearth fireplace in the family room, the snack bar and pass-thru to kitchen and the isolation of the master bedroom and its private bath.

Design 22329 2,268 Sq. Ft.; 25,492 Cu. Ft.

● Brick privacy walls create for this design an inviting entrance court. Such an area provides a pleasing view from the kitchen and the nook. Front porch sitting will have its privacy as well as an appealing atmosphere. The center entrance is but a few steps from the main areas of the plan. Four bedrooms and two baths will serve the growing family well. Note that two of the bedrooms have direct access to the terrace. Closet space is outstanding. The living and dining rooms encompass a large area with the living room well-defined by being sunken one step. The sloped ceiling family room with its commanding fireplace is off by itself. The laundry and wash room are well situated.

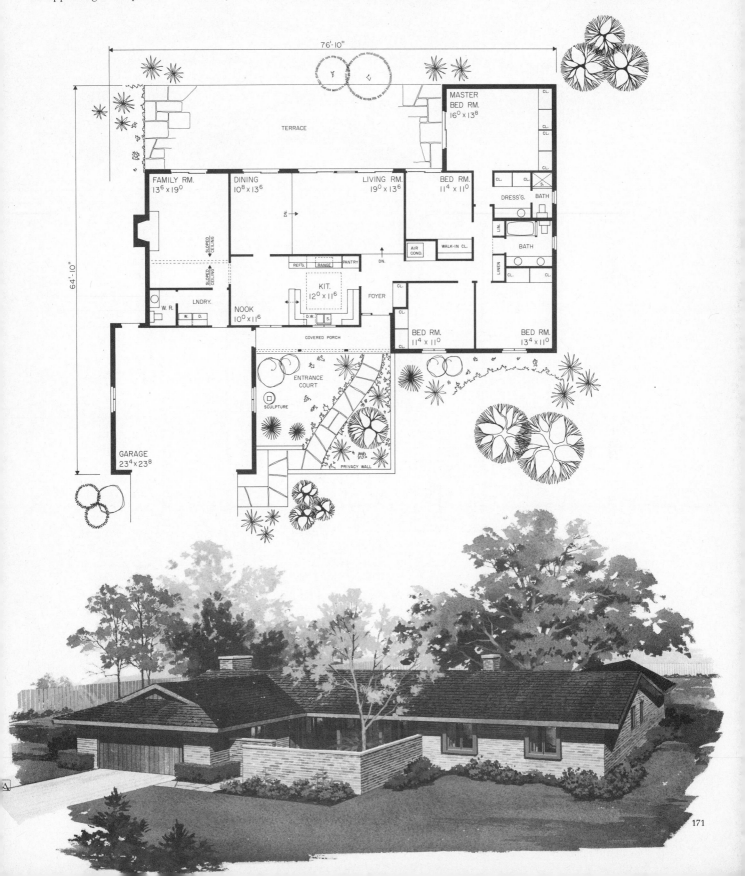

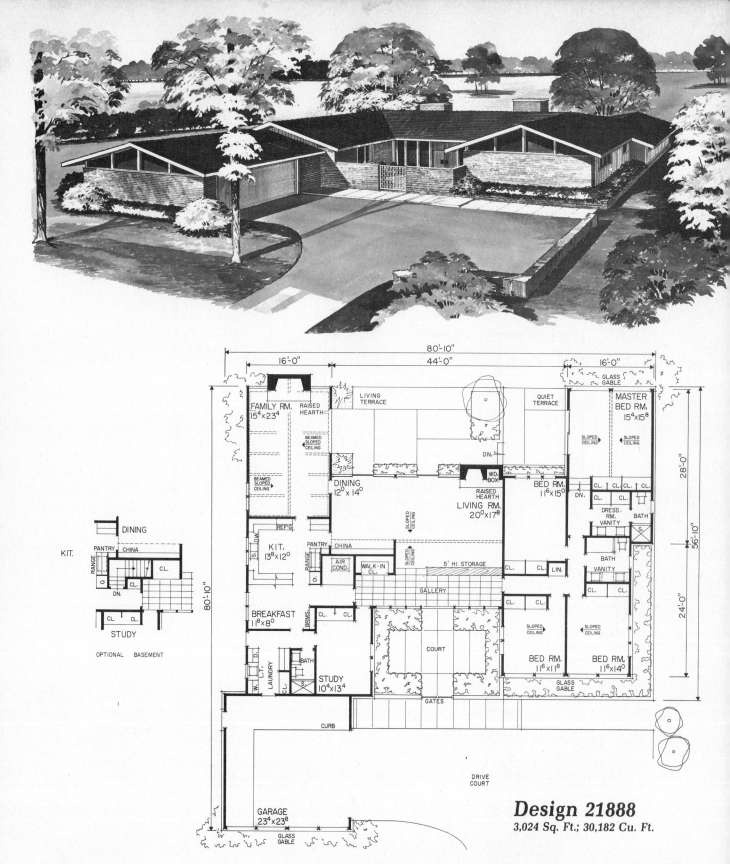

Design 21888
3,024 Sq. Ft.; 30,182 Cu. Ft.

● If you have a big, active family that needs plenty of well-defined space in which to move around, then this modified H-shaped house may be just perfect. With all that space, you should be happy to know that you won't have to buy the biggest piece of property in town to build on. The shape of the house keeps the overall dimension small enough to fit a modest sized lot. However, there is nothing modest about the inside. The list of features will be king size, indeed. Which features will be at the top? The court, the gallery or the 32 foot living/dining area? How about the study, the huge family room or the master bedroom? Note the details of the optional basement and non-basement included with blueprints for this design.

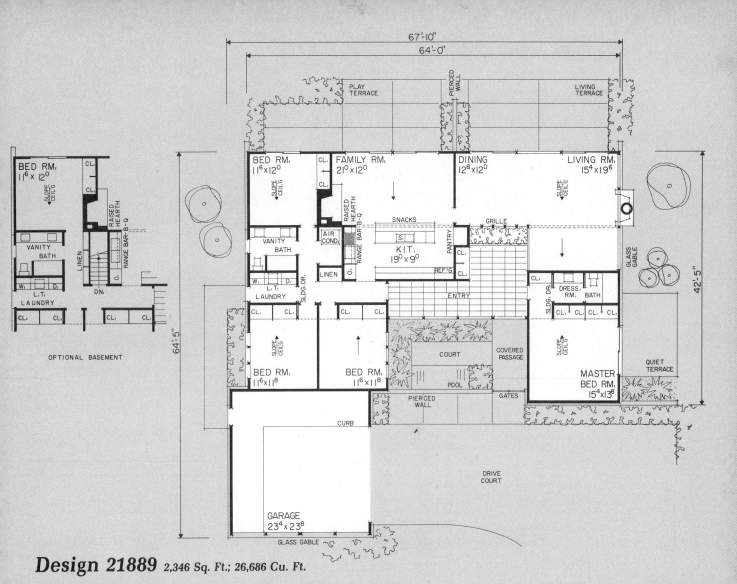

Floor plan labels:

Optional Basement:
- BED RM. 11⁶ x 12⁰ — SLOPE CEILG
- RAISED HEARTH — RANGE BAR-B-Q
- VANITY BATH
- LINEN
- W. L.T. D.
- LAUNDRY
- DN.
- CL. CL. CL. CL.
- OPTIONAL BASEMENT

Main Plan:
- 67'-10"
- 64'-0"
- 42'-5"
- 64'-5"
- PLAY TERRACE
- PIERCED WALL
- LIVING TERRACE
- BED RM. 11⁶ x 12⁰ — SLOPE CEILG
- CL.
- FAMILY RM. 21⁰ x 12⁰
- RAISED HEARTH — RANGE BAR-B-Q
- DINING 12⁸ x 12⁰
- LIVING RM. 15⁴ x 19⁶ — SLOPE CEILG
- GLASS GABLE
- SNACKS
- GRILLE
- AIR COND.
- VANITY BATH
- KIT. 19⁰ x 9⁰
- S.
- PANTRY
- CL.
- LINEN
- REF'G
- CL.
- W. L.T. D.
- LAUNDRY
- SLDG. DR.
- ENTRY
- CL.
- DRESS. RM. BATH
- SLDG. DR.
- CL. CL. CL. CL. CL.
- BED RM. 11⁶ x 11⁸ — SLOPE CEILG
- BED RM. 11⁶ x 11⁸
- COURT
- COVERED PASSAGE
- MASTER BED RM. 15⁴ x 13⁸ — SLOPE CEILG
- POOL
- GATES
- QUIET TERRACE
- PIERCED WALL
- CURB
- DRIVE COURT
- GARAGE 23⁴ x 23⁸
- GLASS GABLE

Design 21889 *2,346 Sq. Ft.; 26,686 Cu. Ft.*

● Where your list of favorite features would begin and end would be difficult to predict correctly. You might start with the distinctive character of this contemporary exterior and finish with the great idea of having the master bedroom enjoying its full measure of peace and quiet. Then, again, you'd hardly be in error were you to commence with the dramatic court, and close with spaciousness of the living areas. Whatever the sequence, try to fill-in the myriad of other features. They will all go together to help guarantee years of fine livability. Don't miss the optional partial basement. This area which extends below the bedrooms will be fine for development of a work shop and an additional recreation area. Notice the popular sloping ceilings.

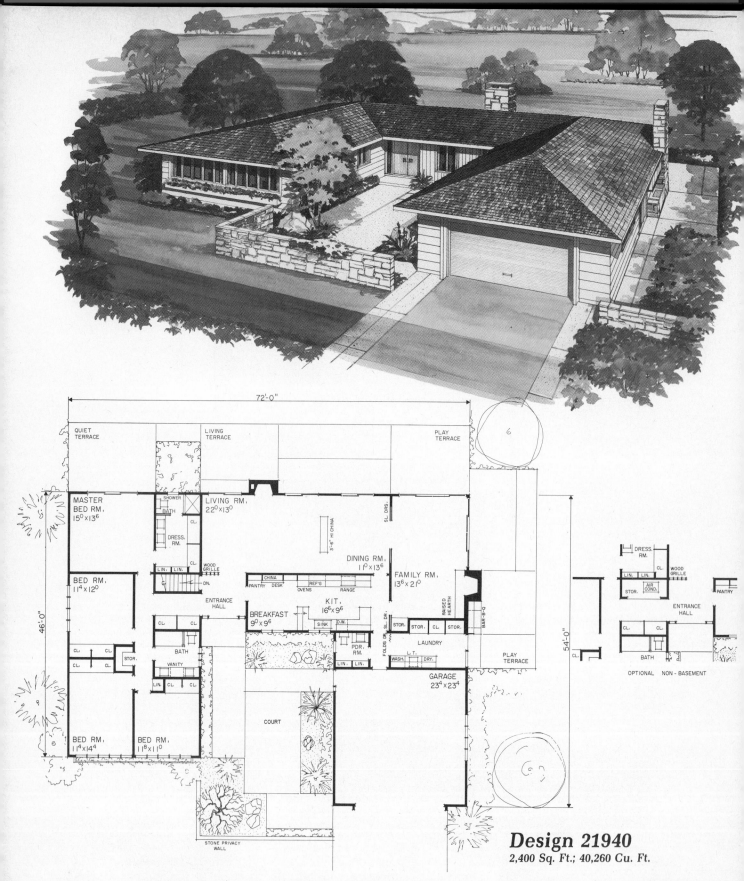

Design 21940
2,400 Sq. Ft.; 40,260 Cu. Ft.

● Let us just list the features of this trim, hip-roofed, U-shaped home. 1. Four large bedrooms; 2. Two full baths, extra powder room; 3. Exceptional storage facilities; 4. Handy, first floor laundry with storage closets; 5. Two fireplaces, one with raised hearth; 6. Pleasant breakfast room; 7. Wonderfully spacious living and dining area; 8. Partial basement for bulk storage; 9. Efficient and strategically located kitchen; 10. Recessed sliding doors; 11. Big all-purpose family room; 12. Sliding glass doors leading to; 13. Functional outdoor terraces; 14. Large built-in desk and china units; 15. Oversized two-car garage; 16. Stone privacy wall creating; 17. Front court garden; 18. Outdoor window planter; 19. Double front doors; 20. Built-in barbecue unit outside.

● The front entrance court with its planting areas and surrounding accents of colorful quarried stone (make it brick, if you prefer), provide a delightful introduction to this interesting contemporary home. The spacious entry hall leads directly to a generous L-shaped living and dining area. Sliding glass doors provide direct access to the outdoor terrace. An efficient, interior kitchen will be fun in which to work. It could hardly be more strategically located — merely a step or two from the formal dining area, the breakfast nook, and the family room. Although this home has a basement, there is a convenient first floor laundry and an extra washroom. The four bedroom sleeping wing has two full baths. Two of the rooms have access to the outdoor terraces. Notice garage storage.

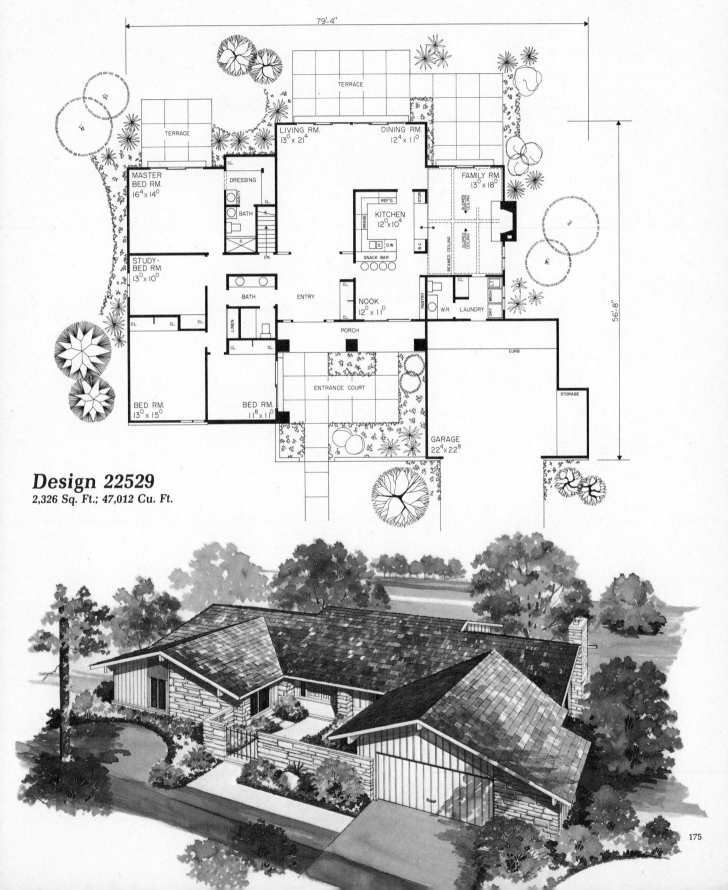

Design 22529
2,326 Sq. Ft.; 47,012 Cu. Ft.

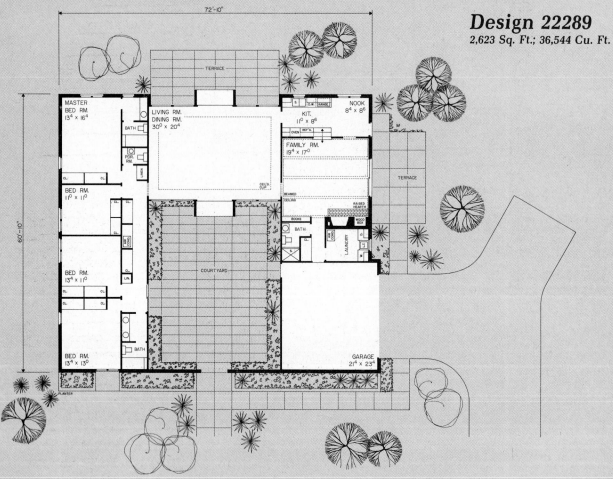

Design 22289
2,623 Sq. Ft.; 36,544 Cu. Ft.

● Impressive? You bet it is! And, as a matter of fact, it looks almost palatial. It is easy to guess that there will be as much fun (and maybe more) in that huge court yard as in any other part of the unique plan. The formality of the exterior is derived from the trim plant- ing areas and the contemporary adap- tation of the French Mansard roof. The two-story effect of the front entrance is, indeed, dramatic. Separating the peaceful sleeping wing is the formal living-dining area. Measuring 30 x 20 feet, this will be a real joy to furnish. With all that glass and the 17 foot ceil- ing, spaciousness will be the byword. The kitchen — family room — laundry area functions well. Don't miss the three full baths, the raised hearth fire- place or the breakfast nook. Note the pass-thru from kitchen to family room.

ALL the "TOOLS" you and your builder need...

... to, first select an exterior and a floor plan for your new house that satisfy your tastes and your family's living patterns ...

... then, to review the blueprints in great detail and obtain a construction cost figure ... also, to price out the structural materials required to build ... and, finally, to review and decide upon the specifications to which your home is to be built. Truly, an invaluable set of "tools" to launch your home planning and building programs.

1. THE PLAN BOOKS

Home Planners' unique Design Category Series makes it easy to look at and study only the types of designs for which you and your family have an interest. Each of five plan books features a specific type of home, namely: 1½ and 2-Story, One-Story Over 2000 Sq. Ft., One-Story Under 2000 Sq. Ft., Multi-Levels and Vacation Homes. In addition to the convenient Design Category Series, there is an impressive selection of other current titles. While the home plans featured in these books are also to be found in the Design Category Series, they, too, are edited for those with special tastes and requirements. Your family will spend many enjoyable hours reviewing the delightfully designed exteriors and the practical floor plans. Surely your home or office library should include a selection of these popular plan books. Your complete satisfaction is guaranteed.

2. THE CONSTRUCTION BLUEPRINTS

There are blueprints available for each of the designs published in Home Planners' current plan books. Depending upon the size, the style and the type of home, each set of blueprints consists of from five to ten large sheets. Only by studying the blueprints is it possible to give complete and final consideration to the proper selection of a design for your next home. The blueprints provide the opportunity for all family members to familiarize themselves with the features of all exterior elevations, interior elevations and details, all dimensions, special built-in features and effects. They also provide a full understanding of the materials to be used and/or selected. The low-cost of our blueprints makes it possible and indeed, practical, to study in detail a number of different sets of blueprints before deciding upon which design to build.

3. THE MATERIAL LIST

A list of materials is an integral part of the plan package. It comprises the last sheet of each set of blueprints and serves as a handy reference during the period of construction. Of course, at the pricing and the material ordering stages, it is indispensable.

4. THE SPECIFICATION OUTLINE

Each order for blueprints is accompanied by one Specification Outline. You and your builder will find this a time-saving tool when deciding upon your own individual specifications. An important reference document should you wish to write your own specifications.

THE PLAN BOOKS

The Design Category Series . . .

. . . A great selection of five plan books specially edited for ease in studying specific design types. Features most of the house plans shown in other current titles. The five book Complete Collection guarantees many enjoyable hours of happy house hunting. A fine set of books for the home or office reference library.

1. 400 1½ and TWO-STORY HOME PLANS - Those interested in studying a wide variety of 1½ and two-story exteriors and floor plans need look no further. New England Gambrels, Salt Boxes, Tudor, French Mansards, Georgians, Southern Colonials, Cape Cods, Virginia Tidewater, Farmhouses and Contemporary exteriors are featured. Family living floor plans with two to six bedrooms.

2. 210 ONE-STORY HOME PLANS - Over 2,000 Square Feet - Designs for those who prefer one-story living and all the convenience that goes with it. A selection of homes with varying exterior styles housing practical and efficient family living floor plans. Gathering rooms, family rooms, formal and informal dining areas.

3. 350 ONE-STORY HOME PLANS - Under 2,000 Square Feet - A wide selection of one-story homes for the modest building budgets. Delightful Traditional exteriors as well as exciting Contemporaries. Fine functioning floor plans for both the small and large family. Plans with optional elevations.

4. 205 MULTI-LEVEL HOME PLANS - For those who wish to experience new dimensions in total livability. This fine collection includes split foyer bi-levels and tri-levels for flat and sloping sites. Also, homes with exposed lower levels.

5. 223 VACATION HOMES - A popularly acclaimed vacation and leisure-living book of exteriors and floor plans. A-Frames, Chalets, Hexagons and other interesting shapes with decks, balconies and terraces. 96 exciting full color pages.

1 320 Pages, $5.95

2 192 Pages, $3.95

3 256 Pages, $4.95

4 192 Pages, $3.95

5 176 Pages, $4.25

The Exterior Style Series . . .

. . . Delightfully edited for those who wish to review home plans of their favorite exterior styling. Ideal for those who want to compare the unique appeal of various pleasing facades.

10. 120 EARLY AMERICAN PLANS - This unique plan book is devoted exclusively to Early American architectural interpretations adapted for today's living patterns. Exquisitely detailed exteriors retain all of the charm of a proud heritage.

11. 125 CONTEMPORARY HOME PLANS - An exciting book featuring a wide variety of home designs for the 1980's and far beyond. The exteriors are refreshing with their practical and progressive "new look".

12. 135 ENGLISH TUDOR HOMES - and other Popular Family Plans is a favorite of many. The current popularity of the English Tudor home design is phenomenal and this book is loaded with Tudors for all budgets.

13. 136 SPANISH & WESTERN HOME DESIGNS - Stucco exteriors, tile roofs, courtyards and rambling ranches are characteristics which make this design selection distinctive. These sun-country designs highlight indoor-outdoor relationships. Their appeal is not limited to the Southwest region of our country.

14. 130 DISTINCTIVE HOME DESIGNS - Commencing with the Early American Homes and continuing through the Tudor, French, Spanish and Contemporary, this book will be enjoyed by all. The pleasing exteriors and exciting floor plans assure hours of rewarding home planning.

15. 144 HOME DESIGNS FOR ALL AMERICANS - Here, favorite house styles match geographical regions. The New England section has its Gambrels; South, its stately columns; West, its Spanish charm; Northwest, its dramatic contemporary design; Mid-Atlantic, its historic front porch, etc.

16. 112 TRADITIONAL and CONTEMPORARY FAMILY HOMES - A delightful collection of designs for varying tastes. All sizes and types of designs for family living. Over 300 exterior and floor plan illustrations.

17. 102 HOME PLANS - An excellent selection of home designs featuring a wide variety of exterior styles. There are Early American, Tudor, Spanish, French and Contemporary facades. A special 16 page section in full color.

10 112 Pages, $2.95

11 112 Pages, $2.95

12 104 Pages, $2.95

14 112 Pages, $2.75

15 128 Pages, $2.95

16 96 Pages, $2.75

The Budget Series . . .

. . . Construction costs are influenced to a significant extent by the size of the house. The houses and plans in this series have been edited according to square footage ranges. Each book highlights a wide variety of design styles and types.

6   96 Pages, $2.75

7   112 Pages, $2.95

8   112 Pages, $2.75

9   112 Pages, $2.75

175 LOW BUDGET HOMES - The house designs in this book average 1505 square feet. From 1165 square foot average for the one-story houses to an 1812 average for two-stories. 1½-Story and tri-level averages fall within this range, too. Many designs have expansive potential where sleeping areas may be finished off later. Wide selection of styles. Two to five bedrooms. Family rooms, extra baths, formal and informal dining rooms. This book is a must for those with a restricted building budget.

165 AFFORDABLE HOME PLANS - Designs averaging 2052 square feet are featured in this collection of houses. They range from a 1581 square foot average for the one-stories, to 2261 for the two-story homes, to 2381 for the tri-levels. Tudor, French, Early American, Spanish and Contemporary exteriors are featured throughout the book. Efficient, family living floor plans. This wide selection of houses and plans will fit the medium budget. Basement and non-basement designs.

142 HOME DESIGNS FOR EXPANDED BUILDING BUDGETS - This selection of designs highlight houses with an average square footage of 2551. One-story plans average 2069; two-stories, 2735; multi-levels, 2825. As the family's size and income grows so does its need for, and ability to finance, a larger home grow. A fine group of designs for all exterior style tastes and livability requirements. Spacious homes featuring raised hearth fireplaces, beamed ceilings, open planning and efficient kitchens.

110 HOME PLANS FOR VARYING BUILDING BUDGETS - Edited in appealing two-color featuring designs for all budgets. One, 1½, two-story and multi-levels. Colonial, Tudor, Spanish, French and Contemporary exteriors, among the most popular, are featured. Special section of energy-oriented designs with solariums, atriums, skylights, collectors, etc. Trend houses and history house designs. Houses designed for flat and hillside sites. Exposed lower levels are also available.

Three Great Books in Full Color . . .

For Plan Book Order Form Kindly turn to page 189.

18   96 Pages, $5.95

19   96 Pages, $5.95

20   96 Pages, $5.95

13   96 Pages, $2.95

116 TRADITIONAL and CONTEMPORARY PLANS - A beautifully illustrated home plan book in complete, full color. One, 1½, two-story and split-level designs featured in all of the most popular exterior styles.

122 HOME DESIGNS - This book has delightfully dramatic full color throughout. More than 120 eye-pleasing, colored illustrations. Tudor, French, Spanish, Early American and Contemporary exteriors.

114 TREND HOMES - Heritage Houses, Energy Designs, Family Plans - these, along with Vacation Homes, are in this exciting, new plan book in full color. A potpourri of designs cater to a variety of tastes.

Popular Designs . . .

17   96 Pages, $2.75

166 MOST POPULAR HOMES - A book of best-selling house plans containing over 400 illustrations. Houses range in size from 1,050 to 5,308 square feet. Tudor, Early American, Spanish and French exteriors plus Contemporary elevations and floor plans.

172 MOST POPULAR HOMES - The second book in this series. These designs are selected from Home Planners esteemed portfolio of over 1400 different home plans. An excellent book to gauge the tastes in styles and preferences in floor plans from the past readers of Home Planners' books.

21   112 Pages, $2.95

22   128 Pages, $2.95

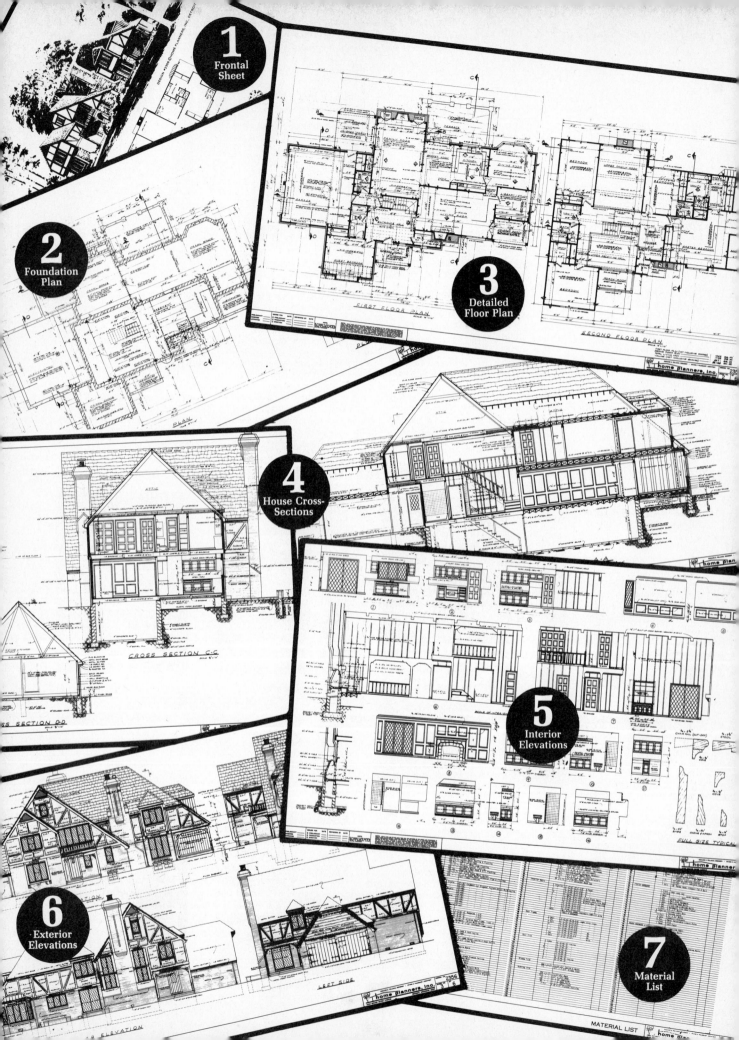

1
Frontal Sheet

2
Foundation Plan

3
Detailed Floor Plan

4
House Cross-Sections

5
Interior Elevations

6
Exterior Elevations

7
Material List

FIRST FLOOR PLAN

SECOND FLOOR PLAN

CROSS SECTION C-C

CROSS SECTION D-D

LEFT SIDE

MATERIAL LIST

The Blueprints. . .

1. FRONTAL SHEET.
Artist's landscaped sketch of the exterior and ink-line floor plans are on the frontal sheet of each set of blueprints.

2. FOUNDATION PLAN.
¼" Scale basement and foundation plan. All necessary notations and dimensions. Plot plan diagram for locating house on building site.

3. DETAILED FLOOR PLAN.
¼" Scale first and second floor plans with complete dimensions. Cross-section detail keys. Diagrammatic layout of electrical outlets and switches.

4. HOUSE CROSS-SECTIONS.
Large scale sections of foundation, interior and exterior walls, floors and roof details for design and construction control.

5. INTERIOR ELEVATIONS.
Large scale interior details of the complete kitchen cabinet design, bathrooms, powder room, laundry, fireplaces, paneling, beam ceilings, built-in cabinets, etc.

6. EXTERIOR ELEVATIONS.
¼" Scale exterior elevation drawings of front, rear, and both sides of the house. All exterior materials and details are shown to indicate the complete design and proportions of the house.

7. MATERIAL LIST.
Complete lists of all materials required for the construction of the house as designed are included in each set of blueprints.

THIS BLUEPRINT PACKAGE
will help you and your family take a major step forward in the final appraisal and planning of your new home. Only by spending many enjoyable and informative hours studying the numerous details included in the complete package, will you feel sure of, and comfortable with, your commitment to build your new home. To assure successful and productive consultation with your builder and/or architect, reference to the various elements of the blueprint package is a must. The blueprints, material list and specification outline will save much consultation time and expense. Don't be without them.

The Material List. . .

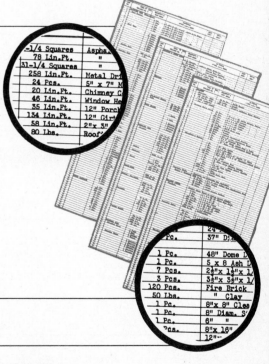

With each set of blueprints you order you will receive a material list. Each list shows you the quantity, type and size of the non-mechanical materials required to build your home. It also tells you where these materials are used. This makes the blueprints easy to understand.

Influencing the mechanical requirements are geographical differences in availability of materials, local codes, methods of installation and individual preferences. Because of these factors, your local heating, plumbing and electrical contractors can supply you with necessary material take-offs for their particular trades.

Material lists simplify your material ordering and enable you to get quicker price quotations from your builder and material dealer. Because the material list is an integral part of each set of blueprints, it is not available separately.

Among the materials listed:

- Masonry, Veneer & Fireplace • Framing Lumber • Roofing & Sheet Metal • Windows & Door Frames • Exterior Trim & Insulation • Tile Work, Finish Floors • Interior Trim, Kitchen Cabinets • Rough & Finish Hardware

The Specification Outline. . .

This fill-in type specification lists over 150 phases of home construction from excavating to painting and includes wiring, plumbing, heating and air-conditioning. It consists of 16 pages and will prove invaluable for specifying to your builder the exact materials, equipment and methods of construction you want in your new home. One Specification Outline is included free with each order for blueprints. Additional Specification Outlines are available at $3.00 each.

CONTENTS
• General Instructions, Suggestions and Information • Excavating and Grading • Masonry and Concrete Work • Sheet Metal Work • Carpentry, Millwork, Roofing, and Miscellaneous Items • Lath and Plaster or Drywall Wallboard • Schedule for Room Finishes • Painting and Finishing • Tile Work • Electrical Work • Plumbing • Heating and Air-Conditioning

Before you order

1. STUDY THE DESIGNS . . . found in Home Planners current publications. As you review these delightful custom homes, you should keep in mind the total living requirements of your family — both indoors and outdoors. Although we do not make changes in plans, many minor changes can be made prior to the period of construction. If major changes are involved to satisfy your personal requirements, you should consider ordering one set of blueprints and having them redrawn locally. Consultation with your architect is strongly advised when contemplating major changes.

2. HOW TO ORDER BLUEPRINTS . . . After you have chosen the design that satisfies your requirements, or if you have selected one that you wish to study in more detail, simply clip the accompanying order blank and mail with your remittance. However, if it is not convenient for you to send a check or money order, you can use your credit card, or merely indicate C.O.D. shipment. Postman will collect all charges, including postage and C.O.D. fee. C.O.D. shipments are not permitted to Canada or foreign countries. Should time be of essence, as it sometimes is with many of our customers, your telephone order usually can be processed and shipped in the next day's mail. Simply call toll free 1-800-521-6797, (Michigan residents call collect 0-313-477-1854).

3. OUR SERVICE . . . Home Planners makes every effort to process and ship each order for blueprints and books within 48 hours. Because of this, we have deemed it unnecessary to acknowledge receipt of our customers orders. See order coupon for the postage and handling charges for surface mail, air mail or foreign mail.

4. A NOTE REGARDING REVERSE BLUEPRINTS . . . As a special service to those wishing to build in reverse of the plan as shown, we do include an extra set of reversed blueprints for only $25.00 additional with each order. Even though the lettering and dimensions appear backward on reversed blueprints, they make a handy reference because they show the house just as it's being built in reverse from the standard blueprints — thereby helping you visualize the home better.

5. OUR EXCHANGE POLICY . . . Since blueprints are printed up in specific response to your individual order, we cannot honor requests for refunds. However, the first set of blueprints in any order (or the one set in a single set order) for a given design may be exchanged for a set of another design at a fee of $10.00 plus $3.00 for postage and handling via surface mail; $4.00 via air mail.

TO: HOME PLANNERS, INC., 23761 RESEARCH DRIVE
FARMINGTON HILLS, MICHIGAN 48024

Please rush me the following:

____ SET(S) BLUEPRINTS FOR DESIGN NO(S). _____ $_____
    Single Set, $95.00; Additional Identical Sets in Same Order $25.00 ea.
    4 Set Package of Same Design, $145.00 (Save $25.00)
    7 Set Package of Same Design, $180.00 (Save $65.00)
    (Material Lists and 1 Specification Outline included)
____ SPECIFICATION OUTLINES @ $3.00 EACH . . . . $_____

Michigan Residents add 4% sales tax $_____

| FOR POSTAGE AND HANDLING PLEASE CHECK ✔ & REMIT | ☐ $3.00 Added to Order for Surface Mail (UPS) – Any Mdse.
☐ $4.00 Added for Priority Mail of One-Three Sets of Blueprints.
☐ $6.00 Added for Priority Mail of Four or more Sets of Blueprints.
☐ For Canadian orders add $2.00 to above applicable rates | } $_____ |

☐ C.O.D. PAY POSTMAN
(C.O.D. Within U.S.A. Only)   **TOTAL in U.S.A. funds** $_____

PLEASE PRINT
Name _____
Street _____
City _____ State _____ Zip _____

CREDIT CARD ORDERS ONLY: Fill in the boxes below   Prices subject to change without notice
Credit Card No. [ ][ ][ ][ ][ ][ ][ ][ ][ ][ ][ ][ ][ ][ ][ ][ ]   Expiration Date Month/Year [ ][ ][ ][ ]

CHECK ONE: ☐ VISA ☐ MasterCard
Order Form Key CV2   Your Signature _____

BLUEPRINT ORDERS SHIPPED WITHIN 48 HOURS OF RECEIPT!

TO: HOME PLANNERS, INC., 23761 RESEARCH DRIVE
FARMINGTON HILLS, MICHIGAN 48024

Please rush me the following:

____ SET(S) BLUEPRINTS FOR DESIGN NO(S). _____ $_____
    Single Set, $95.00; Additional Identical Sets in Same Order $25.00 ea.
    4 Set Package of Same Design, $145.00 (Save $25.00)
    7 Set Package of Same Design, $180.00 (Save $65.00)
    (Material Lists and 1 Specification Outline included)
____ SPECIFICATION OUTLINES @ $3.00 EACH . . . . $_____

Michigan Residents add 4% sales tax $_____

| FOR POSTAGE AND HANDLING PLEASE CHECK ✔ & REMIT | ☐ $3.00 Added to Order for Surface Mail (UPS) – Any Mdse.
☐ $4.00 Added for Priority Mail of One-Three Sets of Blueprints.
☐ $6.00 Added for Priority Mail of Four or more Sets of Blueprints.
☐ For Canadian orders add $2.00 to above applicable rates | } $_____ |

☐ C.O.D. PAY POSTMAN
(C.O.D. Within U.S.A. Only)   **TOTAL in U.S.A. funds** $_____

PLEASE PRINT
Name _____
Street _____
City _____ State _____ Zip _____

CREDIT CARD ORDERS ONLY: Fill in the boxes below   Prices subject to change without notice
Credit Card No. [ ][ ][ ][ ][ ][ ][ ][ ][ ][ ][ ][ ][ ][ ][ ][ ]   Expiration Date Month/Year [ ][ ][ ][ ]

CHECK ONE: ☐ VISA ☐ MasterCard
Order Form Key CV2   Your Signature _____

How many sets of blueprints should be ordered?

This question is often asked. The answer can range anywhere from 1 to 7 sets, depending upon circumstances. For instance, a single set of blueprints of your favorite design is sufficient to study the house in greater detail. On the other hand, if you are planning to get cost estimates, or if you are planning to build, you may need as many as seven sets of blueprints. Because the first set of blueprints in each order is $95.00, and because additional sets of the same design in each order are only $25.00 each (and with package sets even more economical), you save considerably by ordering your total requirements now. To help you determine the exact number of sets, please refer to the handy check list.

How Many Blueprints Do You Need?

___ OWNER'S SET

___ BUILDER (Usually requires at least 3 sets: 1 as legal document; 1 for inspection; and at least 1 for tradesmen — usually more.)

___ BUILDING PERMIT (Sometimes 2 sets are required.)

___ MORTGAGE SOURCE (Usually 1 set for a conventional mortgage; 3 sets for F.H.A. or V.A. type mortgages.)

___ SUBDIVISION COMMITTEE (If any.)

___ TOTAL NO. SETS REQUIRED

Blueprint Ordering Hotline –

Phone toll free: 1-800-521-6797. Orders received by 11 a.m. (Detroit time) will be processed the same day and shipped to you the following day. Use of this line restricted to blueprint ordering only. Michigan residents simply call collect 0-313-477-1854.

Kindly Note: When ordering by phone, please state Order Form Key No. located in box at lower left corner of blueprint order form.

In Canada Mail To:
Home Planners, Inc., 20 Cedar St. North
Kitchener, Ontario N2H 2W8

Swimming Pools
For an Extra Measure of Fun

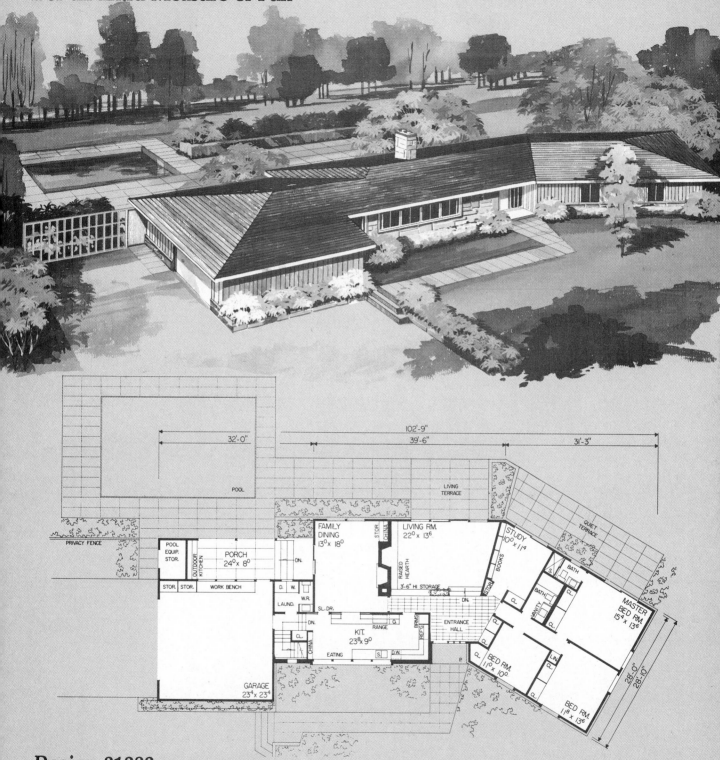

Design 21232 *2,050 Sq. Ft.; 27,756 Cu. Ft.*

● This angular, hip-roofed ranch home has all the exterior appeal and all the interior livability one could ask for. Its trim, interesting lines are accentuated by the wide overhanging roof. The spacious entrance hall is a fine spot from which to view the

sunken living room. Looking over the low built-in storage room divider your guest will be taken by the spaciousness. The dramatic raised hearth fireplace and delightful expanse of glass will be favorite features. Adjacent to this formal living area is the

all-purpose family room. It too, has an impressive fireplace wall. The kitchen has extra eating space and will be fun in which to function. Study the sleeping wing. It has three bedrooms and two baths to serve the family ideally. Note laundry.

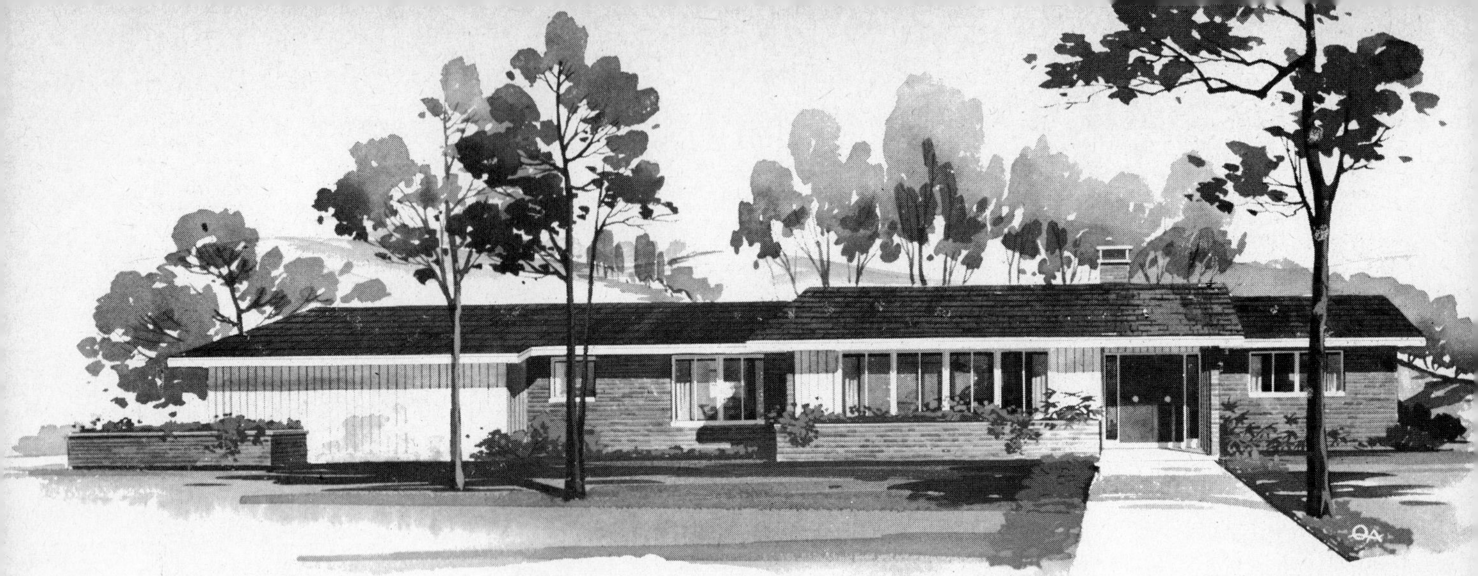

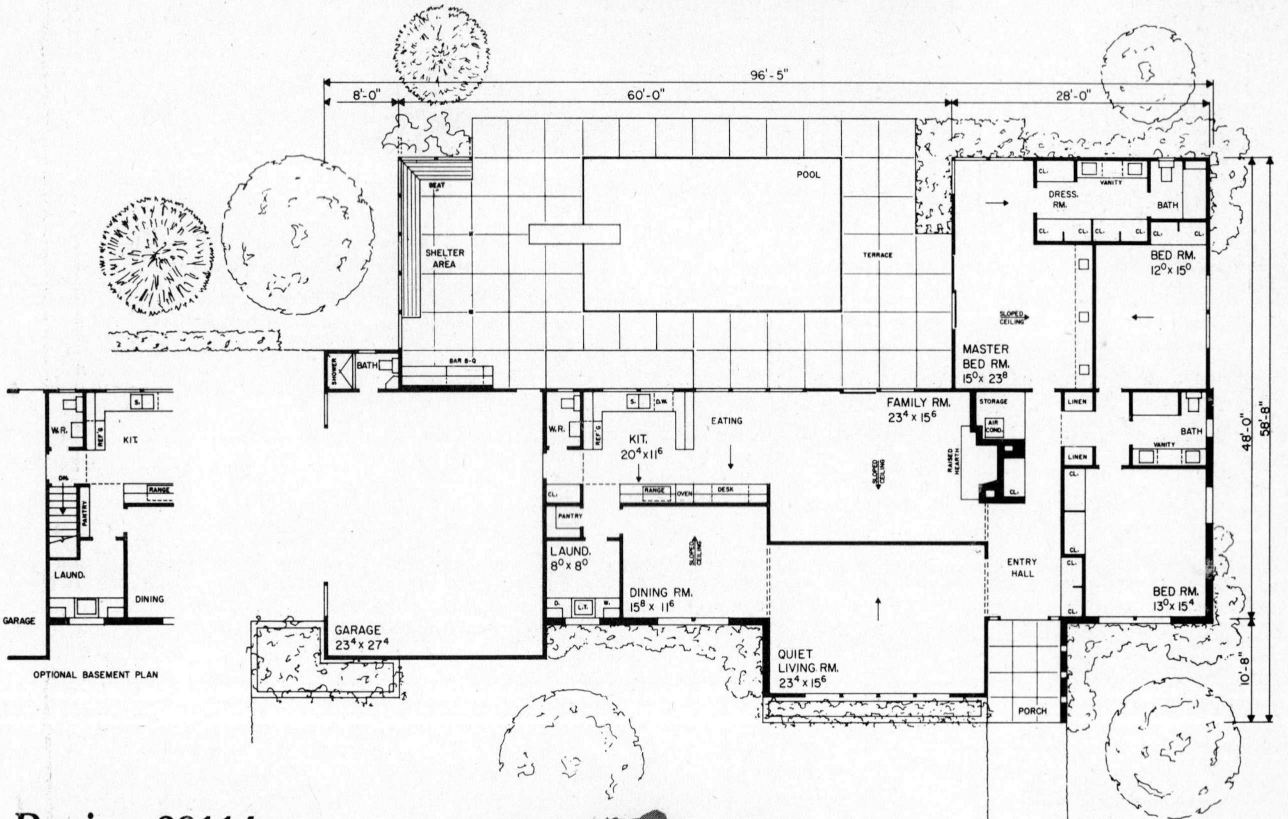

96'-5"
8'-0"
60'-0"
28'-0"
POOL
SEAT
SHELTER AREA
TERRACE
BAR B-Q
SHOWER
BATH
DRESS. RM.
VANITY
BATH
BED RM. 12⁰ x 15⁰
SLOPED CEILING
MASTER BED RM. 15⁰ x 23⁸
FAMILY RM. 23⁴ x 15⁶
STORAGE
AIR COND.
RAISED HEARTH
LINEN
EATING
KIT. 20⁴ x 11⁶
W.R.
RANGE
OVEN
DESK
PANTRY
LAUND. 8⁰ x 8⁰
DINING RM. 15⁸ x 11⁶
GARAGE 23⁴ x 27⁴
QUIET LIVING RM. 23⁴ x 15⁶
ENTRY HALL
PORCH
BED RM. 13⁰ x 15⁴
48'-0"
58'-8"
10'-8"
KIT.
DINING
GARAGE
OPTIONAL BASEMENT PLAN

Design 22114 *2,665 Sq. Ft.; 29,819 Cu. Ft.*

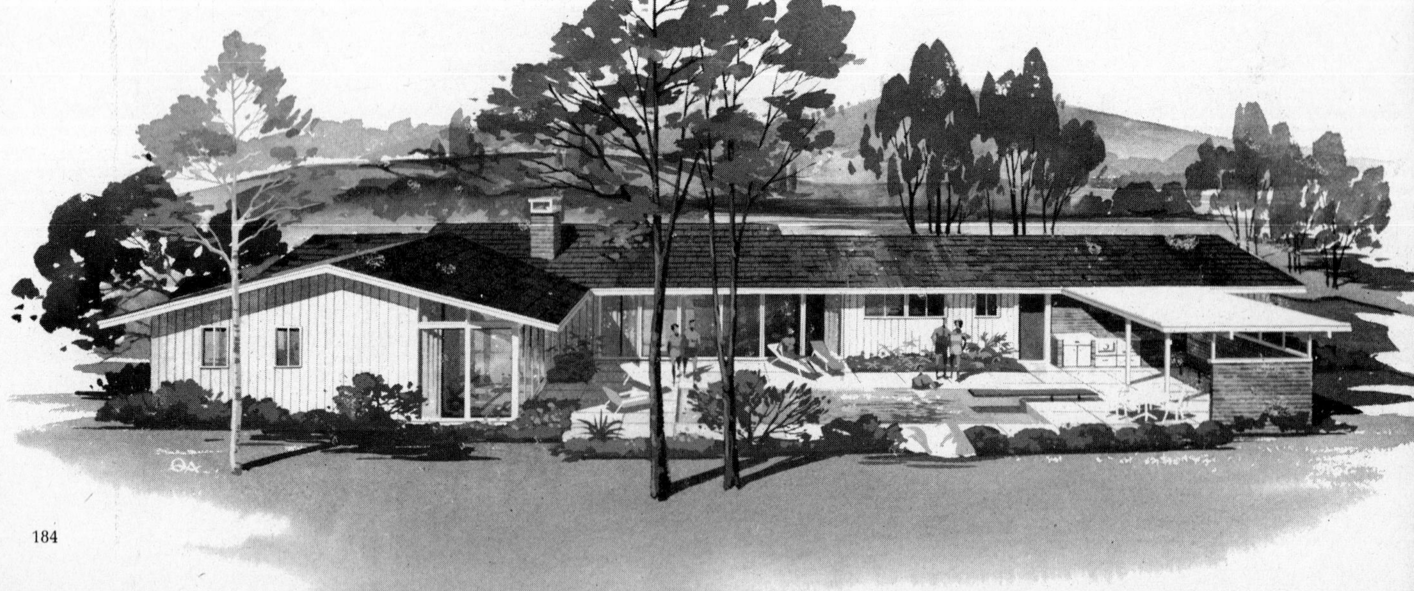

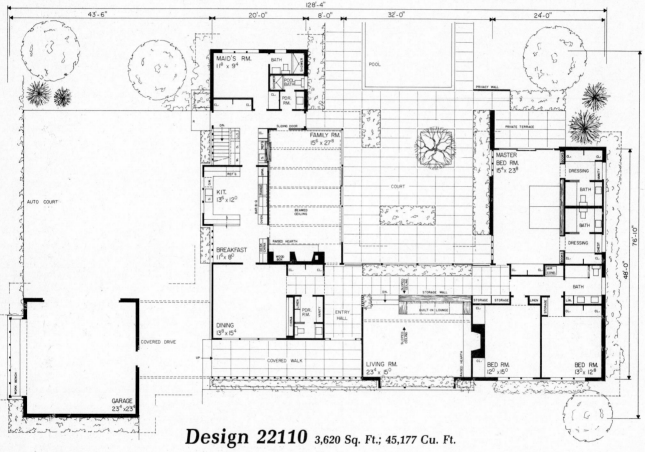

Design 22110 3,620 Sq. Ft.; 45,177 Cu. Ft.

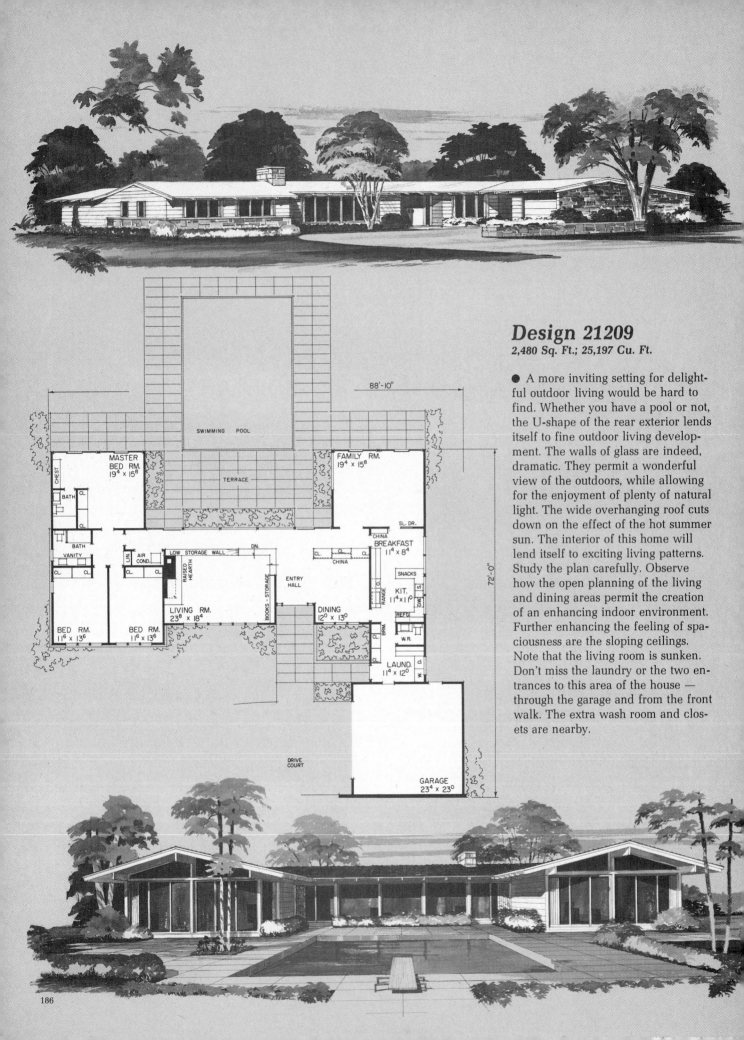

Design 21209
2,480 Sq. Ft.; 25,197 Cu. Ft.

● A more inviting setting for delightful outdoor living would be hard to find. Whether you have a pool or not, the U-shape of the rear exterior lends itself to fine outdoor living development. The walls of glass are indeed, dramatic. They permit a wonderful view of the outdoors, while allowing for the enjoyment of plenty of natural light. The wide overhanging roof cuts down on the effect of the hot summer sun. The interior of this home will lend itself to exciting living patterns. Study the plan carefully. Observe how the open planning of the living and dining areas permit the creation of an enhancing indoor environment. Further enhancing the feeling of spaciousness are the sloping ceilings. Note that the living room is sunken. Don't miss the laundry or the two entrances to this area of the house — through the garage and from the front walk. The extra wash room and closets are nearby.

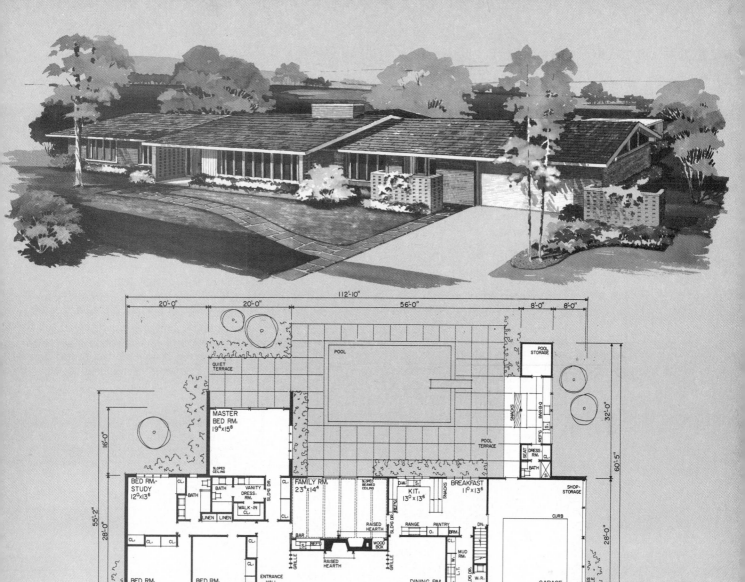

Design 21926
2,946 Sq. Ft.; 45,835 Cu. Ft.

● A home which will surely guarantee delightful living patterns for the whole family. The fine indoor/outdoor relationships will provide fun for all. Should you not wish to have a swimming pool there would be an abundance of terrace area for games to be enjoyed by children and parents alike. The floor plan is positively outstanding. There are four bedrooms, two full baths, and plenty of closets in the sleeping zone. Located to the front are the formal living and dining rooms. The big family room has a sloping beamed ceiling, a separate snack bar and an attractive raised hearth fireplace with wood box. The kitchen which overlooks the rear yard development is separated from the convenient breakfast room by another snack bar. A pass-thru between the upper and lower cabinets facilitates the serving of meals. Just inside the service entrance is the mud room which features the laundry equipment and a handy wardrobe closet. An extra wash room is nearby. Don't overlook the garage storage area and the outdoor kitchen. Observe dressing room and bath with stall shower. The front exterior highlights brick, double front doors, pleasing window treatment and a wide overhanging roof.

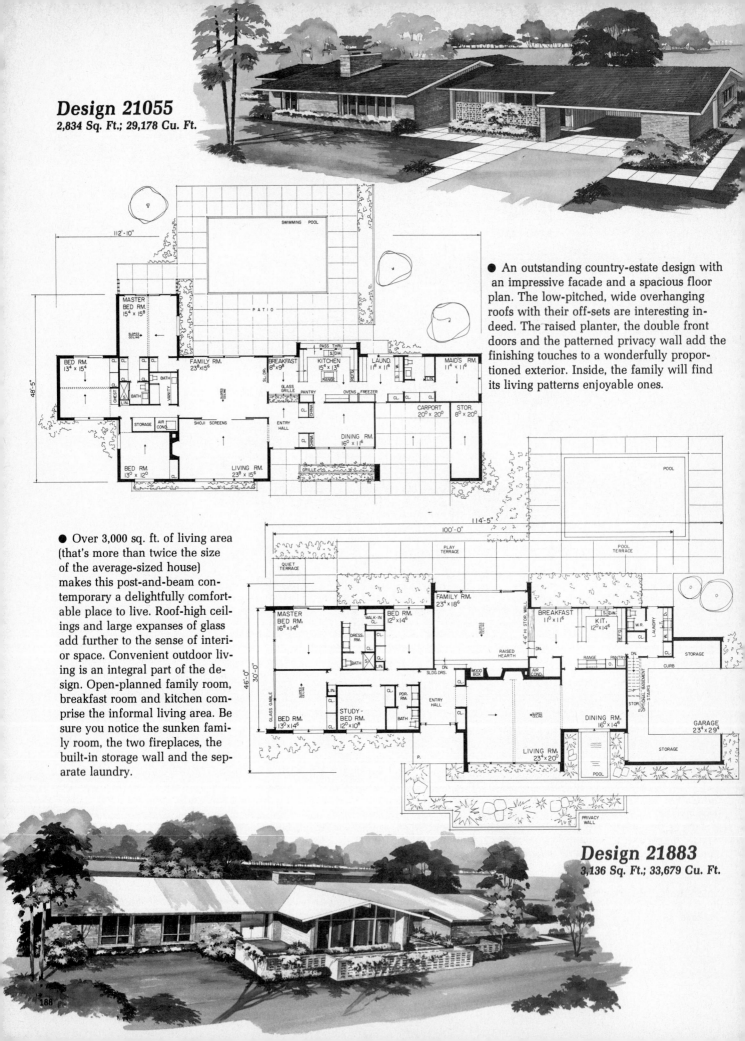

Design 21055
2,834 Sq. Ft.; 29,178 Cu. Ft.

● An outstanding country-estate design with an impressive facade and a spacious floor plan. The low-pitched, wide overhanging roofs with their off-sets are interesting indeed. The raised planter, the double front doors and the patterned privacy wall add the finishing touches to a wonderfully proportioned exterior. Inside, the family will find its living patterns enjoyable ones.

● Over 3,000 sq. ft. of living area (that's more than twice the size of the average-sized house) makes this post-and-beam contemporary a delightfully comfortable place to live. Roof-high ceilings and large expanses of glass add further to the sense of interior space. Convenient outdoor living is an integral part of the design. Open-planned family room, breakfast room and kitchen comprise the informal living area. Be sure you notice the sunken family room, the two fireplaces, the built-in storage wall and the separate laundry.

Design 21883
3,136 Sq. Ft.; 33,679 Cu. Ft.

... Three More Popular Titles —

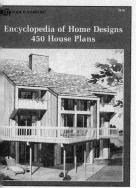

23 320 Pages, $8.95

24 128 Pages, $2.95

25 192 Pages, $3.50

450 HOUSE PLANS - An encyclopedia of home designs for those who wish to review and study perhaps the largest selection of designs available in a single volume. This book features sections on Heritage Houses from our architectural past along with Trend Houses, one, 1½ and two-story homes, multi-levels and vacation homes. Of particular interest are designs with optional exteriors and floor plans. Also, homes for country-estate living.

152 HOUSE PLANS - An appealing use of second color tones effectively compliments the wide variety of exterior styles and practical floor plans. From one, 1½, two-story and multi-level house plans. From 936 to 4509 square feet. For small, medium and large families. Included are houses with second floor lounges, secluded master suites, country kitchens, gathering rooms, exposed lower levels, indoor and outdoor balconies and energy-oriented solariums and greenhouses.

255 HOME DESIGNS FOR FAMILY LIVING - This exciting two-color plan book has over 700 illustrations of contemporary and favorite traditional exteriors. Tudor, French, Spanish and Early Colonial are among the popular styles. In addition to the plans which cater to a wide variety of family living patterns and budgets, there are special feature sections on: Vacation Homes, Earth-Sheltered Designs, Sun-Oriented Living and Shared Livability.

THE PLAN BOOKS

... are a most valuable tool for anyone planning to build a new home. A study of the hundreds of delightfully designed exteriors and the practical, efficient floor plans will be a great learning and fun-oriented family experience. You will be able to select your preferred styling from among Early American, Tudor, French, Spanish and Contemporary adaptations. Your ideas about floor planning and interior livability will expand. And, of course, after you have selected an appealing home design that satisfies your long list of living requirements, you can order the blueprints for further study of your favorite design in greater detail. Surely the hours spent studying the portfolio of Home Planners' designs will be both enjoyable and rewarding ones.

Kindly note: For detailed information about the complete home planning package, see pages 177 through 182.

Kindly note: For detailed information about the complete home planning package, see pages 177 through 182.

HOME PLANNERS, INC.
Dept. BK, 23761 Research Drive
Farmington Hills, Michigan 48024

Phone Toll Free:
1-800-521-6797

PLAN BOOK ORDER FORM

Please mail me the following:

THE DESIGN CATEGORY SERIES - A great series of books specially edited by design type and size. Each book features interesting sections to further enhance the study of design styles, sizes and house types. A fine addition to the home or office library. Complete collection - over 1275 designs.

		Unit Price	
1. _____	400 1½ & Two-Story Home Plans	$5.95	$_____
2. _____	210 One-Story - Over 2,000 sq. ft.	$3.95	$_____
3. _____	350 One-Story - Under 2,000 sq. ft.	$4.95	$_____
4. _____	205 Multi-Level Home Plans	$3.95	$_____
5. _____	223 Vacation Homes	$4.25	$_____

OTHER CURRENT TITLES - The interesting series of plan books listed below have been edited to appeal to various style preferences and budget considerations. The majority of the designs highlighted in these books also may be found in the Design Category Series.

The Budget Series-

6. _____	175 Low Budget Homes...................................	$2.75	$_____
7. _____	165 Affordable Home Plans	$2.95	$_____
8. _____	142 Home Designs for Expanded Bldg. Budgets	$2.75	$_____
9. _____	110 Home Plans...	$2.75	$_____

The Exterior Style Series-

10. _____	120 Early American Home Plans	$2.95	$_____
11. _____	125 Contemporary Home Plans	$2.95	$_____
12. _____	135 English Tudor Homes	$2.95	$_____
13. _____	136 Spanish & Western Home Designs (July '85)	$2.95	$_____
14. _____	130 Distinctive Home Designs............................	$2.75	$_____
15. _____	144 Home Designs For All Americans	$2.95	$_____
16. _____	112 Traditional & Contemporary Family Homes	$2.75	$_____
17. _____	102 Home Plans...	$2.75	$_____

Three Great Books In Full Color-

18. _____	116 Traditional & Contemporary Plans	$5.95	$_____
19. _____	122 Home Designs	$5.95	$_____
20. _____	114 Trend Homes	$5.95	$_____

Two Books Of Most Popular Designs-

21. _____	166 Most Popular Homes	$2.95	$_____
22. _____	172 Most Popular Homes	$2.95	$_____

Encyclopedia Of Home Designs-

23. _____	450 House Plans	$8.95	$_____

Two More Outstanding New Titles-

24. _____	152 House Plans	$2.95	$_____
25. _____	255 Home Designs for Family Living	$3.50	$_____

MAIL TODAY

SATISFACTION GUARANTEED!
Your order will be processed and shipped within 48 hours

	Sub Total	$_____
Michigan Residents kindly add 4% sales tax		$_____
TOTAL-Check enclosed		$_____

Name _____

Address _____

City _____ State _____ Zip _____

In Canada Mail To: Home Planners, Inc. 20 Cedar St. N., Kitchener, Ontario N2H 2W8
CV2

Design 22251
3,112 Sq. Ft.; 36,453 Cu. Ft.

● It will not matter at all where this distinctive ranch home is built. Whether located in the south, east, north or west the exterior design appeal will be breathtakingly distinctive and the interior livability will be delightfully different. The irregular shape is enhanced by the low-pitched, wide overhanging roof. From the main living area of the house two wings project to help form an appealing entrance court. Variations in grade result in the garage being on a lower level. The plan reflects an interesting study in zoning and a fine indoor-outdoor relationship of the various areas.

Design 22227
2,263 Sq. Ft.; 20,367 Cu. Ft.

● Here is a contemporary home which gives a clue to just how much fun day-to-day living can really be. With, or without, the pool and the cabana with its excellent facilities, the occupants of this home will enjoy their newly formed living patterns immensely. The covered patio provides an interesting backdrop for each of the three rooms with which it functions. The convenient kitchen is but a step or two from: the laundry with its adjacent wash room and storage facilities; the separate dining room with its attractive room divider and the ever-popular family room with its snack bar. An appealing, open-end fireplace is a focal point of the living room. Fine wardrobe storage and bath facilities are the highlights of the bedroom area. Skylights permit extra light into the house.

Design 22343 3,110 Sq. Ft.; 51,758 Cu. Ft.

● If yours is a growing active family the chances are good that they will want their new home to relate to the outdoors. This distinctive design puts a premium on private outdoor living. And you don't have to install a swimming pool to get the most enjoyment from this home. Developing this area as a garden court will provide the indoor living areas with a breathtaking awareness of nature's beauty. Notice the fine zoning of the plan and how each area has its sliding glass doors to provide an unrestricted view. Three bedrooms plus study are serviced by three baths. The family and gathering rooms provide two great living areas. The kitchen is most efficient.

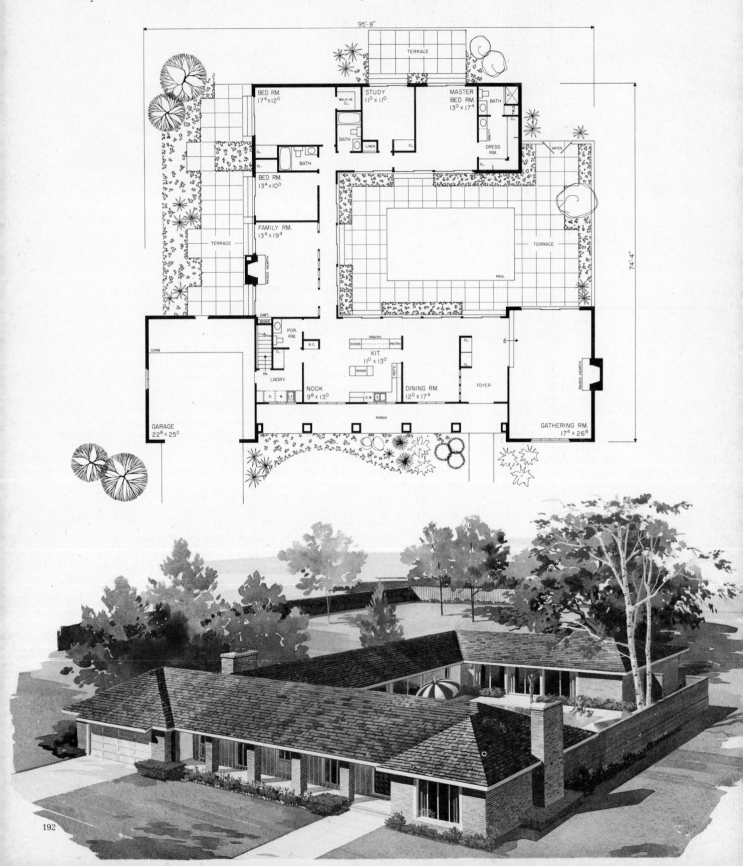